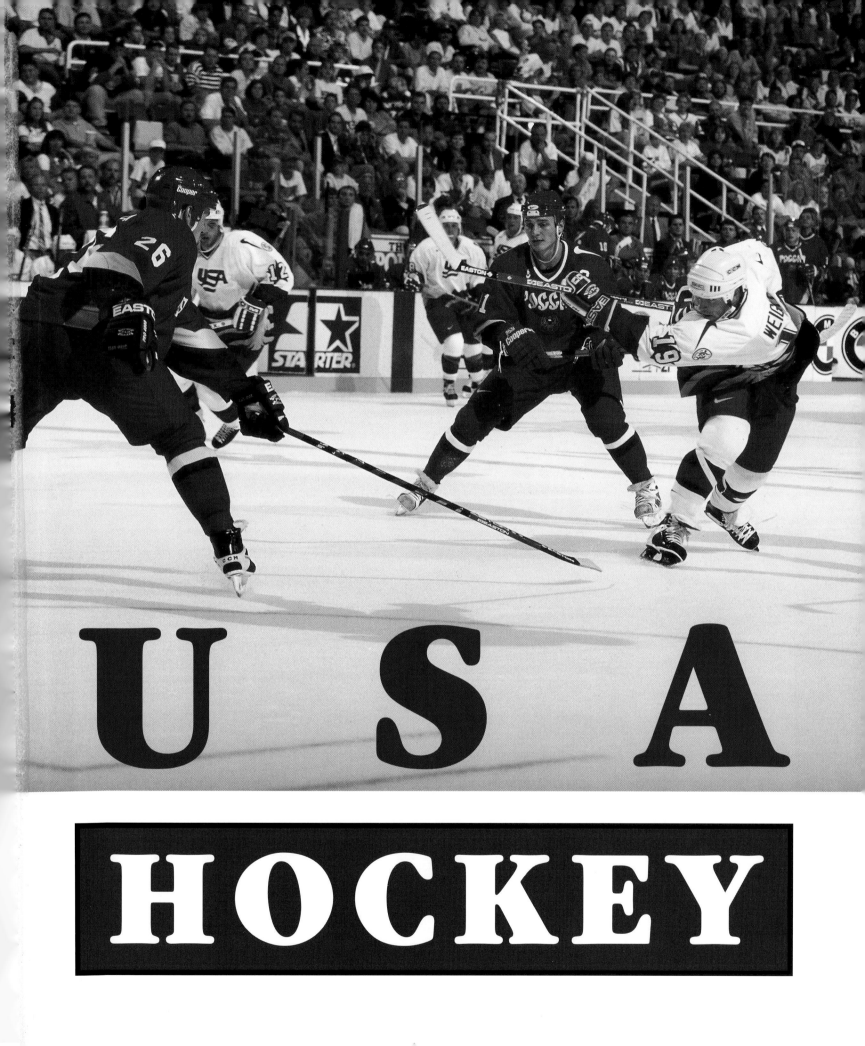

USA
HOCKEY

USA
HOC

KEY

A Celebration of a Great Tradition

The Official Commemorative Book

KEVIN ALLEN

Produced and distributed by Triumph Books.

This book is available in quantity at special discounts for your group or organization. For further information, contact:

Triumph Books
644 South Clark Street
Chicago, Illinois 60605
(312) 939-3330
Fax (312) 663-3557

Printed in the United States of America.

ISBN 1-57243-236-5

Book design by Bob Moon

Cover design by Mike Mulligan

Dedicated to the memory of Margaret Allen
whose influence on her son was never
appreciated enough.

ACKNOWLEDGMENTS

Early in this project it became clear that summing up more than one hundred years of American hockey history in 60,000 words was like trying to shoehorn all of your worldly belongings into a two-car garage.

It can be accomplished, but not without angst. The agonizing over this book wasn't spent deciding what to include, but rather what to leave out.

For a country that is only now really discovering hockey in a national way, America has a plethora of hockey tradition. Over the several months it took to complete this research, more than one hundred people provided me with interviews. Not all could be included in the book, but each one provided me with a greater understanding of hockey's culture in the United States. For that insight, I'm forever grateful.

Many debts are owed on this book, most too large to repay. But some people deserve special mention. A day or two into the research, the realization came that one of the foremost authorities on American hockey history was actually a Canadian named Bob Duff, a sportswriter for the *Windsor Star* (Ontario). He became my supermarket of hockey information, providing me with dates, newspaper clippings, and amazing insight into the pre-1950s hockey world. Without Duff as one of my guides, this literary journey would have been far more arduous and far less enjoyable.

Thanks is also due to Don Clark, the unofficial historian of U.S. hockey history, whose dedication to the sport cannot be surpassed, and to Tom Karakas, who let me see Eveleth and Mike Karakas through the eyes of someone who knew them both intimately. My gratitude also goes to USA Hockey officials, particularly Walter Bush, Dave Ogrean, Brian Petrovek, and Art Berglund, for opening their doors and hearts to this project.

I owe Bush more than just thanks. I owe him a Great Big Bertha graphite driver. I broke his on the first tee of our interview site. The look on everyone's face when that mammoth club head sailed fifty yards down the fairway is one I'll never forget. I'm a writer, not a golfer.

I'm also unlikely to forget the honor I felt interviewing Frank Brimsek, the pure enjoyment of interviewing Herb Brooks, or the enlightment I received talking to Murray Williamson, Jack Riley, Whitey Campbell, John Mayasich, Mike Eruzione, and Ron Wilson.

Most of the support material I used for this book is mentioned throughout the text, but four books helped more than others: Trent Frayne's *Mad Men of Hockey*, Stan and Shirley Fisher's *Everybody's Hockey Book*, Michael McKinley's *Hockey Hall of Fame Legends*, and Fishler and Duff's *Hockey Encyclopedia*.

The great bulk of the research for this project came from newspapers, primarily the *New York Times*, *Montreal Gazette*, *Windsor Star*, *Detroit News*, *Boston Globe*, and the *Toronto Globe*. The *New York Times* was the primary source for most of the information about Hobey Baker. Some information for this book was gleaned from articles that had been saved by families and friends of early hockey heroes. In some cases, it was impossible to determine from what publication they had been clipped.

My gratitude also goes to *USA TODAY* hockey editor Mike Brehm who rummaged through the newspaper's computerized library to find articles for my project, and who gave me flexibility on my work schedule to complete the project. Thanks also to my attorney, Greg Graessley, who helped edit my work.

Special thanks is also owed to Darryl Seibel, who is USA Hockey's public relations chieftain and a good friend who managed to get through this project without hating me. He's the winger who works ferociously in the corners to get the puck in front of the net so the center can tap it in and get all the glory.

Final thanks go to my wife, Terri, and children, Erin, Kelsey, and Shane, whose contributions on this book were second to none.

I will always remember the vacation we took in 1996 when my kids killed time in the car by helping me organize all of my research material into files, nor will I forget that ten-year-old Kelsey would ask me daily how many pages I had written. When my answer fell short of her expectation, she would mockingly give me the look I give her if her homework isn't completed.

Terri is the Hobey Baker of wives; she's noble, talented, adventuresome, and is a big-play performer. I needed her often on this book; she helped me sift through the clutter in my mind to find the focus of this work. She's also the only editor of my work with whom I never argue.

CONTENTS

The readers of *American Hockey Magazine* selected the All-Time USA Hockey team during USA Hockey's 60th anniversary season in 1996-97. Clockwise (from top): Frank Brimsek (#1), Tom Williams, Brett Hull, Neal Broten, Chris Chelios, Brian Leetch, Mike Richter, Bill Cleary, Joe Mullen, Pat LaFontaine, John Mariucci, and John Mayasich.

INTRODUCTION

Montreal, September 14, 1996

On the morning of its most important hockey game since Lake Placid in 1980, the USA's coach, Ron Wilson, was searching for his Sir Galahad. The deciding game of the World Cup of Hockey was to be fought in the enemy's castle. In the lower region of Montreal's Molson Centre, America's knights prepared for the looming battle with Canada. Wilson's legion would be ready. Skates were sharpened. Helmet screws were tightened. Sticks were checked and rechecked. Goalies fussed over their pads the way King Arthur's men had probably readied their shields so many years before.

The Canada-USA hockey rivalry had been a 100-year war. Since the first international contest staged by American and Canadian college players in 1895, the Canadians had ruled America on ice. The great Hobey Baker, American hockey's first knight, might have been as talented as any Canadian player in the years before World War I, but even he couldn't break the chains of Canadian domination. Canada had too many talented players, too much pride in being the best. The Americans were victorious in some significant battles, such as the USA's 2-1 win against Canada en route to the Olympic gold medal at Squaw Valley in 1960. But the successes were few, and the frustrations many.

The National Hockey League had also been Canada's domain. During the first fifty years of the league's existence, only a small number of Americans had worn an NHL uniform. General managers, coaches, and scouts were all Canadian. Hence, players were Canadian. Only the persistence and exceptional talent of Taffy Abel, Frank Brimsek, Mike Karakas, John Mariucci, Doc Romnes, Tommy Williams, and a few others prevented the NHL from being an exclusive Canadian club. But prejudices remained. Mariucci fought more than once during his NHL career when his citizenship was insulted, and a Canadian-born general manager once told Williams that Americans didn't have the mental toughness required to be NHLers.

Times changed. By the 1996-97 season, almost 18 percent of NHL players were Americans. Canada's membership had slipped to 64 percent. What hadn't changed was Canada's domination over the U.S. in international hockey competition. At the world championships for players under the age of twenty, at the senior men's World Championships, and at the Canada Cup, the U.S. remained subservient.

The American players in the World Cup dressing room that morning in 1996 were confident they could overthrow Canadian rule. They didn't specifically think about the U.S.'s hockey pioneers, but they understood they were playing for them as well as for themselves. From day one of training camp, Wilson had asked them to win this tournament for the many American players who had never known the thrill of beating Canada in a championship set-

ting. In 1960, when the USA had downed the Canadians at Squaw Valley, their best players were in the NHL. This championship was different.

At a press gathering on the day before the deciding game three, Wilson talked about how the Canadians had developed consistency in their program through the art of storytelling. Each successful generation of Canadian players passed along stories to the next generation so that every Canadian player knew how previous teams had risen to the occasion to keep the country's pride intact. Wilson said he longed for the day when the U.S. had a winning tradition to pass down.

When Wilson surveyed his dressing room on the morning of game three, he was drawn to right wing Tony Amonte. Amonte wasn't the USA's best player or even one of its leaders. But in the previous six games, the Massachusetts native had proven himself a warrior. Amonte had played as if he had jets on his skates and nitro in his veins. Whenever the USA needed a lift, Amonte had scored, created a scoring chance, or stapled an opponent against the boards with a well-timed check. Sometimes just the sight of Amonte flying down the ice at Mach 2, with his long hair flowing and his USA jersey flapping behind him, was enough to rally his teammates to greater glory. Amonte had played this tournament with moxie and conviction. Most important, he had played it to win.

Wilson was looking for someone who would pick up the flag and inspire the troops if it became necessary that night. He thought Amonte might be the heroic knight.

"Tony," Wilson said, "you are going to be America's Paul Henderson."

"Who the hell is Paul Henderson?" joked Amonte.

Most of the 28 million people in Canada, and Amonte, knew Henderson scored the game-winner to beat the Soviet Union in the famous 1972 Summit Series. In the U.S., men and women over forty know where they were when John F. Kennedy was assassinated. In Canada, men and women over forty know where they were when Henderson fired the puck past Vladislav Tretiak in Moscow.

Boston University alum Tony Amonte had always possessed a scorer's "knack." But he never scored a goal as important as the one he netted for Team USA in the deciding game of the 1996 World Cup.

But if Amonte was to be anointed as hero in waiting, he preferred his model made in America. To U.S. hockey players of Amonte's generation, the list of fabled hockey heroes was restricted to the U.S. team that captured the gold medal at the 1980 Olympics in Lake Placid. When Amonte contemplated his destiny, he immediately thought of the man whose goal had vanquished the Soviets sixteen years before.

"Can I just be Mike Eruzione?" Amonte asked.

"Yea," said Wilson. "You are both ugly, you are both Italian, and you are both from Boston University. You can be Eruzione and score the big goal for us tonight."

Neither man realized how prophetic their conversation would be.

Chapter 1

In the idyllic days before the Great War, journalists viewed Hobey Baker as the embodiment of America—or at least what they thought America should be. The golden-haired Princeton star athlete was as handsome as he was talented, as noble as he was fearless, as daring as he was cunning. With his lion's heart and poet's soul, he was bursting with confidence, yet stardom humbled him in a way that no one quite understood. Hobart Amory Hare Baker was the favorite son for whom all Americans longed. Whether returning a punt or flying up ice with the puck on his stick, Baker persevered with a passion and courage that hadn't been seen on college campuses before he arrived at Princeton in 1910.

Newspapers weren't content to merely report Baker's hockey and football exploits; they glorified them through headlines and prose that brought romance and idealism to all that he accomplished. To the media, Baker was an artist whose runs with the football or dashes with the puck were like lines of poetry to be savored and enjoyed. They were smitten with Hobey Baker like amorous teenagers doting upon first loves.

HOBEY BAKER

Hockey's First American Knight

"If it is possible to say of any man that he was beautiful, it may be said of Hobey Baker because he was beautiful of body, soul and spirit," *New York Herald Tribune* writer Al Laney wrote more than forty years after Baker had graced Princeton's ice.

Baker may have been the model for the all-American boy. He was F. Scott Fitzgerald on skates, minus the highbrow cynicism. Novelist Fitzgerald was actually Baker's contemporary at Princeton. Legend suggests that he used Baker as a model for characters in his books, though he probably needed to dress down Baker, who was too flawless for a good fictional tale. Baker dominated college hockey from 1910 to 1914 the way Wayne Gretzky dominated the NHL in the early 1980s. In his sophomore season, Baker had 92

Everyone on the Princeton campus from 1910-14 knew Hobey Baker. His charm went beyond his athletic ability. He was a handsome man—golden blond and stylishly dressed—who always placed a high premium on friendship and manners. Said to be uncomfortable with his stardom, Baker detested the occasions when his friends exaggerated his accomplishments.

In addition to being America's finest hockey player from 1910-14, Hobey Baker was also an All-American football player. He was a fearless punt returner whose reckless style often left Princeton fans fearing for his safety.

points to help unbeaten Princeton win what would have been the national championship.

At a time when America had finally grown accustomed to flying machines roaring overhead, Baker's skates must have seemed as if they were powered by warp drive. He was a dazzling skater with speed that amazed those who witnessed it for the first time. When the puck found the blade of his stick and he began his trek up ice, a buzz would move through the crowd, as if they were about to witness magnificence born before their eyes.

"Here he comes," they would yell in unison, like children noting the start of a parade.

The rules of seven-man hockey were perfect for Baker's talents. With no forward passing allowed, Baker, playing rover, had license to carry the puck coast to coast many times during the game. As a youngster, he had perfected his stickhandling by practicing on darkened rinks. The puck clung to his stick as if attached by a magnet.

The *Boston Herald* couldn't have imagined the level of talent that players such as Gordie Howe, Rocket Richard, Wayne Gretzky, and Mario Lemieux would bring to hockey in coming years. But at the time, the newspaper unabashedly called Hobey Baker "the greatest hockey player who ever lived."

Baker played hockey the way he played football—with an open throttle and a refusal to recognize that his playing style might be dangerous. In 1912, he was named an all-American halfback, putting him on the same team with the legendary Jim Thorpe. Like Thorpe, Baker was also an accomplished drop kicker whose skill was invaluable in a football era where the forward pass was just becoming a part of strategy. His kicking skill resolved several gridiron stalemates in Princeton's favor.

Baker's daring style was most apparent as a punt returner. Sure-handed and unafraid, he would stand well beyond where the punt would come down to assure he could be in full gallop when he cradled the ball in his arms. Fans would gasp as the ball, Baker, and the defensive ends would all arrive virtually at the same time. More often than not, Baker would elude the would-be tacklers and dart to the outside for a touchdown romp or long gainer. Sluggish offenses were the norm in that era; hence, Baker had plenty of opportunities to dazzle crowds with his unique and exhilarating punt-return style.

That bravado also showed on the ice when he attempted to stickhandle through defenders, most of whom would resort to physical attacks to slow him down. The news accounts from that era make frequent references to Baker jumping over sticks and legs to fill the opposing net. One report claimed Baker had 30 of Princeton's 42 shots on goal in a game against Yale.

Even the elitist *New York Times* often waxed poetically about Baker. Describing his performance as a rover in a 7-5 win against Yale on January 17, 1913, the *Times* said that Baker "was all over the rink skimming up and down the ice like a shadow."

That game had been tied 5-5 at the end of two regulation, 20-minute halves. In the extra period, Baker scored a goal with a spectacular end-to-end dash during which "he carried the puck to every part of the ice surface without being stopped."

"Baker had regained his second wind and he started as dazzling an exhibition of skating as had ever been seen on the rink," the unnamed *New York Times* correspondent wrote. " He started a series of zigzag dashes across the rink....He was going so fast that the Yale players went down before him." He was clearly like no athlete reporters had

It was often said that Baker was a one-man team at Princeton. The comment rankled Baker, who believed teamwork was essential to any successful sporting venture. Here is the unbeaten Princeton team, victors of the 1911-12 intercollegiate championship. As it was customary to call colleagues by their last name, the team photo didn't include first names. Back row (left to right): Coach Fitzpatrick, Kuhn, Blair, Mathey, Emmons, and Team Manager Davis. Front row (left to right): Kalbfleish, Patterson, Captain Kay, Baker, and McKinney.

ever seen, yet their fascination seemed to transcend his skill. They were disarmed by Baker, intrigued by him.

Baker was a well-spoken lad when he arrived at Princeton in 1910 after establishing himself as a schoolboy legend at St. Paul's School in Concord, New Hampshire. Early accounts of his athletic successes speak of a "twinkle in his eye" and an impish grin that no doubt served him well whether he was wooing the ladies or charming professors, who probably were as fascinated with him as the rest of the Princeton campus.

Born into Philadelphia high society, Baker arrived at Princeton with a well-defined set of values and ideals for his athletic involvement. During four years of hockey at Princeton, he had only two minor penalties, despite the fact that he was manhandled, roughed, and whacked with sticks in almost every game. Most opposing teams correctly figured that the way to stop Princeton was to stop Baker, and some teams resorted to tactics that were on the outside edge of the rule book. But to the astonishment of his teammates, Baker never retaliated. No matter how rough the contest, he shook the hands of opponents after games.

In one football game, Dartmouth all-American Red Louden was rendered unconscious in a failed attempt to stop Baker. Not only did Baker carry Louden off the field

Some hockey historians argue that Francis "Moose" Goheen was as talented a player as Hobey Baker. But Goheen's insistence on staying in Minnesota where he had a high-paying job prevented him from matching the national exposure that Baker enjoyed. Had Baker lived, the two of them might have played together on the 1920 U.S. Olympic team.

himself, he was almost too upset to return to the game. Only the thought of letting down his teammates convinced Baker to return to the contest.

Baker, always nattily attired, usually in a Norfolk jacket, was a dashing figure on campus. He probably looked the way a younger Robert Redford did in the movie *The Great Gatsby*. Baker was a person everyone wanted in their circle of friends. No one knew exactly what Baker was going to do with his life, but they were relatively sure he was going to be a success.

Standing 5-foot-9 and weighing about 160 pounds, Baker wasn't physically imposing. But he was a superbly honed athlete who was said to be as proficient at golf, track, and swimming, as he was football and hockey.

The only other American hockey player drawing a high degree of attention in that era was Francis "Moose" Goheen of White Bear Lake, Minnesota, who created his own hockey legend in the west. He was two years younger than Baker and began making his mark as a rover and defenseman with the St. Paul Athletic Club just as Baker was finishing up at Princeton.

But the fact that Baker's games were usually covered by the *New York Times* gave him a much broader reputation as America's best hockey player. He was, at the very least, on the same athletic level as the great players of Canada, such as Cyclone Taylor, who was known to Americans because he had made tour stops in New York and Boston.

Baker dominated a sport that was relatively new to the American public. Unlike in Canada, where seven-man hockey had known some level of notoriety since the 1860s, hockey was really still in its infancy when Baker began drawing attention as an extraordinary athlete.

In the early 1890s, college athletes were playing what they called "ice polo." The idea was the same, except each team used only five players and the object of their attention was a ball, not a puck. Some American college tennis standouts had brought back hockey after a challenge match between Canada and the U.S. in 1895. The earliest documented college game was between Yale and Johns Hopkins in 1896.

Hockey had also taken hold in Pittsburgh before the turn of the century with the introduction of the Western Pennsylvania League and the Interscholastic League (though a fire that destroyed the Schenley Park Casino rink temporarily stalled the game's growth). The sport was also gaining popularity in Michigan's Upper Peninsula. In 1904, a dentist named

Cyclone Taylor was a Canadian counterpart to Hobey Baker. Like Baker, Taylor was a dazzling skater—agile, swift on the ice, and confident in his athletic abilities. But unlike Baker, Taylor played fifteen professional seasons.

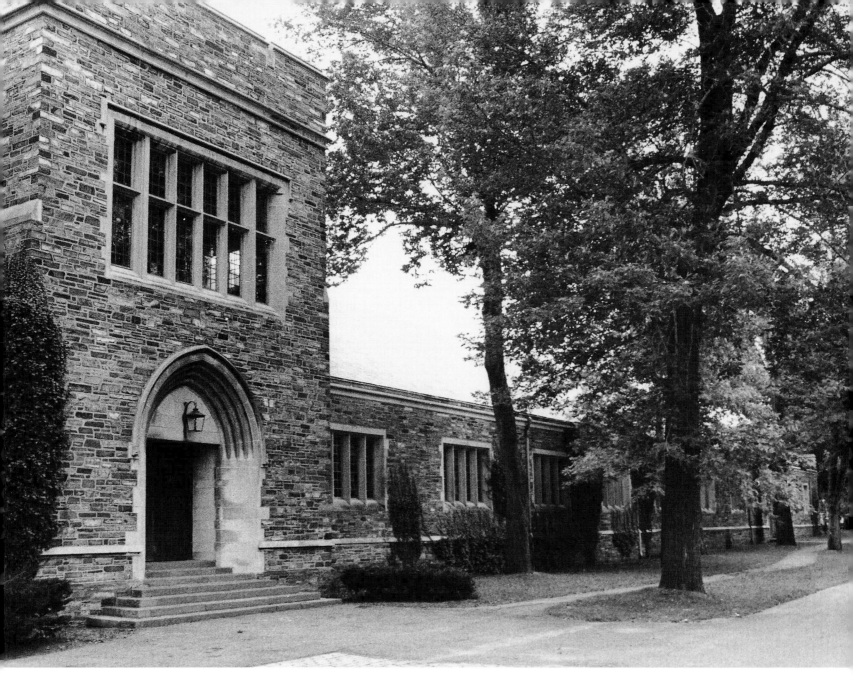

After Hobey Baker was killed in a plane crash in 1918, his friends raised enough money to construct this hockey arena to honor his memory. The Princeton team has played there for the past seventy-five years.

J. L. Gibson began America's first pro league. Called the International Hockey League, it included the Calumet-Larium Miners, the American Soo Indians, Pittsburgh (Pennsylvania), the Canadian Soo, and Houghton.

By the time Baker arrived at Princeton, ice hockey had a strong foothold, especially on the East Coast where Baker's name gained considerable prominence. American "amateur" hockey had been thriving, although the rosters of those teams often included many Canadians who had come south for the promise of under-the-table payments.

According to the *New York Times*, Baker had several offers to turn pro after he left Princeton. Later reports suggested he turned down $3,500 from the NHL's Montreal Wanderers. That would have put him in the salary neighborhood of Taylor, who the *New York Times* had called "the Ty Cobb of pro hockey." Taylor made more than $5,000 when the Renfrew Millionaires lured him to play for that club team.

Baker's decision not to become a professional player following his career at Princeton isn't surprising, given his circumstances. First, professional hockey wasn't viewed as being quite the honorable vocation that it is today. Second, Baker's upper crust background and Princeton degree suggest that the money offered in those days wouldn't overwhelm him.

Third, a professional career would probably have forced him to play in Canada. The Pacific Coast Hockey Association's first American team had arrived that year in Portland, but somehow it just doesn't seem likely that America's greatest player would abandon his East Coast lifestyle to play professionally for a team called the Rosebuds. As much as Baker talked of hockey being a team game, he certainly must have appreciated that his greatest fame was with those who watched him play for four years at Princeton.

The logical choice to further his career was the St. Nick's amateur team out of New York, which he joined after his graduation in 1914. The St. Nicholas team was a major hockey attraction before his arrival, but with Baker on the squad, it drew even more attention. Newspapers made reference to limousines lined up outside St. Nick's arena on the nights Baker would play. With an Ivy League college connection, hockey had become a high-society sport. When St. Nick's won a game from the Montreal Stars in the 1915 Ross Cup series, the *Montreal Press* wrote: "Baker cooked our goose so artistically that we enjoyed it."

But soon Baker began showing signs of restlessness. He toured Europe and wrote of his experiences for the *New York Times*. While Baker was in Europe, Archduke Ferdinand, heir to the Austro-Hungarian throne, was assassinated, triggering World War I. Baker's buddies had a difficult time talking him out of enlisting in the British army. He returned to New York to become a banker and play hockey, although his heart seemed to be only in the latter. But his sense of duty continued gnawing at him, so that, by 1916, Baker was training to become a pilot. After only a short period, his zeal for flying through the air surpassed his desire to fly up ice.

By all accounts, he had a flair for dogfighting, an innate sense of knowing when to make the right moves at the right times. He buzzed through the clouds like he was weaving through defenders on a Saturday afternoon at Princeton.

In 1917, Baker was sent over as a member of the Lafayette Escadrille Squadron, among the first American pilots shipped to France, although much to his chagrin, he didn't enter the war zone immediately. His first assignment in France involved pushing papers, a duty that clearly bored someone who was accustomed to being in the center of the fray.

In April of 1918, he was finally given a chance to fight in his single-seater Spad, painted in orange and black Princeton school colors. By May, he had recorded his first kill of a German aircraft—the first of three he would be credited with before the war's end. He would receive the Croix de Guerre medal for his heroism.

Baker enjoyed the thrill of combat, probably because it provided him with the same adrenaline rush he knew from lugging the football in the open field or stickhandling through the men from Harvard. But Baker might have loved being a pilot more than he should have. He was clearly bothered by the thought that life after football and hockey might be somewhat anticlimactic. According to his biography by John Davies, Baker told friends after he departed Princeton: "I realize my life is finished. No matter how long I live, I will never equal the excitement of playing on the football field."

When the Great War finally ended, Baker seemed more saddened than pleased. Perhaps he felt he hadn't fulfilled his duty or lived up to the measure of his own destiny.

Why he needed to take one last flight over the French soil a month after the war ended is not known. He had been ordered stateside and was to leave that day. When he showed up at the airfield, his subordinates protested his plans for a final flight, some of them undoubtedly believing the superstition that pilots shouldn't test fate by taking a "last flight." Too many stories existed about pilots crashing on their final trip into the sky. Pushing his luck further, Baker decided to climb into a recently repaired plane.

Perhaps sentimentality ruled Baker that day. Perhaps he felt a nostalgic craving to say farewell to the skies where he had fought with honor and dignity. While training to become a pilot in 1916, he had chosen a football Saturday for a flight over the Princeton stadium. Fans recognized him instantly. They would remember that day as his goodbye to them.

Perhaps the same bravado and adventuresome spirit that helped him survive his combat experiences contributed to his death in the end. Baker was always confident in his ability to steer clear of danger. After all, he had avoided monstrous hits by big-chested linemen in football and dodged the high sticks that Canadian players always directed his way.

According to the Canadian wire service report of his death in the *Montreal Gazette*, eyewitnesses said Baker was trying a stunt at an altitude that was too low on December 21, 1918, when the Spad's 220 horsepower engine sputtered, then fell silent. But the *New York Times* report said the engine simply died 600 yards above the earth. Baker could have simply kept flying straight and crash-landed the plane a few miles away from the airfield. Many pilots, including Baker himself, had walked away from crash landings in the durable Spad. But Baker probably didn't want to scuttle his aircraft, which would have been an embarrassment considering the flight didn't need to be taken. Maybe he had time to think all this, or maybe he merely acted instinctively, as had been his style in the athletic arena.

For whatever reason, Baker immediately engineered a difficult maneuver that instantly put him in peril because the nose of his plane was pushed further down. Though Baker struggled to keep the nose up, he ran out of sky before the task was completed. He died as his colleagues raced to take him to the field hospital. He was twenty-six.

Hobey's relatives and friends were left to ponder his death. Had he been distraught over the prospect of entering a life where there would be no war or sports to test his mettle? Not even his closest friends knew for sure. The tragic circumstances of his death somehow fit the theatrical nature of his life. The memories of Baker's friends and family would have him weaving up ice on skates or dancing through the clouds in his Spad. This was a Greek tragedy at its tear-invoking best. Not Homer, not Fitzgerald, not even Hemingway could have written a more tragic climax to Baker's story.

U.S. President Woodrow Wilson, the former Princeton president, who chose to watch Baker practice on the day he was elected, was among those to issue condolences. Almost immediately, friends set about establishing a fund for an ice rink to be built at Princeton to carry Baker's name. It was put up in 1922 and still bears his name today.

Would Baker have returned to hockey had he arrived safely home from the war? Although professional hockey was garnering greater recognition, it probably would not have been palatable to Baker, who preferred more sportsmanship and less anger in his sports endeavors. Had he survived the war, he might have joined the 1920 U.S. Olympic team. Moose Goheen was on that team, and that tandem would have been difficult to stop. If Baker had been a member of the team, the Americans might not have waited until 1960 to land an Olympic gold medal.

Today, the Hobey Baker Memorial Award honors the top college player each season. The winners are all talented, but probably not quite as dashing as Hobey was in his heyday.

In 1981, the Decathlon Club of Minnesota began presenting the Hobey Baker Memorial Award to the Outstanding Collegiate Hockey Player in the United States. Past winners include Dallas Stars' center Neal Broten, Washington Capitals' general manager George McPhee, Mighty Ducks of Anaheim winger Paul Kariya, and St. Louis Blues' winger Scott Pellerin.

HOBEY BAKER MEMORIAL AWARD

PRESENTED ANNUALLY TO THE OUTSTANDING COLLEGIATE HOCKEY PLAYER
IN THE UNITED STATES BY THE
DECATHLON ATHLETIC CLUB OF BLOOMINGTON, MINNESOTA

Chapter 2

Dashing and daring Hobey Baker probably would have had a significant impact had he chosen to play in the National Hockey League. Clarence "Taffy" Abel became the player who helped open the NHL door for Americans by playing for the New York Rangers and the Chicago Blackhawks. When 6-foot-2, 245-pound Abel arrived in the National Hockey League in 1926, he was as imposing as one of the 350-pound black bears that roamed near his hometown of Sault Ste. Marie, Michigan. Opponents must have looked at him the way climbers gaze at Mount Kilimanjaro. Even with a pocketful of change, many forwards of that era struggled to weigh 165 pounds. Pitting themselves against Abel was a formidable challenge. Abel protected the goal and his teammates the way a father would protect his children.

HOCKEY IN THE 1920s

Willing and Abel

Born in 1900, Abel was the grandson of the chief of the Cherokee tribe. He was a legend around the Soo until his hometown ice rink burned to the ground. To continue his hockey career, Abel moved to the St. Paul Athletic Club, where he started to draw the attention of the NHL and organizers of the 1924 U.S. Olympic team. He made the Olympic team and was chosen to be the American flag bearer at the Winter Games in Chamonix, France.

In an era when it was considered blasphemy for defenders to stray from their own blue line, Abel managed to net 15 goals in five games as the USA won the silver medal in France. Word of his exploits reached Conn Smythe, then the manager of the New York Rangers. He had been interested in Abel prior to the Olympics because he had heard Abel was as big as a house, but could still skate with reasonable quickness.

Several newspapers have erroneously reported that Abel was the first American to play in the NHL. Actually, Eddie Carpenter, born in Hartford, Michigan, played for the Quebec Bulldogs in the 1919-20 season; Bobby Benson of Buffalo, New York played eight games for the Boston Bruins in the 1924-25 season; and Jerry Geran, who played briefly for the Montreal Wanderers before they folded in 1918, played again for the Boston Bruins in the 1925-26 season.

Clarence "Taffy" Abel was probably America's first National Hockey League standout. Feared by opponents, Abel was a ferocious bodychecker who weighed as much as 245 pounds in an era when many forwards weighed about 150. Despite his size, he was reputed to be an accomplished skater.

Some historians might count Billy Burch, born in Yonkers, New York, among the first Americans. But Burch, a member of the Hall of Fame, grew up in Hamilton, Ontario, and was far more Canadian than American. Herb Drury, who played five years for Pittsburgh, has some credibility as an American because he played for the 1924 U.S. Olympic team, but he was actually born in Midland, Ontario. In those days, Canadians migrated south of the forty-ninth parallel to earn extra money. U.S. teams often paid top Canadian players for their services. Drury was on the Pittsburgh "amateur" team, which turned professional when it joined the NHL in 1925.

Also in the 1925-26 season, goaltender Alphonse Lacroix, who played for the 1924 U.S. Olympic team, signed to play five games for the Montreal Canadiens because regular goaltender George Vezina contracted pneumonia. Lacroix was 1-4 with a 3.20 goals-against average and never played another NHL game.

The American player the NHL wanted most in the 1920s was Francis "Moose" Goheen, a rushing defenseman from White Bear Lake, Minnesota, known for his end-to-end dashes with the puck. He played football and baseball at Valpraiso University and then went on to play hockey for the St. Paul Athletic Club. He played for the 1920 U.S. Olympic team, but rejected an invitation to play for the 1924 squad. He also said no to contract offers from the Toronto Maple Leafs and Boston Bruins because he didn't want to give up his excellent job at the Northern States Power Company.

"Had he gone to Canada or other outposts in North America where the game flourished, Goheen would have been sainted years ago," Don Riley wrote in the *St. Paul Pioneer Press* in 1978.

Goheen was a wickedly fast skater with large, powerful thighs and sculpted shoulders. According to writings of the time, Goheen clearly had an advanced understanding of hockey tactics and puck movement. Goheen seemed to be a thoroughbred in a field of plow horses. Crowds would endure below-zero temperatures in the unheated Minnesota State Fairgrounds to see Goheen perform his hockey magic act.

"The team could be sluggish and then Moose would make one of those rink-long trips, split the defense, leaving falling bodies behind, and pour in goal," teammate Emy Garrett said years later. "From that point on, bedlam tore up the house and his team would become unbeatable."

Don Clark, one of the foremost authorities on American hockey history, is convinced Goheen and Baker were peers in terms of their hockey ability.

Abel couldn't match the pure hockey skill of those two, but his defensive ability and toughness made him just as attractive to professional coaches. Since he wasn't immediately enamored with the idea of an NHL career, he went back to St. Paul after the 1924 Olympics, resisting the idea of an NHL career with the same fierce stubbornness that made him one of the league's better defenders. Smythe's method for locking Abel into his first National Hockey League contract in 1926 was literally locking him in.

Or at least that's what Smythe threatened to do.

Smythe had heard his hockey buddies gush about the 245-pound American defenseman for several years and was more than annoyed to discover Abel wasn't overly impressed by the NHL's offers and was as stubborn as Smythe when it came down to money.

Abel rejected several Rangers offers before Smythe convinced him to at least show up for a face-to-face meeting in the Pullman train car. Abel wouldn't budge on his stance, and when the conductor announced the train was about to roll, he began to head for the door. Smythe raced ahead of him and locked him in.

"The money's good, you won't do better, and the next stop is two hundred and fifty miles away," Smythe said. "If you don't sign, you won't be getting off until then."

Abel, a powerful man with a quick temper, must have been amused by Smythe's style because on another day he might have thrown Smythe through the window. Instead, he

A member of the 1924 U.S. Olympic team, Herb Drury is sometimes considered one of the first Americans to play in the National Hockey League. But Drury was a Canadian who moved to the United States to make money as a hockey player. Drury played six NHL seasons (1925-26 to 1930-31), scoring 24 goals in 207 games.

When pudgy Taffy Abel refused to lose weight, the New York Rangers traded him to the Chicago Blackhawks. Just as he had in New York, Abel helped his new team win the Stanley Cup in 1934. He then quit after a salary dispute. At retirement, he had 359 penalty minutes in 327 NHL games.

signed the contract, shook Smythe's hand, and jumped from the train as it was pulling out of the station.

The Rangers immediately proclaimed Abel to be the NHL's largest player, which would be both a curse and a blessing for Abel. Although opponents feared Abel's girth, coaches felt he would have been more effective if he was better conditioned and twenty pounds lighter.

According to the media reports of that era, Abel was a gum-chewing, rough-and-tumble competitor whose body checks often sent opposing forwards airborne. He was also adept at pushing his opponents into the boards and draping over them until the referee whistled the play dead. His size and his willingness to use it made him an intimidating presence. When he was playing for the Blackhawks, the fans in New York, Boston, and Detroit loved to rain boos and insults down on him and razz him unmercifully about his girth.

Meal money didn't go to waste on Abel. At various points in his career, Abel weighed more than 260 pounds. When he played with the New York Rangers early in his career, he was paired with Ching Johnson, another beefy defenseman. At a combined 430 to 460 pounds—depending upon when they had last been fed—they were probably the heaviest defensive duo in the game. Johnson, although born in Winnipeg, actually had some American roots. He had come down to Eveleth, Minnesota, as a teenager to play senior hockey. He was still playing senior hockey in Marquette, Michigan, when he was in his forties.

In his rookie season, Abel's eight goals made him the Rangers' fourth-highest goal scorer and one of the league's top-scoring defensemen. That level of production put him in the company of Ottawa Senator King Clancy, New York American Lyle Conacher, and Boston Bruin Eddie Shore, all of whom were considered elite-level defensemen.

Shore was considered among the best ever to play the position. But it certainly wasn't his offensive touch that endeared him to fans; he never had more than three goals or six points in any future NHL season. He was known as an immovable object and quickly earned a reputation for doing whatever was required to achieve a win.

People in the Soo knew Abel had that same intense drive to win. According to local folklore, the legend of Abel's competitive spirit was established by a well-timed right cross.

Abel's team, the Soo Indians, had just lost a 1-0 decision against a bitter rival when the team manager strolled into the dressing room and said: "Well, there's always the next game." The sentence was barely finished when Abel's fist caught the manager flush on the jaw. It was a one-punch TKO, and Abel was suspended for the remainder of the season.

"He was two different personalities," says Bill Thorn, Abel's second cousin. "Off the ice, he was easygoing. But on the ice, you didn't want to meet him. He hated to lose."

He also didn't like anyone taking advantage of him on or off the ice. A Canadian newspaper carried the story of Abel, then playing for the Rangers, being rolled for $100 by a Manhattan con artist who had convinced the kindhearted Abel to loan him $2. When Abel removed his money clip from his trousers, the thief snatched it and escaped into the streets before Abel could react.

Shocked and then enraged by the mugging, Abel returned to his room and plotted revenge. He pulled a gun from its hiding place in his room and set out to bring vigilante justice to his assailant. It didn't take long to locate him. The con man hadn't been smart enough to know he shouldn't be spending Abel's money within a few blocks of where the fleecing took place. It's not difficult to imagine the combination of fear and surprise the petty thief must have felt as he found himself staring at the business end of Abel's revolver. He immediately returned the ill-gotten cash to Abel. However, it was short the money he already had spent, so Abel escorted his new "friend" around town until he managed to borrow enough money to repay the original amount.

Bill Thorn spent many hours listening to Abel's stories, and among those he enjoyed most was the tale of Abel's participation in one of the most famous games in Stanley Cup finals history. Abel was on defense when 45-year-old coach and general manager Lester Patrick was forced into action as a New York Rangers goalie when starter Loren Chabot was injured. In those days, NHL teams didn't carry a backup goaltender and the Montreal Maroons, the Rangers' opponent, were rather unsympathetic to the Rangers' predicament. They saw the situation as assuring them a badly needed win.

"Taffy told me neither he or Ching Johnson was going to allow any shots to get through to the net," Thorn said. "He thought there was only a few [dangerous] shots on goal on Patrick."

Although Abel had served the Rangers well for three seasons and helped them win their first Stanley Cup in 1928, team management became concerned with the fluctuation of Abel's weight. When Abel refused to shed his excess pounds, the Rangers sold him to flamboyant Chicago Blackhawks' owner Major McLaughlin for a whopping $15,000, a sizable sum for a hockey transaction.

"He was comfortable the way he was, and he told them that," Thorn said. "At that weight, he could still skate very fast."

Abel's popularity was instantaneous in the Windy City. Fans loved the way Abel could use his massive body as a weapon of terror. Much of the time, the sight of Abel racing toward opponents like a charging rhino would be enough to force a turnover. But those brave hearts who stood up to Abel found that he was willing to use his body as an instrument of destruction. In the 1932-33 season, his seventh NHL season, he registered more penalty minutes than he had since his rookie season with the Rangers.

In his fifth season with the Blackhawks, Abel showed up at training camp in the best shape of his career. Newspaper articles state Abel was fifteen to twenty pounds lighter than during his previous seasons with the Hawks.

Sportswriter Jim Gallagher of the *Chicago American* newspaper wrote: "Montreal fans find it hard to understand why the Rangers even parted with Abel. Taff has trimmed his huge bulk a bit, although he still retains enough weight to render him a stone wall that is almost impervious to enemy attacks."

A writer for the *Chicago American* said: "Rated strictly on his defensive ability, there's no better left defenseman in the league."

Hall of Fame defenseman Art Coulter, who was Abel's teammate in Chicago, said Abel probably should have been elected to the Hall of Fame. "He was a very good skater," Coulter said. "When he would start up ice, the defense would just converge on him. They would be hanging all over him. He would be like a mother ape with five baby apes hanging off him."

After Abel had been in the league a few years, not many opponents challenged him. "You would have had to be pretty stupid to do that," Coulter said. "And guys weren't that stupid."

At age thirty-two, Abel helped the Blackhawks win their first Stanley Cup. That summer, he had a contract squabble with McLaughlin and decided to retire when it wasn't resolved.

"He told me it was only a matter of $100," Thorn said. "He had been promised more money if they won the Stanley Cup, and [if] McLaughlin wasn't going to give it to him, he was going home. And he did. He believed a promise was a promise."

Abel returned home to Sault Ste. Marie where his legend had begun.

Chapter 3

THE 1937-38 STANLEY CUP

One Rebel and a Few Yankees

Triumphant Blackhawks wear their Sunday best as they carry the Stanley Cup through the streets of Chicago following their 1937-38 NHL championship. It was the second of three titles the Blackhawks have won since their inception in 1926-27. The others were in 1933-34 and 1960-61.

W hen Abel retired to Sault Ste. Marie to launch a supper club, Elwin "Doc" Romnes was the only standout American left in the league. Mike Karakas would show up in two years, but Cully Dahlstrom was still a few years away. Dahlstrom had jumped right from Minneapolis South High School to the American Hockey Association, but the next step to the NHL took time.

"I just didn't have the natural talent like some kids had to jump directly," Dahlstrom told writer Randy Schultz years later.

Dahlstrom failed his first tryout with the Boston Bruins, who were starting to pay attention to the Americans. He failed it badly, according to his own words. "Those guys were skating circles around me," he said. "It was as if I was going in slow motion."

Two years later, his feistiness earned him a spot on McLaughlin's Blackhawks, although McLaughlin wasn't his biggest fan. However, McLaughlin was inexplicably

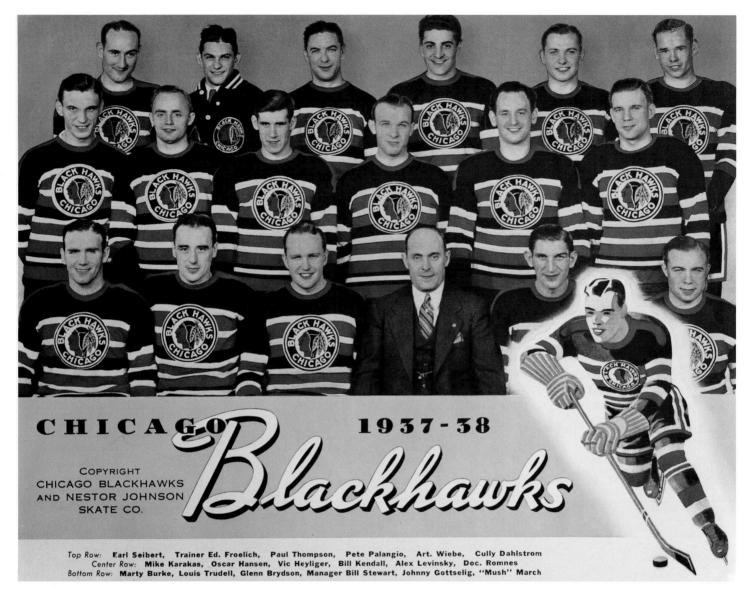

Top Row: **Earl Seibert, Trainer Ed. Froelich, Paul Thompson, Pete Palangio, Art. Wiebe, Cully Dahlstrom**
Center Row: **Mike Karakas, Oscar Hansen, Vic Heyliger, Bill Kendall, Alex Levinsky, Doc. Romnes**
Bottom Row: **Marty Burke, Louis Trudell, Glenn Brydson, Manager Bill Stewart, Johnny Gottselig, "Mush" March**

The 1937-38 Stanley Cup champion Chicago Blackhawks–Top row (left to right): Earl Seibert, trainer Ed Froelich, Paul Thompson, Pete Palangio, Art Wiebe, and Cully Dalhlstrom. Center row (left to right): Mike Karakas, Oscar Hansen, Vic Heylinger, Bill Kendall, Alex Levinsky, and Doc Romnes. Bottom row (left to right): Marty Burke, Louis Trudell, Glenn Brydson, Coach Bill Stewart, Johnny Gottselig, and Mush Marsh.

becoming a fan of American hockey talent, maybe because he had witnessed the way fans worshipped Abel. Although never particularly liked by his players, McLaughlin could be considered one of the pioneers of American hockey. He did more for American players than any other owner in that era.

The Major, as he was called, was a cantankerous businessman who frequently jousted at league meetings with Conn Smythe, Lester Patrick, and James Norris. He was an idea man, a mover and shaker, far more aggressive than the conservative men who sat in the governors chairs for the other NHL teams. On some nights, he came across like the ringmaster at a Barnum and Bailey circus. That was especially true in 1937 when he announced he was planning to fill his roster entirely with American-born players, telling the *New York Times* he was going to create the "Chicago Yankees."

Since only a few American-born players had ever been thought worthy of NHL consideration, McLaughlin's idea was met with howls of laughter. Norris and Patrick filed

protests with the league, claiming this practice would create an unfair advantage for the teams that were lucky enough to have the Blackhawks on their schedule late in the season.

The Blackhawks already boasted four American-born players on their roster, although only Karakas and winger Romnes had spent all of their lives in the U.S. The other two, Alex Levinsky and Louie Trudel, were born in the United States and then moved to Canada as youngsters.

For the final five games of the 1936-37 season, Blackhawks coach Clem Louglin added defenseman Ernest "Ike" Klingbeil of Hancock, Michigan, and winger Ben "Bun" Laprairie of Sault Ste. Marie, plus defenseman Paul "Butch" Schaefer, center Milt Brink, and winger Al Soumi, all of Eveleth, Minnesota.

The all-American team had a 1-4 record during McLaughlin's experiment, recording the only win on a 4-3 decision against the New York Rangers. Patrick, who had plenty to say before the experiment, was strangely quiet after his team lost to the American squad. But overall, the American experiment hadn't been a success. The Hawks were outscored 27-14 over the five games, and Klingbeil was the only newcomer to register a point. He had a goal and two assists. None of the late-addition Americans played another NHL game.

Bill Stewart of Jamaica Plain, Massachusetts, is known more for his work as an NHL referee and major league baseball umpire than he is for coaching the 1937-38 Chicago Blackhawks to the Stanley Cup Finals.

"I think that since his team was in an American city he wanted American-born players," Dahlstrom told *The Hockey News* years later. "But he soon found out there weren't enough Americans to build one team around. I don't think it took him long to discover that."

But McLaughlin didn't surrender the idea immediately. Miffed that he had been subjected to ridicule, he made his experiment more interesting by hiring an American-born coach. That coach and several Americans, including Dahlstrom and Romnes, would help McLaughlin exact some revenge with one of the most unlikely Stanley Cup championship runs in NHL history.

The foundation of the Chicago Blackhawks' 1937-38 Stanley Cup championship season was a dusty infield, not a clean sheet of ice. Blackhawks owner McLaughlin was basking in the sun at Wrigley Field in the summer of 1937, enjoying a game between the Chicago Cubs and St. Louis Cardinals, when he realized the home plate umpire was Bill Stewart, who spent his winters as an NHL referee.

McLaughlin was keenly interested when Cardinals' manager Frankie Frisch started chirping at Stewart from the dugout. Frisch apparently didn't like Stewart's read on balls and strikes and wasn't timid about voicing that opinion.

Finally boiling over, Frisch, known as the Fordham Flash, stormed from the dugout and made a charge toward home plate. The diminutive, barrel-chested Stewart peeled off his mask and pointed it at Frisch, as if it possessed the power to stop Frisch in his tracks.

"Franklin," Stewart growled. "Turn around and head back to that dugout because I don't want to listen to you. I'll throw you right out of this game."

Frisch scowled for another moment or two before deciding retreat was his best course of action. He had scrapped with "Stumpy" Stewart before and knew Stewart didn't threaten unless he intended to follow through.

McLaughlin was clearly amused by what he had seen. "That's the man I need to run my hockey team," McLaughlin reportedly told folks who were with him. "Anyone who can handle Frankie Frisch is tough enough to handle my team."

A few days later, McLaughlin offered Stewart, forty-three, a one-year contract for $6,500 to coach the Chicago Blackhawks. But Stewart, a sharp businessman, told McLaughlin he wouldn't do it unless McLaughlin gave him a two-year deal and a promise not to meddle in coaching decisions. He knew the Major liked to tell coaches who should be playing and who shouldn't. McLaughlin was the George Steinbrenner of hockey in the 1930s. He agreed to both of Stewart's stipulations, although Stewart would discover later those promises weren't made in full earnestness.

McLaughlin knew more about Stewart's toughness than he had witnessed at Wrigley. Stewart had been a highly respected NHL referee since 1929. In 1934, Stewart had awarded the only forfeit in NHL history during a playoff game after Blackhawks coach Tom Gorman hit him. Before awarding the forfeit, Stewart jumped over the boards and chased Gorman through the Boston Garden lobby.

But Stewart's toughness was only part of the lure to McLaughlin. Stewart, from Jamaica Plain, Massachusetts, was an American, and a respected American at that. If anyone could help him develop an all-American team and keep ridicule to a minimum, it was Stewart.

Although Stewart did not bring back any of the late addition Americans from the previous season,

> After registering 10 goals and 9 assists in 48 games, Minneapolis native Cully Dahlstrom won the Calder Trophy as the NHL Rookie of the Year in 1937-38.

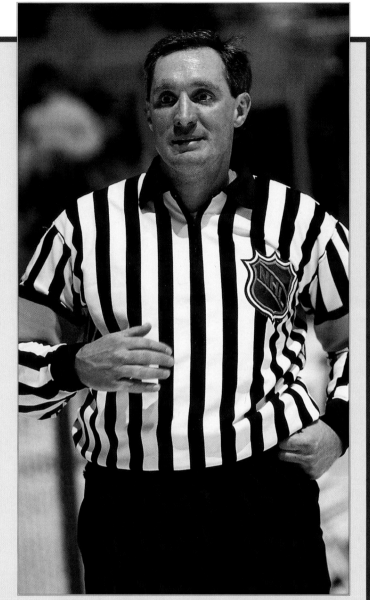

Paul Stewart appreciated the irony when his first penalty in the World Hockey League was a two-minute minor for elbowing Craig Patrick. Stewart was the grandson of Bill Stewart, the long-time NHL referee and short-time coach who guided the Chicago Blackhawks to the 1938 Stanley Cup. Patrick was the grandson of Lester Patrick, the legendary coach and general manager of the New York Rangers in the 1920s and 1930s.

Craig Patrick's father, Lynn, had been general manager of the Boston Bruins for many years. Craig's uncle, Muzz, had been the Rangers' GM in the 1950s.

"Our families had been so intertwined that it seemed right that it was an interesting coincidence," said Stewart.

Known mostly as a tough guy, Stewart's professional hockey career lasted from 1976-80. At that point, he began to seriously consider following his grandfather's career path as a pro referee. His background as a brawler certainly worked against him: there was sentiment around the league that his history would make it difficult for him to earn respect as an official. That would prove to be inaccurate.

He made it into the NHL trainee program, and worked his first NHL game March 27, 1986, as a replacement for injured Dave Newell. But his major break came that summer when an injury forced him into service as a referee in the Canada Cup championship series between Russia and Canada. The Russians had won the first game in Montreal, and Game 2 in Hamilton would be pressure-filled.

Perhaps bolstered by his deceased grandfather's legacy, Stewart had what he considers one of the best games of his life. Just as his grandfather had been, Stewart was bold enough to put the Canadians down two men with

PAUL STEWART

his penalty calls. Canada won the game 6-5, but after the game Russian defenseman Slava Fetisov skated up to Stewart and said: "Good ref."

After the game, NHL officiating director John McCauley came into the dressing room and found Stewart with tears welled up in his eyes. He knew he had made the big time, just as his grandfather had done.

"You did great," McCauley said, and then proceeded to tell him that the Russians and tournament director Alan Eagleson were talking about having Stewart do the deciding game because both teams were happy with Stewart's handling of the game.

Much to Stewart's surprise, McCauley told him: "But you aren't going to do that game because you are going to limp out of here like you are hurt, because after that game I can use you in the NHL. And we don't want anything to get in the way of that."

Stewart hadn't worked a single NHL game in the 1986-87 season and he understood some didn't want him in the league. He also remembered his father had always told him to trust McCauley. "I knew he was protecting me," Stewart said.

Stewart limped out of the arena that night, feeling better than he had ever felt before.

he ended up with a roster that was about 50 percent American-born. Goaltender Mike Karakas, forwards Roger Jenkins, Elwin "Doc" Romnes, Carl Voss, Louis Trudel, Virgil Johnson, and Cully Dahlstrom, and defenseman Alex Levinsky were all born in America. Of course, their red, white, and blue lineage wasn't exactly pure; Trudel, Levinsky, Jenkins, and Voss had spent much of their younger days in Canada.

Despite Stewart's background, he probably didn't like McLaughlin's "American-born player" concept all that much. "He believed if you could play, you could play and it didn't matter where you were from," said Paul Stewart, his grandson, who would later play and officiate in the NHL.

Ironically, the first of several arguments Stewart had with the owner was over McLaughlin's desire to trade one of the American players. McLaughlin wanted to dump Dahlstrom because he didn't believe he was talented enough. Stewart kept him anyway, and Dahlstrom went on to win the Calder Trophy as Rookie of the Year after netting 10 goals and 9 assists in forty-eight games. "My grandfather loved Cully Dahlstrom's grit," Bill Stewart III said.

The McLaughlin-Stewart relationship was probably akin to the Steinbrenner-Billy Martin relationship in the 1970s in terms of their ability to push one another's hot buttons. "When it came to final control over the players, it was stubborn versus stubborn," Bill Stewart III recalled.

Stewart undoubtedly knew what he was getting into when he took the job. But he was a tough man who believed correctly that he could handle anything McLaughlin could throw at him. Stewart viewed McLaughlin as having "a lot of dough and nothing to do with it."

Coping with McLaughlin's style was just part of being a member of the Chicago Blackhawks. Karakas once approached the Major with some suggestions about how to restructure the team to make it more competitive.

"We can be better organized," Karakas had said.

"Organized? What are you, a communist?" McLaughlin had replied.

Stewart's arrival didn't instantly trigger any magical transformation of the Hawks into a championship caliber team. Chicago's 14-25-9 record was only two points better than its mark the season before, and the Blackhawks had given up more goals than any team in the league except the Montreal Maroons.

No one anticipated what was to happen in the playoffs, least of all the players, who knew they had been outclassed in the regular season. The best-of-three quarterfinal against the Canadiens began as expected, with a 6-4 loss at Montreal. But then the Blackhawks' fortunes began to turn in game two when Karakas posted a 4-0 shutout

Goaltender Alfie Moore played a major role in the Blackhawks' 1937-38 championship. After spending the 1937-38 regular season in the minors, Moore wasn't considered a topflight goaltender. He entered the Chicago net under controversial circumstances and beat Toronto 3-1 in Game 1 of the Stanley Cup Finals.

Bill Stewart embraces the Stanley Cup at the Graemere Hotel in Chicago where some of the Chicago Blackhawks lived. With the 1937-38 Blackhawks' victory, he became the first true American to coach an NHL team to the Stanley Cup title. However, Stewart was fired the next season for not following team owner Major McLaughlin's direction on player moves.

I do know [my grandfather] said he went wild because he was really mad. He said, 'Conn Smythe screwed me.'"

Imagine the anger on the Hawks bench after the Maple Leafs scored on their first shot against Moore. But then, as it had during the entire playoffs, fortunes changed for the Blackhawks. Moore buckled down and Chicago posted a 3-1 win. Once, when Moore thought the puck was behind him, it actually hit him in the seat of his pants: that's how dramatically the Blackhawks' fortunes had changed during the playoffs.

All the screaming started anew before game two when NHL president Frank Calder ruled Moore was now ineligible because he had a contract with another team and the Hawks would have to use rookie Paul Goodman. The Maple Leafs hammered the rookie 5-1.

The Blackhawks had other problems heading into game three in Chicago. Several players had been cut by high sticks in game two. Dahlstrom had injured his knee, and Toronto's Red Horner had broken Romnes's nose in three places with the butt end of his stick. Romnes would play game three wearing a Purdue football helmet and face mask to protect the injury. Stewart asked the players not to take revenge on Horner, but he probably knew they wouldn't listen. The only good news for the Chicago Hawks heading into game three was that Karakas was going to play, although his toe wasn't close to being healed.

"It was the roughest, wildest series I ever saw," Levinsky would say years later. "The games were completely out of the referee's control and everybody skated around with his stick a mile in the air."

A record crowd of 18,402 showed up for game three at Chicago Stadium. Fans were frisked at the door because it was expected they would bring in objects to hurl at the Maple Leafs, who had bruised their Blackhawks so badly in the previous game. The fact that McLaughlin had convinced the local newspaper to publish a photograph of all the injured players at the hospital helped rile Hawks fans even more. First and foremost, McLaughlin was a showman.

Romnes, who had won the Lady Byng trophy in 1936 as the league's most gentlemanly player, wasn't gentlemanly in game three. In the first minute, the 160-pound Romnes clubbed the 200-pound Horner and knocked him out, or at least that's what the Toronto media reported. The Chicago media said Romnes missed and Horner fainted. Stewart's son, Bill II, was at the game, however, and he would tell his sons that

THE 1937-38 STANLEY CUP

Romnes "just tweaked his nose, kind of clipped him." In a letter to sportswriter Jim Proudfoot almost thirty years later, former NHL president Clarence Campbell seemed to support the notion that Horner was overcome more by fear than the actual hit.

"Without being touched, he fainted dead away and was only revived by a goodly supply of Tim Daly's smelling salts," Campbell wrote.

He also didn't seem to blame Romnes much for the incident. "In the second game, the Chicago team took a pretty good physical beating and poor Doc had his nose spread all over his face by Horner," Campbell added. "That night it was a mass of ugly green and purple and Doc was in no Lady Byng mood."

Also in that game, Romnes waylaid 200-pound Toronto defenseman Harvey Jackson. "He really laid into him," recalled former NHLer Art Coulter, who watched the game. "He knew what he was doing."

Adding insult to Horner's alleged injury, Romnes ended up scoring the game-winning goal with 4:05 remaining to give the Hawks a 2-1 victory.

Two days later, the Chicago Blackhawks won 4-1 to finish off their improbable drive to the Stanley Cup championship. The players kissed Karakas and carried Stewart on their shoulders, but in keeping within the spirit of their season, they almost dropped him.

The Blackhawks weren't able to drink from the Stanley Cup because the Detroit Red Wings, who had won it the year before, had shipped it to Toronto, fully convinced the Maple Leafs would win easily. McLaughlin was beside himself, proud that he could thumb his nose at those who said he couldn't win with American players. Nobody was laughing at him now.

When the NHL season was completed, Bill Stewart's son would meet him at the train with his umpire equipment so he could begin his baseball season.

Stewart also felt a sense of pride because, as he would tell his family later, "They were laughing at us because of our mediocre year." He is recognized as the first true American coach to win the Cup. Though Hall of Famer Leo J. Danderand, born in Bourbonnais, Illinois, was part owner and coach of the Montreal Canadiens when they won the Stanley Cup in 1924, he wasn't considered a true American because he had moved to Canada as a teenager.

But the Cup didn't resolve the differences between Stewart and McLaughlin. Even while the Hawks were polishing off the Maple Leafs, there were rumors that McLaughlin was planning to fire Stewart. He had obviously decided he didn't like a man who had the courage to stand up to him as often as Stewart did.

The Major fired Stewart in January the next season. Stewart immediately headed for Florida to wait for the start of spring training. He used the $13,000 of pay to buy a beautiful home in Jamaica Plain that still belongs to his family. He came back to the NHL as a referee and worked until 1943.

Blackhawks management wanted to announce that Stewart had resigned to keep the team's image intact—after all, they were firing a guy who took them to the championship the year before. But Stewart told the *Boston Globe* he was fired for not following McLaughlin's orders about personnel. "I've never quit on the job," Stewart said, "and I'm sure not going to start now."

The Blackhawks played poorly the next season. McLaughlin found some other American players he liked, but he never found a collection quite as good as Dahlstrom, Romnes, and especially Karakas, whose importance to the Blackhawks' triumph is often overlooked.

Chapter 4

While the world was busy extracting pure iron ore out of the countryside around Eveleth, Minnesota, the National Hockey League had began to mine a different mother lode. Eveleth's production of elite-level players is one of the great stories, if not mysteries, of American hockey history. How could this immigrant community of five thousand people send several players to the NHL at a time when American NHLers were as scarce as unchipped teeth? Crazier still, how could Eveleth High School graduates Mike Karakas and Frank Brimsek have claimed two of the NHL's six goaltender positions? A third would go to Sam Lopresti when he succeeded Karakas in the Chicago net.

"We had two indoor ice rinks and the city had tremendous interest in the sport," said Tommy Karakas, Mike's younger brother. "And baseball had a lot to do with the goaltenders. We played a lot of baseball and all had good glove hands."

Canadians never quite knew what to make of Eveleth residents entering their exclusive NHL domain. "We just considered Eveleth a province of Canada," joked *Toronto Star* hockey writer Jim Proudfoot. "In terms of climate, it was very similar."

Eveleth was actually 100 miles from Canada and 60 miles from Duluth, where pure iron ore could be shipped to all parts of the world and molded into

EVELETH'S MOTHER LODE

Entering an Exclusive Domain

Boston Bruins' All-Star netminder Frank Brimsek makes a toe save. The Eveleth, Minnesota native was named the NHL's Rookie of the Year in 1938-39 after posting a 1.58 goals-against average and recording 10 shutouts. In consideration of his high shutout total, teammates stuck him with the nickname "Mr. Zero." Brimsek played 9 seasons with the Bruins before finishing with the Chicago Blackhawks in 1949-50.

PPODROME ICE RINK
T PAUL - MINN APRIL

LARGEST IN THE WORLD
270 x 119 FEET

The Eveleth hippodrome ice rink, constructed in the early 1920s, was an ice palace in its day with seating for 3,000 spectators.

everything from automobile parts to steel casings. At one point, the Mesabi Iron Range in northern Michigan was producing 80 percent of the world's iron ore. In the 1930s, Eveleth began exporting hockey talent, as well.

Eveleth's hockey history might have begun earlier, but the first recorded game for the town was against Two Harbors on January 23, 1903. Fan response to the game led to the creation of four outdoor rinks by 1914. An indoor rink, begun in 1919, would have been finished if World War I hadn't interfered with plans.

By 1920, the Eveleth team was competing in the United States Amateur Hockey Association. Eveleth enjoyed some of the best amateur hockey in the country until 1926 when high operating costs and raids by professional teams forced teams such as Eveleth to take a lower profile.

But during the early 1920s, hockey thrived in Eveleth. The Eveleth Reds even attracted some future NHL players from outside of town, such as Manitoban Ching Johnson, who would eventually have a Hall of Fame NHL career with the New York Rangers, and Perk Galbraith, who would sign with the Boston Bruins in 1926. Sault Ste. Marie native Vic Desjardins, one of the first Americans to play in the NHL, was also on that team.

Eveleth won the USHA Group 3 title that season with a 13-1 record. Though Eveleth lost the national title to Cleveland, they did defeat the American Soo for the McNaughton Cup. Interest in hockey was so intense during that period that an estimated crowd of one thousand stood in frigid temperatures outside the Western Union office to await results of the Eveleth playoff games in Pittsburgh and Cleveland.

The scene outside the Western Union office inspired the Eveleth mayor to push for the construction of the 3,000-seat hippodrome rink, which opened January 1, 1922. On game nights, the hippodrome would be jammed with spectators, many of the youngsters sneaking in through the coal chute, or through windows or tunnels they had dug themselves. An article by Chuck Muhich in the *State Sport News* in 1953 reminisced about how the hippodrome caretaker would sometimes turn on the lights to the building hours before game time only to find one section of the stands already filled with young boys. Brimsek and Karakas could have been among those boys, watching the players who would one day make it to the NHL.

America usually celebrates Jim Craig's brilliant performance at Lake Placid as the defining moment of U.S. goaltending history, but Karakas and Brimsek won Stanley Cup championships long before Craig was even born.

FRANK BRIMSEK

Brimsek succeeded Karakas in goal at Eveleth High School where they had also been batterymates on the baseball team. Brimsek was the pitcher and Karakas was the catcher. "They were both quiet guys," Tommy Karakas said. "Neither one of them was a Dennis Rodman."

Brimsek's NHL debut would come with the Bruins in the 1938-39 season, but it was the Detroit Red Wings who first showed interest in him the season before. No draft existed in those days, and even if it had, it's doubtful Brimsek would have heard much about it in Eveleth, where people sometimes didn't pay much attention to what was going on outside their mining town. Brimsek later remembered he had been playing in the NHL for several years when a couple of townsfolk stopped him to ask, "Frankie, we haven't seen much of you lately. What have you been up to?"

"Not much, just keeping busy," Brimsek had replied.

When the Red Wings informed Brimsek that he was on their protected list, Brimsek had no idea what that meant. He showed up for their training camp, but quickly decided he wouldn't sign with them "because I didn't like Jack Adams."

Adams was the Red Wings' irascible general manager who controlled his hockey team like a bully might control the neighborhood school yard. Adams liked to rule through intimidation. "Adams had a bad habit of favoritism and I wanted no part of that," Brimsek said.

After spurning the Red Wings, Brimsek decided to play for Pittsburgh in the American Hockey League. In the Steel City, Brimsek first earned his reputation as a man of few words and bushels of toughness. Brimsek once played in Pittsburgh with an eyelid that had been sliced so severely that "I could see through it even when I closed my eyes."

His decision to sign with the Boston Bruins wasn't difficult. He liked Bruin general manager Art Ross, who was the first to sense greatness in Brimsek. But Ross still needed proof, and that was even more true for the players. Brimsek had an impressive athletic build and a ruggedly handsome Errol Flynn look about him, but he seemed too shy to be an NHL goaltender. He was too low-key, too sensitive, too quiet, too much of a brooder and worrier to survive in a world where manhood was tested nightly. How was this shy man going to replace the great Tiny Thompson who had won 233 games, posted 70 shutouts, and won four Vezina Trophies in a decade with the Bruins?

But Ross had run a test before he decided to fire Thompson and replace him with Brimsek. He shot twenty-five pucks at Thompson from ten feet, and Thompson nailed nineteen of them. He did the same with Brimsek, who snagged every puck like he was grabbing apples off a tree limb. After that display, Ross decided to sell Thompson to the Detroit Red Wings for $15,000 and insert Brimsek as the Bruins' new guardian of the corded cottage.

Even though Brimsek had performed well in the test, no one anticipated the impact he would have on the game. In his rookie season, he had a record of 33-9-1 with a

1.58 goals-against average and 10 shutouts. He also won the Calder, plus the first of his two Vezina trophies. He was tagged with the nickname "Mr. Zero" because he recorded six shutouts in his first eight NHL starts. His teammates later shortened the moniker to "Zee."

His performance shocked teammates, most of whom had never heard of Brimsek before he arrived in Boston. "His hands were like lightning—the fastest I ever saw," Ross would say later.

Brimsek played his first NHL game on December 1, 1938, at the Montreal Forum and beat the Canadiens 2-0 to start a string of four consecutive shutouts. The New York Rangers finally fired two pucks past him in his fifth game, but the Bruins still won 3-2.

Brimsek later recalled the feeling of tension he had in his first game in the Boston Garden after replacing Hall of Famer Thompson. "The crowd was so quiet that first night," he said. "I could hear them breathe and could feel their cold eyes on my back."

The Boston Bruins sold Tiny Thompson to the Detroit Red Wings during the 1938-39 season to make way for Frank Brimsek. Brimsek, from Eveleth, Minnesota, was a quiet man with many quirky habits and plenty of goaltending talent.

His teammates quickly became fond of their quiet colleague and eventually learned to be amused by his idiosyncrasies, especially his frequent medical maladies. Brimsek's pregame health was usually a barometer for how well he would play. "When Frankie said he wasn't feeling well, we knew he was going to have a good night in goal," said Hall of Famer Milt Schmidt.

Fifty years after the fact, Brimsek recalled that gamblers would ask him how he felt as he entered Boston Garden.

On more days than not, Brimsek would complain of scratchiness in his throat or sinus trouble or achiness in his body or a throbbing headache, and predict he was just hours away from coming down with the grippe.

One by one, Bruins would stop by Brimsek's locker and inquire of his health. Coach Dit Clapper had the honor of doing the final Brimsek medical update.

"How you feeling tonight, Frankie?"

"Rotten," Brimsek would say, which meant his teammates would wink at each other and congratulate one another on their good fortune.

Brimsek had many nights of feeling poorly and playing well en route to 252 career wins and a lifetime 2.70 goals-against average. "Goaltending is mostly luck," the humble Brimsek would say often.

Maurice "Rocket" Richard said Brimsek was the toughest goaltender he ever faced. "I had a lot of trouble against him," he said. "He was a stand-up goaltender and there didn't seem to be any room to shoot the puck."

Players from that era described Brimsek as being technically flawless. "You had to beat

Brimsek, because he never beat himself," said Emile Francis, who played in goal for the Chicago Blackhawks and New York Rangers.

Francis admired Brimsek enough to seek his counsel when he was struggling to keep the puck out of his net early in his career. Fraternization with opposing players was considered sinful in those days; players could be fined $100, a sizable sum in the 30s, for talking to rivals. But there were also no goaltending coaches, and Francis was concerned about his slump. He decided to take a chance, and when the two goalies passed each other in Boston Garden one night, he quietly asked Brimsek to meet him after the game.

Brimsek picked the Ironhead, a bar near the Boston Garden. When Francis arrived, he found Brimsek sitting alone in a booth near the back of the bar. The conversation went like this:

"What do you need?"

"I'm getting beat to my glove side."

"Did you play baseball?"

"Yeah, I played shortstop."

"I thought so. You're charging the puck like you're playing the infield. You have to slow down. What lie stick are you using?"

"An 11."

"Use a 13. It will stand you straighter."

Francis and Brimsek chatted briefly after that, but then quickly departed, not wanting to risk being seen. Francis said he never spoke to Brimsek again, but he appreciated the advice. "That was the answer," he said. "I started playing better right after that."

As was the case with many NHLers, Brimsek lost some time to the service during World War II. He missed the 1943-44 and 1944-45 seasons while in the U.S. Coast Guard. During his ninth NHL season in 1948, he began to hear some boo birds in the Garden even though he had a 2.72 goals-against average that season. The boos mostly reflected the fact that the Bruins weren't playing as well as they had at the beginning of his career. That season the *New York Times* carried a story suggesting Brimsek, called by *Sport Magazine* "the best goaltender in NHL history," might be slipping as he headed toward his thirty-fourth birthday. That kind of criticism was insensitive, given that Brimsek was coping with the death of his one-year-old son.

When Clapper resigned at the end of the 1948-49 season, Brimsek surprised the hockey world when he sent a telegram to *Boston Herald* sportswriter Henry McKenna in which he asked the Bruins to move him to another club.

"I was stunned to hear of Dit Clapper's resignation," Brimsek said in the telegram. "You know my high personal regard for him. Now with Dit gone, I sincerely hope management will let me go."

Today, Brimsek says the Bruins weren't really surprised by his request for a trade. He had told them two years before that he wanted to go to Chicago, where his brother John had a blueprint business.

After serving on a supply ship in the South Pacific during the war, Brimsek found that he didn't enjoy playing as much as he had before the war. "When Art Ross told me when to report after I got back, I told him I'm going deer hunting," Brimsek said.

Brimsek had occasionally talked of trying to get closer to Eveleth, and sportswriter McKenna speculated correctly that Brimsek would be sent to the Chicago Blackhawks. The Bruins wanted to trade Brimsek, not sell him, but the Hawks' general manager wouldn't part with any top player, so the two sides settled on a cash payment that was said to be largest since the Toronto Maple Leafs paid $35,000 to get King Clancy from Ottawa in 1930.

Brimsek played one season with the Blackhawks and posted a 3.49 goals-against average before heading back to Eveleth. He was elected to the Hall of Fame in 1966.

MIKE KARAKAS

Mike Karakas was known as "Iron Mike" long before Mike Ditka came to Chicago. A product of Eveleth, Minnesota, Karakas posted a 1.88 goals-against average and had two shutouts to help the Blackhawks win the 1937-38 Stanley Cup Championship. The 147-pound netminder had catlike agility around the crease.

Mike Karakas, born in 1912, was one of six brothers, five of them hockey players—four of them goaltenders. His older brother George, born in 1908, played for Eveleth in senior-league competition. But at twenty-four, he suffered an appendicitis attack. It ruptured while the family was taking him to the hospital in Duluth. He died shortly thereafter. "We thought he was even better than Mike," said younger brother Tommy.

Luke, born in 1916, played minor-league hockey in Muskegon, Michigan, and Omaha. The only winger, John, born in 1919, played for the Baltimore Blades in the American League and the Los Angeles Monarchs of the Pacific Coast League. Tommy, born in 1923, played minor-league hockey for five years, primarily in Minneapolis, Milwaukee, and Portland, Oregon. His career was interrupted by World War II. While he could have been sharpening his skills for a shot at the NHL, he was analyzing the movements of the Imperial Japanese army as a member of the U.S. Army's military intelligence. When the U.S. Marines hit the beach at Okinawa, Tommy Karakas was there with them.

Mike Karakas was signed by the Blackhawks for the 1935-36 season. He posted nine shutouts and boasted a 1.91 goals-against average, earning the Calder Trophy as NHL Rookie of the Year. As the NHL's first number-one American goaltender, his sphere of recognition expanded beyond the normal bounds of hockey. Several media outlets, including the uppity *Colliers* magazine, took notice of his arrival. *Colliers* did a four-page spread on Karakas entitled "Yankee Invasion." His notoriety also prompted General Mills to put his face on a Wheaties box. "It wasn't like today, getting a deal with Nike," brother Tommy said. "I think we just got to eat a lot of Wheaties."

The highlight of Karakas's hockey career was the 1937-38 championship when he helped the Blackhawks win the Stanley Cup after a disastrous regular season. Karakas didn't enjoy his finest regular season either. In the playoff series against Montreal and the New York Americans, Karakas posted a shutout in both second games after the Blackhawks lost game one. He had a 1.88 goals-against average in the playoffs and 1.00 goals-against average in the finals. He might have been the playoff's most valuable player had an award been given. (Awarding the Conn Smythe Trophy didn't begin until 1966.) "I think they had to be the worst team in NHL history to win the Stanley Cup," Tommy Karakas said.

Neither Brimsek nor Karakas were large goalies: Brimsek was 5-foot-9, 170 pounds, and Karakas was probably an inch taller and weighed 15 to 20 pounds less. They came from the same program, but their styles were different. Brimsek relied on his positional play and the excellent glove hand he had developed on the Eveleth diamond.

"Mike was a little more adventurous," Tommy Karakas said. "He would go halfway to the blue line to get the puck, and he had a tremendous glove hand. When it came to crunch time, he could always do it."

During the 1936-37 season, Boston Bruins' great Eddie Shore said Karakas was the NHL's best goaltender. Karakas had 22 career shutouts for the Blackhawks in an era when the team's talent level was not impressive. Chicago sportswriters nicknamed him "Iron Mike," presumably because he didn't miss a regular season game in his first four seasons.

Away from the rink, Karakas was best known for having the world's only golf ball–retrieving cocker spaniel. The dog's name was Goalie, and Karakas trained him to fetch golf balls thrown under the bed. Eventually, Karakas realized Goalie could be extremely valuable on the golf course.

Karakas would pretend to throw a ball in the woods, and Goalie would fly into the woods and hunt until he found a lost golf ball. If a ball went in the water, Karakas would throw a stone into the water, and Goalie would paddle out, then go under to get the ball. "A golf pro in Hershey, Pennsylvania, offered him $2,500 for the dog," Tommy Karakas said.

Mike rejected the offer and eventually raised other cocker spaniels to do the same work.

Karakas took his NHL life in stride until the Blackhawks sent him first to Montreal and then to the minors in Providence. When he was first sent to the minors, they asked him to play for $75 a week. He had been making five times that as an NHLer for the abbreviated worked year. He knew he was paying the price for the Hawks' poor performance because it was easier to move him than the other fifteen guys. "He was ticked," his brother Tommy remembered.

Mariucci may have been particularly incensed that game because Gordie Howe had checked Doug Bentley into the boards after the whistle. Max Bentley went after Howe, and Red Wings captain Sid Abel had gone after Max. That scenario probably didn't sit well with Mariucci, who was very protective of his teammates.

His fight with Stewart resumed in the penalty box and spilled into the players' corridor. When it was over, Mariucci had to pass the Red Wings' bench to get to the Chicago Stadium dressing room. Detroit coach Jack Adams cussed him out every inch of the way, but when Adams's assistant, Johnny Mowers, started riding him, Mariucci had heard enough.

"He had one punch left and he landed it on Mowers," Francis said.

Not many in his era were tougher or as loyal to teammates as Mariucci. After he left the NHL, he ended up playing for St. Louis in the American Association, where every young tough guy wanted to prove himself against Mariucci. One incident occurred during an exhibition game in Barrie, Ontario. A rookie rapped him on the head with his stick, but Mariucci, probably growing weary of having to whip every gunslinger on the planet, didn't respond. When the young pup smacked him again, Mariucci dropped his stick and went after him. Mariucci was in such a rage that the rookie fled for his life. Sugar Jim Henry opened the door to the bench to offer the kid safety, and the guys kept Mariucci at bay until he was cooled off.

After the game, Mariucci told Springfield coach Earl Seibert, whom he knew from his days with the Hawks: "Do me a favor and don't play that kid against us tomorrow, or there will be a dead pigeon on your hands."

Shortly thereafter, there was a knock at Mariucci's door, and Mariucci found the rookie standing before him. "I want to apologize for my actions, Mr. Mariucci," he said. "And my coach said I should ask you if it would be all right for me to play against your club tomorrow. I promise to behave myself."

Mariucci retired after the 1947-48 season and went on to leave a more significant imprint on the game as a coach than he did as a player. He fought for the advancement of the American player just as ferociously as he fought Stewart that day.

Other players from Eveleth include Joe Papike, who played part of three seasons with the Blackhawks but never quite earned the status of full-time player. In the 1940-41 season, he managed two goals and two assists in 10 games with Chicago.

Eveleth-born Aldo Palazzari's career ended prematurely and tragically when the speedy left winger lost his left eye as a result of an injury suffered at the New York Rangers' training camp in Winnepeg just prior to the 1944-45 season.

Defenseman Manny Cotlow, a Minnesota native who was trying out for the Rangers, was on the ice when the accident occurred. "Hank Goldup went around him and his stick came up and got him," Cotlow said. Palazzari's eyeball had ruptured.

Cotlow said he turned away. "I couldn't stand to look at something like that," he said.

In Palazzari's one NHL season, split between the Bruins and Rangers, he had eight goals in 35 games, a respectable total for a first-year player. His son, Doug, would carry on the Eveleth tradition by making the St. Louis Blues roster in 1974.

Eveleth was also the home to John Mayasich, a member of the gold medal–winning 1960 U.S. Olympic team, and Mark Pavelich, who played for the 1980 gold medal team. Goaltender Willard Ikola, a star at the University of Michigan and goaltender on the silver medal-winning 1956 U.S. Olympic team, was also from Eveleth. Other Eveleth players, Milt Brink, Rudy Ahlin, Al Souci, and Butch Schaefer, had brief tours of duty with the Blackhawks.

American hockey talent today is stretched across the map. But fifty years ago, there was no question that Eveleth, Minnesota, was the hockey capital of America.

Yale, or St. Lawrence could go to the NCAA tournament. Boston University and Boston College officials believed they should go because their teams had more wins. But Jeremiah noted that all four teams had similar loss totals and ordered the playoff. Boston University and Boston College refused to participate.

"[Jeremiah] held to this honest, courageous stand despite some violent opposition," Princeton coach Dick Vaughn said at the time.

Snooks Kelley, coach at Boston College, was overcome with emotion the night he and Jeremiah faced each other for the final time as adversaries during the 1966-67 season. Jeremiah was dying from cancer in his final season at Dartmouth.

"I really feel badly about Jerry leaving the game," Kelley told Boston reporters. "When they made him, they threw the mold away. He's to college hockey as Ted Williams was to baseball. I call him Mr. Dartmouth."

JOHN MARIUCCI

Mariucci's fighting days weren't over when he hung up skates for the last time. He began using words instead of his fists.

Mariucci became coach at the University of Minnesota in 1952 and won 215 games there before leaving fifteen years later. He then took a job with the Minnesota North Stars. His rough-and-tumble demeanor often masked what his friends considered his gentle soul and kind heart. He was a strange blend of intellect and toughness, a man who could speak four languages, yet still seemed to enjoy a good scrap now and then.

"He loved art and knew a lot of history," remembered Jack McCartan, who played for him at Minnesota and on national teams. "We would be in Europe, riding on the bus, and he would be lecturing us on the history of the area, just like he was a teacher."

The University of Minnesota's new ice rink, named after legendary coach John Mariucci, opened in 1993.

But Mariucci's lifelong fight, the crusade that consumed the last thirty-eight years of life, was the battle to gain respect for the American hockey player. No coach in America fought that battle with more passion and ferocity than Mariucci. He brought a missionary zeal to his work, whether he was preaching the importance of the Minnesota high school program or explaining yet again why he primarily recruited Americans.

"People thought he was anti-Canadian," said Herb Brooks, who played and coached under Mariucci. "But he wasn't. He was a visionary. He believed in the American player."

His close friend, Bob Ridder, called Mariucci "the noblest Roman of them all," a line borrowed from Shakespeare's "Julius Caesar." And yet, Mariucci didn't mind poking fun at himself. He would talk about how many of his ex-players were all making plenty of money in the real world.

"Why don't I make any of the money," he would muse. "I should have listened to myself."

One of his players' favorite memories of Mariucci came when he coached the 1956 U.S. Olympic team. Before the team landed in Europe, Mariucci spent an inordinate amount of time preaching the importance of keeping track of one's own luggage. Mariucci said he didn't want to have to wet-nurse anyone on this trip. Every man should keep track of his own belongings. He didn't want to wait for someone who couldn't keep track of his own stuff.

"Of course, when all of the bags came down," player John Mayasich remembered, "the bag that was missing belonged to Mariucci."

As a coach, Mariucci was more of a motivator than a strategist. His temper would sometimes get the best of him on the bench. If a player made a mistake, he would bench him, putting him in the back row.

Former Minnesota player Lou Nanne recalled a game against Michigan when Mariucci called for the next pair of defensemen, and nobody jumped on the ice.

"Where are my defensemen?" Mariucci bellowed.

"We are all here in the back row," Nanne replied. Mariucci had forgotten that he had benched all of his remaining defensemen.

Nanne said many times that Mariucci influenced his life more than any other person except his parents. He loved Mariucci like a father, which meant they did not always agree.

John Mariucci (center) was known as the "Godfather" of Minnesota hockey. He is one of four players elected to both the Hockey Hall of Fame and the U.S. Hockey Hall of Fame. The others are Hobey Baker, Frank Brimsek, and Moose Goheen.

Five for the Ages

At the 1975 World Championship in Vienna, the two men fought on the bench during the game. Mariucci didn't like the way Nanne was playing, and for some inexplicable reason, he began swatting him on the back of the head. Nanne took it for several seconds before he began wrestling with his mentor. While the game went on around them, the players pulled them apart. Realizing the press was going to quiz him about it, Nanne called Mariucci and asked him what he should tell the media.

"Tell them the truth," Mariucci said. "Tell them that's just the way our relationship works."

Nanne also remembered when Mariucci was an assistant coach with the North Stars and Wren Blair was coach. After the team had arrived home from a long West Coast road trip, Blair ordered a practice for nine o'clock in the morning. That morning, Mariucci put all of his players on the bench and launched into a round of storytelling, interrupting himself with a whistle he blew every minute. Finally one of his players asked him why he was blowing the whistle.

"In case Wren is listening I want him to think I'm putting you guys through stops and starts," Mariucci said.

Mariucci was most proud of his allegiance to the Minnesota high school hockey program. He's considered the Godfather of Minnesota hockey. In 1952, when Mariucci started trumpeting the state's high school tournament, it was drawing 15,000 fans. At the time of his death in 1988, the state tournament attendance had topped more than 100,000.

During his tenure with the Minnesota Gophers, he brought in only a handful of Canadian players, insisting it would destroy high school hockey if he didn't give the vast majority of scholarships to Minnesotans.

"If I didn't give scholarships to Minnesota kids where would they go to play?" Mariucci would say.

At Mariucci's funeral, Nanne said: "You can talk about Clarence Campbell, Rocket Richard, Gordie Howe, and Walter Brown. Mariucci is right up there with them when it comes to having an influence on the game."

In nominating Mariucci for the Hall of Fame, USA Hockey president Walter Bush said, "In 1952, if we had gone to Madison Avenue to find a way to spread the growth of hockey in the United States, we would have hired John. But we were lucky. He did it all for the love of the game."

JACK KELLEY

Coach Jack Kelley

Jack Kelley was to college hockey in the 1960s what Vince Lombardi was to the NFL. Kelley was probably the toughest, most competitive, and most successful coach in college hockey. He ran his practices like a drill sergeant preparing troops for combat. In fact, Pittsburgh Penguins owner Howard Baldwin, an ex-Marine who had tried unsuccessfully to play for the Boston University team, said of his first Kelley practice: "I felt like I was back in basic training on Parris Island."

Most players started out detesting Kelley and his marathon practices, but gradually they learned to respect his methods. He was professional in his preparation and relentless in his dedication.

"He was tougher than anyone imagined," said Boston University coach Jack Parker, who played for Kelley from 1965 to 1968. "The all-out work ethic, the duration of

Herb Brooks led the University of Minnesota to three NCAA championships before being named the head coach of the U.S. Olympic team.

practices, the number of wind sprints. He was a pain, but most of us understood we weren't going to get better coaching."

In 10 seasons at Boston University, starting in 1962, Kelley had a record of 208-80-8. Of those 80 losses, 29 came in the first two seasons when Kelley was implementing his program.

"When he came on the ice, the jabber, the noise, it all stopped," said his son David E. Kelley, a Hollywood writer and producer. "A hush fell over everyone."

Kelley and Cornell's Ned Harkness are credited with ending the western teams' dominance of college hockey. Kelley finished his career at Boston University by winning NCAA titles in 1971 and 1972, the last college team to win back-to-back titles.

At the time Kelley was winning his second title, 28-year-old Baldwin, whom Kelley jokingly insists "cut himself" at Boston University years earlier, was financing a new team in the World Hockey Association called the New England Whalers. He brazenly asked one of college hockey's most successful coaches to join this new league that NHL executives were arrogantly predicting would drown in a sea of red ink.

"He was a big name in Boston," Baldwin said. "I felt he was a very innovative coach. He was the kind of man I wanted."

The WHA was turning to many college coaches. Bob Johnson had said no thanks to the Raiders. The Philadelphia Blazers had offered 1972 U.S. Olympic coach Murray Williamson $60,000 to coach; Williamson thought the situation was too unstable. But Kelley, who really had nothing left to prove at the college level, agreed to a two-year contract with Baldwin and the Whalers.

"I remember the only argument was I wanted the payroll to be $650,000 and he wanted it to be $700,000. Now you couldn't get a second-rate defenseman for that," Baldwin said.

Kelley did bring along his Boston University captain, John Darby, but he didn't load up on college players the first year. He had some NHL veterans, including Boston Bruins standout Teddy Green. By his own admission, Kelley needed to adjust his style for the pros. He tells the story of the Whalers making their first road trip, and he gathered the players all around him and gave every one a rundown of what time the buses would be leaving, when meals would be served, and when curfew would be.

As he was wrapping up his itinerary, Rick Ley, who had already played four seasons in the NHL, raised his hand with a question.

"Coach," he deadpanned, "what kind of pajamas should we wear?"

Kelley later chuckles at the memory. "They let me know quickly that pros expected to be treated differently than college players," he says.

In his first season of professional hockey, Kelley guided his team to the World Hockey Association championship. But the following season, he turned the team over to Ron Ryan and went to Colby College to coach because he liked the college game better than the pro game.

"My father loved to teach as much as he loved to coach," David Kelley said. "His frustration was that he never got to teach enough. He could never get his power play to be as effective as he wanted it because he couldn't have enough practices. There were too many games."

Now sixty-nine, Kelley is still active in hockey, working for Baldwin again as a consultant for the Pittsburgh Penguins.

HERB BROOKS

While Kelley was making his pro debut in the WHA, Herb Brooks was establishing himself as a rising star among American hockey coaches.

After succeeding Glen Sonmor as head coach of the high-profile Minnesota program at the start of the 1972-73 season, Brooks led the Gophers to NCAA championships in 1974, 1976, and 1979. Along the way, he earned a reputation as an innovative coach whose style seemed to combine the best of North American and European hockey.

But even with his impressive credentials, Brooks wasn't the first choice to coach the 1980 U.S. Olympic squad. At best, he was the third choice, and even that is open to debate. First, Harvard's Bill Cleary turned down the job, then Michigan Tech's John MacInnes declined for health reasons. But even then, it was no "lock" that members of the selection committee would appoint Brooks, even if he did have impressive credentials.

Brooks never liked the politics of hockey and had battled with the Amateur Hockey Association of the United States over how to develop players. Brooks always liked to set his own brisk cadence, figuring correctly that success was the best defense of his methods. Ironically, USA Hockey president Walter Bush, who in recent years has debated with

Coach Herb Brooks

Brooks about the direction of American hockey, was among those who supported Brooks. Having watched Brooks win the three national titles at Minnesota, Bush was confident Brooks was the man for the job. He certainly hadn't seen a more organized coach.

"When Herb came in for an interview, he already had a folder an inch thick full of information he had compiled," Bush said.

What Brooks would accomplish for the United States over the next year—culminating in the gold medal triumph at Lake Placid—was clearly the most high-profile coaching achievement in American hockey history. He molded a team of college players into a unit that would beat the world's best team. His 1980 Olympic team beat the Soviets, who may have been as talented as any NHL team with the exception of the New York Islanders.

Brooks bullied his players, cajoled them, dazzled them, and occasionally even made them laugh. But what he did primarily was prepare them to play the best game of their life at precisely the right time. The Soviets were known for their conditioning, but Brooks skated his players to the point where they could have skated from Lake Placid to Moscow if the world had frozen. In fact, if all the skating done during the pre-Olympic practices was added together, the American players may have actually skated that far. Brooks also developed a style of hockey that was designed to counter whatever the Soviets threw at the Americans.

"It was a hybrid," Brooks said. "It was the best of the Europeans and the best of the Canadians. In the worst case scenario, you always had the North American style in your back pocket. If it all unraveled, we could still play dump and chase."

Sometimes players hated Brooks for the mind games he played with the team. But in the end, they realized that he had mentally hardened them for the impending battle. Brooks always had a reason for doing what he did, whether it was threatening to cut Mike Eruzione or riding Rob McClanahan. Mostly, he was looking for ways to unify the team, even if that unification came at the expense of liking him as a coach. "I was always looking for the moment to solidify this team," Brooks said.

When the United States defeated the Soviets in the semifinals, he showed a brief moment of emotion and then left the ice, saying later that the moment belonged to his players.

After the U.S. defeated the Finns to win the gold medal, it was presumed that Brooks would end up in the NHL. Rumors circulated that he would replace Fred Shero in New

York, but instead Brooks went to Switzerland to coach where the pace would be less strenuous. "I was dead tired, out of gas," Brooks said. "I needed to recharge my batteries."

In 1981, Rangers general manager Craig Patrick, who had been Brooks's assistant in Lake Placid, hired Brooks as head coach. Even though this ascension was expected, it was still noteworthy. The NHL still hadn't embraced the idea of a coach stepping directly from college to the big leagues. Jack Kelley had enjoyed some success in the World Hockey Association, but Ned Harkness's move from Cornell to the Detroit Red Wings coach and general manager hadn't worked as well.

Rangers veterans were certainly skeptical about the move, especially since Brooks brought in a style that was completely foreign to most of them. With Shero, practices had been short and conditioning had been lax. With Brooks, practices were long and conditioning was torturous.

Rangers' players didn't initially accept Brooks's ideas on conditioning and offense. One of his favorite practice exercises was to get his players to skate three laps around the rink in 45 seconds. "Reijo Ruotsalainen would lap me," former NHLer Tom Laidlaw recalled.

Players, especially veterans such as Carol Vadnais and Eddie Johnston, had trouble adjusting to Brooks's offensive style, which required players to circle back to get the puck.

Laidlaw, who was in his second season with the Rangers in 1981, was quickly singled out for special abuse by Brooks. When Laidlaw arrived at training camp fifteen pounds overweight, Brooks skated him mercilessly.

Laidlaw's attempts to lose weight to please Brooks became a source of team humor. Once he opened his door to find a room service meal with one slice of white bread and a glass water. His teammates, who sent him the meal, were laughing hysterically down the hall.

Brooks wanted to transform Laidlaw into one of the NHL's best stay-at-home defensemen. "Tommy," Brooks said at one practice, "if you ever have the puck, give it to someone else, because you shouldn't have it."

Brooks had plenty of rules that were difficult for some of the veterans. For example, he liked his players to be in the dressing room forty-five minutes before a practice was to begin. That rule in particular drove Ron Duguay batty. Even though he would arrive forty-five minutes before practice, he would wait in his car until he was officially late. That was his form of protest.

Early in the season, Duguay had written a check for $1,000 and given it to Brooks. "This is for the fines I know I'm going to get," Duguay said. "When I use that all up, let me know and I'll write you another check."

Brooks also liked to conduct a 45-minute meeting after practice. He knew darn well he didn't always have an attentive audience. Privately, he joked about the players' complaints that he used forty-five minutes to say what should take two minutes.

Behind the bench or in practice, Herb Brooks motivated his players mentally and emotionally to obtain the maximum effort required to beat the Soviets.

The hockey community was stunned when the Calgary Flames hired American college coach Bob Johnson to be their new coach in 1982-83. Before Johnson and Herb Brooks landed NHL head coaching jobs a year apart, the league had rarely given college coaches a chance at the professional level.

"When someone asks me what time it is," Brooks said, "I usually tell them how to build a watch."

Brooks lasted until his fourth season with the Rangers before Patrick went behind the bench to replace him. But Brooks left a mark on the game, and other coaches paid attention to what he was doing with his offensive game plan.

"I hated him when he first got there," Laidlaw said. "But I realize now how much he helped me become a better player. He was just ahead of his time. If he came along today, he would be a great NHL coach."

BOB JOHNSON

The season after Brooks started in New York, his archrival, Bob Johnson, left the University of Wisconsin to become coach of the Calgary Flames. The hiring raised some eyebrows because this was a Canadian team hiring an American coach. And Johnson wasn't like Brooks, who for all of his modern approaches to the game didn't spare the rod when dealing with the players. Instead, Johnson was a rah-rah guy who tried to get the most out of his players by making practices fun and entertaining.

"He was the most positive man I ever met," said Cliff Fletcher, who made the decision to hire Johnson.

Like Brooks, Johnson came to the NHL with three NCAA championships to his credit. He had won in 1973, 1977, and 1981, endearing himself to Wisconsin fans forever. They called him Badger Bob, which through the years was shortened to just Badger. He had also coached the USA Olympic team at Innsbruck in 1976, losing a bronze medal through a loss to the Germans.

When he arrived at Calgary, his players didn't know what to think of a coach who looked at each practice session as if it were one of life's great adventures. Was he for real? Could anyone be this infatuated with hockey? What they discovered was that Johnson adored being at the rink. His passion for hockey was second to none, and his meticulous notes scribbled on legal pads were as much a part of his coaching look as a coat and tie.

"He loved the game," said Ken Johannson, a close friend of Johnson's for thirty-five years. "If there was as much written about hockey as other sports, Bob would be listed with John Wooden or Bobby Knight or Don Shula—coaches of that ilk."

Johnson was a master motivator. He dressed up practice goaltenders in Oilers attire so the players could visualize knocking the puck past Edmonton nemesis Grant Fuhr. He took them to see the "Karate Kid" movie to show them someone overcoming adversity to succeed. He planned bowling tournaments and used animal parables to explain the importance of conditioning.

"The lion is king of the beast," Johnson would say. "But if you go to the zoo, you see when he wakes up, the first thing he does is stretch. We can learn from the animals."

When the Flames were having difficulty containing the jet-propelled rushes of Oilers' defenseman Paul Coffey, Johnson surprised the team at practice by commanding his players to leave the ice and take off their skates. With three players left on the ice ready to simulate how Coffey and his teammates were breaking out of their zone, he led the group on a forced march to the upper reaches of the Saddledome so they could get a better perspective on Coffey's breakout rushes. Johnson figured that from 100 feet up, the Flames could see what Coffey was doing.

Johnson also liked to take his team to movies on the day before a game. "It was like a big field trip to him," said *Toronto Sun* writer Steve Simmons, who knew Johnson as well as any member of the media. "That's when I think he was happiest. He always considered himself a teacher."

He brought players together frequently for meetings, often to talk about the power play, which he considered the difference between winning and losing.

Bob Johnson (left) and long-time friend Ken Johannson (right).

Bob Johnson's Pittsburgh Penguins won the Stanley Cup in 1990-91, making Johnson the first American head coach to win the trophy since Bill Stewart won with Chicago in 1937-38.

"I wore out two sets of goalie pads just going to all of his meetings," Don Edwards said.

Johnson actually had a chance to join the professional ranks ten years before he signed with the Flames. In 1972, the New York Raiders of the World Hockey Association tried to coax him away from Wisconsin with a lucrative contract. Johnson opted for the security over the quick hit.

"My lawyer advised me that it was a shaky situation," Johnson told a *Calgary Herald* hockey writer in 1982. "I had no desire to coach pro then and I guess I didn't miss anything. I understand the Raiders moved three times in one year."

Johnson hadn't actually set out to be a hockey coach. He had been an excellent baseball prospect in Minneapolis, signing with the Chicago White Sox organization. When he didn't make it in baseball, he turned to hockey. He never lost his love for the sport.

"Truth is, Bob may have been an even better baseball coach than he was a hockey coach," said two-time Olympic hockey coach Dave Peterson.

If that's true, Johnson probably could have been another Tommy Lasorda or Sparky Anderson. People enjoyed hearing him talk and appreciated his optimism.

At one point, in 1986, the Flames had just lost their 10th consecutive game on a 3-1 decision. Chins were on the floor, faces were glum, and attitudes stunk. Lanny McDonald said it seemed as if the weight of the world was on every player's shoulders when Johnson bounded into the dressing room like he had just won the lottery.

"Boys," he said, "the slump is over because Jim Peplinski scored our goal tonight. That's our breakthrough."

The next game, Peplinski scored the winning goal, and the slump was broken.

In 1986, Johnson was faced with a difficult choice. He was sixty years old, and USA Hockey had offered him a chance to be the organization's executive director. Though he wasn't ready to stop coaching, he knew the job probably wouldn't be open when he was ready.

Johnson resigned in Calgary and threw himself into the office work, just as he had the coaching. He waved the U.S. flag proudly, often pontificating about how hockey would be changed if the sport could attract more premium athletes. He would watch a Monday Night Football game and wonder how the football players would fit into an NHL team's hockey lineup.

"What kind of hockey player would Bo Jackson make?" Johnson would ask. "Probably, a tough, high-scoring center. Three out of four kids who try hockey like it. But most of them never get exposed. We need more rinks in this country."

But Johnson really didn't enjoy being strapped to a desk, and more important, he wasn't done coaching. "He was like a caged lion in an office," said Brad Buetow, who was coaching Colorado College at the time.

When Craig Patrick offered Johnson the job as Pittsburgh Penguins coach, he jumped at the opportunity. He thought from the beginning that this Mario Lemieux-led team could win the Stanley Cup quickly. The Penguins were a veteran team, but they instantly took a liking to Johnson, who knew how to handle stars as well as how to teach young players.

He would walk into the dressing room before a game, spot Lemieux, and commence his speech. "Here's my guy getting a rub down, getting his back ready to go, he'll be banging along the boards, his legs will be going," Johnson would say.

Assistant coach Barry Smith said he sometimes would get frustrated because Johnson always saw the silver lining and never entertained the idea that something was going wrong.

"We're not working that hard today," Smith would say.

"Barry, the ice is bad," Johnson would say. "Bad ice. We can't handle the puck. We can't move the biscuit the way we want to."

Detroit Red Wings coach Scotty Bowman, the winningest coach in NHL history, said he admired the way Johnson believed that he could turn average or below-average players into good players. Bowman was the director of player development in Pittsburgh when Johnson arrived.

"He loved [Penguins winger] Jay Caufield, even though Jay wasn't a great hockey player," Bowman remembered. "He thought if he could have gotten Jay Caufield earlier in his career, he could have made him into a good player. And maybe he could have."

Johnson made no secret of being pro-American, although it didn't seem to color his coaching, except that he liked to bring in players he knew and he knew plenty of Americans.

"We took a lot of heat for having American players," Barry Smith said. "Every time we would get another player, everyone would say here comes the American flag. But really, he was like most coaches in that he liked good players who could handle the puck."

Johnson liked coaching in a working-class city where the media and fans adored him and his ideas. Often he and Smith would stay late to watch an NHL game on the satellite dish, and then Johnson would drag his assistant out for a late snack. He would always pick a working-class bar where he could get an Iron City beer and a sausage. "This is a steel town and we have go to a steel town bar," Badger would say.

"He would walk in and they would all cheer him," Smith said. "He would sit with all the guys in hard hats and say, 'Let's talk hockey.'"

In the 1990-91 season, Johnson led the Penguins to the Stanley Cup championship, becoming the first American coach to win the trophy since Bill Stewart won in 1938. Johnson was pumped up by the experience and was looking forward to coaching the United States at the Canada Cup. That August, while with the team, he became ill. The diagnosis was a malignant brain tumor.

He never stopped being positive. Less than thirty-six hours after surgery for a brain tumor in August of 1991, he sketched out a strategy for the U.S. team to deal with the Swedish fore-checking system in the opening game of the Canada Cup hockey tournament.

A few months later, he died in Colorado Springs. His motto had always been: "It's a great day for hockey." That certainly wasn't true on the day Bob Johnson passed away.

THE 1948

As athletes from all over the world gathered in St. Moritz to compete in the 1948 Winter Olympics, none realized his or her participation was being jeopardized by a war for dominance. Behind closed doors, Walter Brown, vice president of the Amateur Hockey Association of the United States, had locked horns with International Olympic Committee president Avery Brundage. The issue: which hockey players would represent the U.S. in St. Moritz. In a calculated move, Brundage had knowingly allowed two American teams to show up in St. Moritz, believing it was time for him to battle the AHAUS, a fight he expected to win.

Brundage, a pompous administrator who was often accused of trying to run the International Olympic Committee like a dictatorship, had resented the International Ice

Chapter 6
OLYMPICS

A Defining Moment for AHAUS

The United States scores against home-standing Switzerland in the 1948 Olympic Winter Games.

Hockey Federation's decision to recognize AHAUS as the controlling body for the U.S. Olympic hockey team. In Brundage's opinion, AHAUS's registration of senior men's teams smacked of professionalism. He loathed that senior players were often paid, even if the money was shelled out under the guise of reimbursing players for wages they lost by playing hockey. He wanted the Amateur Athletic Union (AAU) to run the show, even though some players on the AAU team had also played under the same reimbursement plan. "Some of the players on the AAU team can't in good conscience take the Olympic oath, not as we see it," Brown told Brundage.

Although the 1948 U.S. Olympic team unofficially finished fourth, their performance did include victories over Poland, Italy, and Sweden.

Brundage was never timid about initiating a scrap. But he had a worthy opponent in Brown. Brown was the president of the Boston Bruins, Boston Celtics, and the Boston Garden, and more important, he had transacted many deals with European rink owners and was well-known and admired in Europe. In 1931, he had handpicked players to tour Europe. The trip would include playing in the World Championship. Brown's Boston Olympics squad, or the Massachusetts Rangers as they were known in Europe, won the 1933 tournament in Prague. Brown had continued the practice of handpicking players for a European tour through 1936 when he was manager of the Olympic team in Garmish, Germany.

Brown came back to manage the United States entry for the 1947 World Championship in Prague. International Ice Hockey Federation members had voted overwhelmingly that AHAUS, not the AAU, be recognized as the master of USA's Olympic hockey program. Brundage seethed over the vote and sent out word that he didn't intend to accept the IIHF decision.

Controlling the Olympic team was an important issue for AHAUS officials, who were finally starting to feel their clout expanding. Starting in 1920, hockey had been controlled by the United States Amateur Hockey Association, but that group was disbanded in 1926. No organization had seized control until the AAU took over in 1930. In the interim, the United States didn't participate in the 1928 Olympics and 1930 World Championship. The AHAUS organization was founded on October 29, 1937, at Madison Square Garden in New York, when representatives from fourteen teams in the New York Metropolitan, Michigan-Ontario, Eastern Amateur, and International Leagues agreed to a national affiliation. The AHAUS's first president was Thomas F.

Lockhart, who had been coaching the New York Rovers in the Eastern League. During his AHAUS career, Lockhart also served as business manager for the New York Rangers.

Lockhart's vision of a formal national youth program really didn't occur until 1947 when Minnesota formed its own association and joined AHAUS. The addition of Minnesota added credibility to AHAUS and significantly increased membership. (Of the 131 teams AHAUS registered in 1947 and 1948, 36 percent were located in Minnesota.) After Minnesota joined AHAUS, Bob Ridder, who was a radio executive and the Minnesota Hockey Association's first president, quickly became an important figure on the national level.

The Olympic controversy took shape the year before the Games. In 1947, Dartmouth standout Jack Riley read an article in a newspaper stating the winner of the AAU tournament would represent the United States at the 1948 Olympics. He asked his coach Eddie Jeremiah to enter the Dartmouth team, but Jeremiah declined. Riley took matters in his own hands and convinced several Dartmouth players to enter the tournament as the Hanover Indians. They won the tournament and expected to be the Olympic team.

Walter Brown was a kingpin in American hockey from the 1930s into the 1960s. In 1948, Brown was vice president of the Amateur Hockey Association of the United States (AHAUS). He was instrumental in convincing the International Olympic Committee to permit the AHAUS team to play in the 1948 Olympics.

The following year, Riley was surprised to receive a letter inviting him to the AAU's Olympic tryout. He talked to Walter Brown, who told him to put together an AHAUS team to compete in the Olympic Games.

"If you get the players, I guarantee you will play," Brown told Riley.

Riley wanted to bring along his brothers, Billy and Joey, but Brown said he didn't want players with college eligibility remaining. That didn't make Riley happy because he considered his brothers to be two of the best players in the country. His brother Billy is still Dartmouth's all-time leading scorer with 228 points, and Joey totaled 116 points in two seasons. In one game against Princeton, he had six goals and four assists.

Riley's team set sail for Europe three weeks before the Olympics in order to have time to play exhibition games. When Riley arrived, an Associated Press reporter, Ted Smith, informed him there was another U.S. team representing the AAU already there and that his brothers were on the roster.

That was not all true. Billy Riley wasn't there because his wife, knowing Jack's AHAUS team would probably play, wouldn't let him go on what she called "a three-week soiree."

"We were still sure we were going to play because there was no way the Europeans were going to go against Walter Brown," Riley said.

Although Brundage had assured the AAU players that they would be playing, he began saying that maybe both teams should be barred. According to Olympic rules, a team was supposed to play only when it was recognized by its national governing body and its international federation. Each team had only one of the required stamps of approval.

A Defining Moment for AHAUS

Moreover, because the Swiss organizers also backed the AHAUS team, Brundage threatened to pull the entire American delegation out of the Olympic Games if the AHAUS team played. That infuriated the Swiss, who had sided with AHAUS because they badly needed the hockey gate receipts and knew Brown was Pied Piper to the European hockey federations. Brundage's threat to turn the Olympics into a shambles over one team must have seemed ludicrous to the Swiss.

But Brundage's entrenched stand didn't surprise the AHAUS officials. "He didn't seem to like hockey, or the Winter Games," Ridder said. "But he didn't hate us as much as he hated the skiers. He considered them an abomination."

Dartmouth player Whitey Campbell, a member of the AAU team, had seen plenty as a tailgunner in World War II, but he had never seen anything quite as bizarre as this political cesspool. "It was embarrassing," Campbell said. "The whole world was mad because we were doing our laundry internationally."

Brown, an important friend of European rink owners, asked local rinks to deny practice time to the AAU team. Campbell's team was able to secure some practice time on some natural ice, but they were allowed on the ice only after figure skater Dick Button had finished his practice routine.

Meanwhile, Brundage was doing all that he could to make sure the AAU team was recognized as the official Olympic team. Although the AAU team had received shoddy equipment before the trip, they did receive the official Olympic pins and the fine white USA team jackets.

Riley, a U.S. Navy bomber pilot during the war, didn't appreciate the treatment he was receiving. "They are acting as if we are the Japanese navy invading them," he growled.

Ever confident, Riley suggested that the two American teams could play each other, with the winner going to the Olympics. Nobody liked that idea, and the bickering continued until the International Olympic Committee decided two days before the Games that both teams would be banned. That didn't stop the debate. Brown pushed hard against the committee's decision. Just past midnight on the eve of the opening ceremony, the IOC officials finally accepted that the AHAUS team was going to play.

AAU players awakened the next morning not knowing what happened in the middle of the night. They still believed they might compete and were told to march in the athletes' parade.

"We marched to the outside ice arena and there before our eyes was the other [U.S.] team getting ready to play Switzerland," Campbell said. "That's when it dawned on us that we probably weren't going to get to play."

Campbell was one of three Dartmouth players on the AAU team. Four other Dartmouth players were members of the AHAUS team. When the controversy finally ended, Campbell went up into the stands and cheered for the AHAUS. "There was no bad feeling, because they were all our buddies," Campbell said.

The soiree that Billy Riley's wife feared then came to pass. AAU players immediately began to ski and party in the beautiful Swiss Alps. Campbell was there about a week until the Dartmouth athletic department notified his coach that Campbell and his teammates should report back to school.

The AAU players had an easier time on the slopes than the AHAUS team had on the ice. After the first game, the International Olympic Committee decreed that the 1948 hockey games wouldn't be considered an Olympic event. No medals would be awarded. The AAU players were told they would be considered Olympians. But the news didn't surprise or overwhelm the AHAUS players. "What the hell was a gold medal," Riley said. "None of us knew anything about medals. We just wanted to play."

Amid the turmoil, the U.S. team played poorly in their opening game and lost to an inferior Swiss team 5-4. Back in sync, they won over Poland, Italy, and Sweden. By then, emotions had cooled, and the politicians agreed to a compromise that allowed the Olympic results to be counted if the Americans didn't win a medal. On the final day of the hockey competition, the Americans lost 4-3 to the Czechs in a game that decided the bronze medal. The Americans unofficially finished fourth.

"I still think if we would have sent out the Dartmouth team we would have won the tournament," Campbell said.

Jack Riley was a member of the U.S. hockey team that got to play at the 1948 Olympic Games in St. Moritz. His brother, Joey Riley, was on the team that didn't play.

As part of the compromise after the 1948 Games, Brundage insisted that the 1952 Olympic team be formed by an eight-man committee. Four members were named from the U.S. Olympic Committee: Daniel J. Ferris, Asa Bushnell, W. E. Moulton, and Eddie Jeremiah.

Representing AHAUS were Brown, Bob Ridder, Fred Edwards, and Leonard Fowle. The group decided Ridder should be general manager and Eveleth's John "Connie" Pleban should be the coach.

Ridder's take-charge approach strengthened AHAUS's reputation in the hockey world. He organized a very successful, well-financed trip for the 1952 Olympic team, including a string of exhibition games to pay for the USA's participation in Oslo, Norway. Ridder even had the Americans play an exhibition game against the Boston Bruins, which was certainly a novel idea at that time.

Some of the exhibition games were against college teams, who were far less concerned about the bottom line than they are today. This was before NIKE deals, equipment contracts, and logo licensing. This was before colleges distinguished between revenue sports and nonrevenue sports.

"I remember we played Michigan and we were supposed to share the gate," Ridder recalled. "But they said, 'Oh, hell, why don't you take the whole thing?' "

The 1952 team won the silver medal at Oslo, and Ridder and Pleban earned high praise for their efforts. "What I learned in 1952 was that nobody complains about success," Ridder said.

Ridder had become an important player in AHAUS. He was invited back to be general manager of the 1956 team, and he and John Mariucci led the team to the silver medal. The stability of Ridder's leadership, with Brown working in the background, helped the American program recover quickly from the embarrassment of the 1948 mess in St. Moritz. The Americans were now looked upon as a well-organized power on the international circuit.

After the embarrassing controversy in St. Moritz in 1948, Bob Ridder was assigned to keep the peace in the next two Olympic Games.

AHAUS's youth hockey movement was also on the move, although not quite at the same pace. AHAUS president Thomas Lockhart, a former cyclist and track-and-field competitor, had organized the Eastern Amateur Hockey League in 1932 and had correctly realized that hockey wasn't going to grow nationally without a strong governing body. However, it took Ridder's Minnesota Hockey Association to spark the youth movement. By 1949, AHAUS was sponsoring national youth tournaments.

Minnesota's important role in the growth of national youth hockey is ironic, since the state's program wasn't nearly as large as it had been prior to World War II. Hockey historian Don Clark, a pioneer in the Minnesota program and a past president of the organization, said Minnesota was the nation's hockey hub in the mid-to-late 1930s. For example, the 435 teams registered in the state for the 1935-36 season was a number that put Minnesota not far behind some of Canada's major metropolitan areas. But then the war took away coaches, fathers, organizers, players, and interest in the game.

By the 1950-51 season, Minnesota was up to 560 teams again, although only 101 chose to register with the Minnesota Hockey Association and AHAUS. It was still an uphill battle for Lockhart, Ridder, Clark, and others to convince team managers that the two dollar per team cost to join AHAUS was worthwhile. Slowly, teams began to see the benefit of national insurance, unified age groupings, and uniform rules, among the other benefits and services AHAUS offered. But it certainly didn't occur overnight. At one point in the early 1950s, only seven teams were registered in New York. Even by 1959, the AHAUS had only 720 registered teams, and 26 percent were located in

Minnesota. It took about twenty years to reach the then attractive goal of 1,000 registered teams.

One of AHAUS's problems in that time was a lack of publicity—ironic since Brown and Lockhart both had reputations as promoters. Even some of AHAUS's members weren't sure exactly what the organization was doing, or where it was headed.

In 1955, Walter Bush, a former Dartmouth player fresh out of law school, decided to drive from Minneapolis to Duluth to attend an AHAUS meeting at the Spalding Hotel. He attended only to determine why the AHAUS was claiming two percent of the gate receipts for his Minneapolis Culbertson's senior team. He didn't know the meeting would alter the course of his life.

Ridder was impressed with Bush and told Brown that he believed Bush had some potential to be a mover and a shaker

(Left to right) Bill and Bob Cleary, along with Walter Brown, Jack Kirrane, Jack Riley, and Dick Rodenheiser.

in the organization. In 1959, Bush, only twenty-nine at the time, was named general manager of the USA National Team. That same year, he become a member of AHAUS's board of directors, a position he has held continuously since then.

In 1964, the AHAUS suffered a loss when Walter Brown died unexpectedly in Hyannis, Massachusetts. For more than thirty years, Brown had been an important figure in the USA's involvement in international hockey.

To be sure, Brown was a promoter and businessman, a man who once invested $1,000 in the Ice Follies and helped transform it into a national investment. (His minimal investment was worth $100,000 when he finally got around to selling his stock years later.) He helped bring Bob Cousy to the Boston Celtics and broke the color line in professional basketball by bringing in Duquesne's Chuck Cooper.

Brown was a colorful character, full of laughter and savvy in the ways of the world. During the depression, he turned down a gift of a Rolls Royce because he didn't believe it was proper for folks to see him driving a Rolls at a time when many were unemployed. An extremely generous man, he always had a few dollars for every cause.

"Walter Brown was a great, but humble man, one characterized first and last by human kindness," said Asa Bushnell of the U.S. Olympic Committee.

After the announcement of his death, statements of remorse came from all over the world. American League president Joe Cronin called him "one of the finest and greatest men I ever knew."

"If you could model your friends, Walter Brown would be the ideal," Montreal Canadiens' managing director, Frank Selke Sr., said at the time.

Brown's death left a huge hole in the AHAUS organization. Though Brown was officially AHAUS's vice president, he had also been an unofficial guru for the organization. Everyone turned to Brown whenever there was a problem. "He had also financed a lot of teams when there were no funds available," Walter Bush said.

It was impossible to replace Brown, who was loved as much by the Europeans as he was by the Americans. "But after 1964, people started calling Ridder when they had a problem," Bush said.

In 1972, William Thayer Tutt succeeded the retired Lockhart as AHAUS president and pushed the idea that the organization needed to be operated more like a business. Tutt, whose family owned the Broadmoor Hotel, had a strong international background, having spent twenty-seven years as a member of the International Ice Hockey Federation's world council. His international affiliation began in 1959 when he had successfully bid for the 1962 World Championship to come to his Broadmoor World Arena in Colorado Springs. The Americans won the bronze medal that year, although the absence of the Russians and Czechs for political reasons had weakened the field.

Walter Bush is the current guiding force of USA Hockey.

Under Tutt's command, AHAUS brought in Hal Trumble as executive director in 1972. Trumble was a prominent IIHF referee and an experienced administrator. He managed the 1972 U.S. Olympic team before taking the job as AHAUS executive director. The Minnesota North Stars, with Bush as president and as one of the co-owners, provided office space for Trumble at the Met Center. But the following year, Trumble and Tutt moved AHAUS to Colorado Springs, partly to honor the U.S. Olympic Committee's desire to have all the national governing bodies located around the Olympic headquarters and partly because Trumble liked the idea of working in Colorado. Tutt also liked the idea of having his administrator working out of his hotel.

Tutt's keen interest in international hockey helped fuel the organization's increasing involvement in international competition. Tutt had been the first to invite Soviet teams to this country in the 1960s. He also hired Art Berglund, a former Colorado College scoring leader who would play an integral part in the development of American hockey over the next twenty years. In 1977, when AHAUS sent its first official American team to the World Junior Hockey Championship, Berglund, who was then managing Tutt's Broadmoor World Arena, was named manager of that team.

American hockey players' involvement in the tournament for the best teenage players actually began three years before when a Midwest Junior Hockey League All-Star team represented the USA in Leningrad. One of the players on the USA squad was Paul Holmgren, who would go on to play and coach in the NHL. Members of that team were picked by coaches John Mariucci and Murray Williamson, with sportswriters Charlie Hallman and John Gilbert. The second World Junior Tournament was officially held in

Winnipeg in 1978, although four games were played at the Met Center in Bloomington, Minnesota. The American roster was again filled by players from the Midwest Junior Hockey League, which is now the United States Hockey League and was started by Walter Bush and Murray Williamson.

When AHAUS decided to send teams in 1977, it looked to expand the player pool, particularly to the college ranks where many of the top 19-year-olds were already playing. But, as Berglund later recalled, it was a very difficult sell to college coaches, who were reluctant to loan their players to the national team, even though they would miss only a few games. To fill the roster that season, Berglund even had to bring along a player from the Dartmouth junior varsity team.

The World Junior Tournament has aided the development of such prominent NHLers such as Brian Leetch, Doug Weight, Mike Richter, Tony Granato, and others. But the American public still hasn't shown much interest in it, even though it was played in Massachusetts in 1996.

"In Canada, junior hockey means one step from the NHL," Berglund said. "In the United States, junior hockey means young kids playing hockey. People here don't know what it is."

Berglund, who helped start the concept of elite summer camps for the United States top 15-, 16-, and 17-year-old players, has been general manager of twenty United States national teams. He has also helped develop U.S. coaches. NHL and college coaches such as U.S. National and Olympic women's coach Ben Smith, Minnesota's Doug Woog, Yale's Tim Taylor, and Anaheim's Ron Wilson and Walt Kyle, got a boost in their careers when Berglund recommended them for United States National coaching positions.

Berglund received the Lester Patrick Award for his contributions to American hockey. Born in Fort Frances, Ontario, he is an American citizen and no one is more emotional about American hockey than Berglund.

"I'm just starting to heal from the bruises I got watching the USA-Russia game with him at the World Junior Championship in 1995," said USA Hockey's public relations director, Darryl Seibel. "Art Berglund was helping [goaltender] Doug Bonner make every save. He must have pounded on my arm fifty times as Doug Bonner successfully held off the Russians in that game. I guarantee you that the most exhausted member of Team USA after that game was Art Berglund."

One of the ironies of Berglund's passion for American hockey is that his position sometimes makes him the villain, or at least a controversial figure. Because he puts together the USA teams, he has always been open to second-guessing by NHL scouts, all of whom have opinions.

"In our office, it's been said that Berglund is like Jerry Lewis," Seibel said. "He's appreciated more in Europe than he is in his own country."

In 1986, Walter Bush succeeded Tutt as president of AHAUS. "If you had a vote to determine what nonplayer has had the most influence in American hockey in this century, Walter would probably win the thing," said USA Hockey executive director Dave Ogrean.

Bush has an air of aristocracy mixed with a gifted legal mind, a razor-sharp business acumen, and a collegial attitude. He's an idea guy and quite comfortable in social settings. In many respects, he is like his mentor, Walter Brown.

It's difficult not to like Bush, unless you stand in the way of something he is trying to accomplish. On the nineteenth hole, he's gallant, noble, and a first-rate storyteller. Behind closed doors, he's a warrior. At age sixty-seven, when others are drifting into retirement, Bush has actually stepped up his pace on the international front, playing major roles in women's and in-line hockey as the International Ice Hockey Federation Vice President.

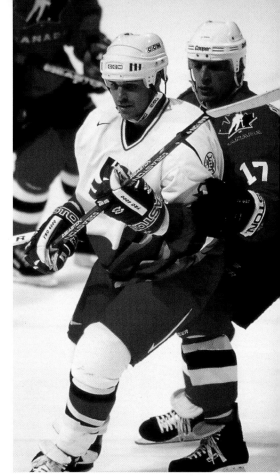

Since 1977, USA Hockey has sent teams to compete in the World Junior Championship, the result of which has been the development of promising National Hockey League players such as Doug Weight.

Bob Johnson remained committed to promoting American hockey at all levels, including youth programs. When he left USA Hockey to coach the Pittsburgh Penguins, he greeted his successor, Baaron Pittenger (above).

"Some have the impression that Walter is a bon vivant who likes to crack a lobster, crack a beer, and crack a golf ball more than 200 yards," Ogrean said. "He does like all of that. But as a president, he's not lost even an inch off his fastball. He's an astute politician whose influence in hockey circles is enormous. It's almost impossible to describe how much he contributes to hockey in America."

USA Hockey vice president Ron DeGregorio, also a close friend of Bush, remembers when he, Bush, and Tony Rossi, a member of the executive committee, discussed hiring Dave Ogrean in 1993. The committee was having difficulty choosing between Ogrean and Brian Petrovek, who had been a vice president of marketing for the New Jersey Devils.

"It's too bad we can't hire them both," DeGregorio said.

Bush mulled it over for just a moment. "Maybe we can," he said. That July, Ogrean and Petrovek came in together as executive director and assistant executive director, respectively, to operate USA Hockey.

In 1996, Bush showed no signs of wanting to retire, although it was clear that he was grooming DeGregorio to eventually replace him.

"[Bush] is a man of boundless energy," DeGregorio said. "I don't like it when I have to be in Toronto and Detroit on consecutive days. He doesn't mind going to Russia for a two-hour meeting."

In 1986, Bush was in Mexico on vacation when he received word that Trumble was leaving AHAUS to join former NFL coach George Allen to set up a sports training academy in California.

When Bush got off the phone, he turned to his wife, Mary, and asked her, "If you could pick one person in the world to be executive director, who would it be?"

"Bob Johnson," she said without hesitation.

The timing couldn't have been much better because Johnson was in the midst of a 10-game losing streak. But he still needed to be talked into the move, even though he had long before viewed the job as one he would like to have later in his career. Johnson's arrival gave the organization increased visibility and perhaps changed the focus ever so slightly toward hockey matters, rather than organizational matters. Johnson was a hockey guy, not an administrator. He was far more concerned about the quality of American goaltenders than about which insurance carrier the organization should choose.

One of his first acts was to get the organization to change the name from Amateur Hockey Association of the United States to USA Hockey, a move his staff applauded.

"I know he was bothered once when he gave his business card to someone on an airplane and they thought AHAUS was a construction firm," Bush said.

It was a simple move, yet it was a step that suggested that the organization was ready for another growth spurt. "When you would call someone and said you were from the Amateur Hockey Association of the United States—by the time you got that all out, you forgot why you had even called," Berglund said.

Another aspect of the name had bothered Berglund for a while. Americans didn't view the word "amateur" with the same hallowed respect that Avery Brundage had for the word. To Brundage, the word meant players weren't paid to be athletes. "But to the public, 'amateur' means not as good," Berglund said. "When you say someone is an amateur in this country, what you are saying is they don't know what they are doing."

Bob Johnson never lost his enthusiasm for promoting American hockey, but it was clear to him early on that he didn't enjoy the politics or the paperwork. More important, he missed coaching. "He was born to be a coach," Bush said. "The only thing I asked him was that if he got a deal he couldn't turn down, to let me know. And he did."

When the Pittsburgh Penguins called, Johnson left in 1990. He was replaced by Baaron Pittenger, who had recently retired from the U.S. Olympic Committee, where he spent 14 years, the last as its executive director. Pittenger held the USA Hockey post until June 24, 1993, when Dave Ogrean took the job. Ogrean had been AHAUS's public relations director from 1978 through 1980, and supervised the official scorers at the 1980 Winter Olympics in Lake Placid. After that, he spent the next thirteen years at ESPN, the College Football Association, and the U.S. Olympic Committee.

An ambitious, progressive administrator with all-star people skills, Ogrean marshalled in a more diversified game plan for the organization. The days of USA Hockey representing only young male ice hockey players were over. Females were starting to play the game with increasing frequency. More and more coaches and referees were joining. And finally, the organization was now registering in-line hockey players.

At the beginning of the 1990s, USA Hockey had a membership of about 200,000. By 1996, that number had risen to more than 500,000. When Trumble had moved the USA Hockey office from Minneapolis to Colorado Springs, all he needed was an office in the Broadmoor for him and a secretary. As of 1996, USA Hockey had forty-five employees.

USA Hockey's program had come a long way since the day Lockhart and his cronies came together in 1937, or even since Ridder and his Minnesota friends met in St. Paul in 1947. With 29,749 registered teams in 1997, USA Hockey had far more teams than anyone had envisioned so many years before. But Ogrean wanted more success from those teams, so he and Vice President and International Council Chairman Ron DeGregorio pushed for the naming of a new national coach whose job would be to improve the international level players. With the support of Bush and DeGregorio and others, membership approved the plan.

Jeff Jackson, who had guided Lake Superior State University to two NCAA championships in the 1990s, was hired as the organization's first permanent national team coach. His plan was to organize and coach two year-round national under-eighteen teams. One of his missions would be putting the USA's program on even ground with the Canadians, who pounded the Americans for many years in international competition.

With more players playing hockey, particularly in the south, there was reason to believe that was possible. It seemed more possible after the 1996 World Cup.

After guiding Lake Superior State University to two NCAA championships in the 1990s, Jeff Jackson became USA Hockey's first permanent national team coach.

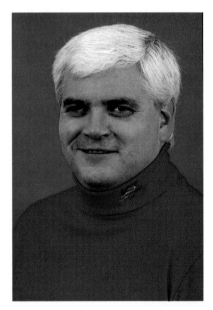

THIS IS USA HOCKEY

USA Hockey, Inc., is the national governing body for the sport of hockey in the United States. As such, its mission is to promote the growth of hockey in America and to provide the best possible experience for all participants by encouraging, developing, advancing, and administering the sport.

Headquartered in Colorado Springs, Colorado, USA Hockey is the official representative to the United States Olympic Committee (USOC) and the International Ice Hockey Federation (IIHF). In this role, USA Hockey is responsible for organizing and training men's and women's teams for international tournaments that include the IIHF World Championships and the Olympic Winter Games.

USA Hockey also coordinates activities with other national hockey federations around the world and, closer to home, works with the National Hockey League (NHL) and the National Collegiate Athletic Association (NCAA) on matters of mutual interest.

USA Hockey is divided into 11 districts throughout the United States. Each district has a registrar to register teams, a referee-in-chief to register officials and organize clinics, a coach-in-chief to administer educational programs for coaches, a risk manager to oversee liability and safety programs, and an initiation program administrator to facilitate learn-to-play programs for youth players and their parents.

For the player, USA Hockey annually conducts regional and national championship tournaments in various age classifications, sponsors regional and national player identification and development camps at the United States Olympic Training Centers and other facilities, studies and makes recommendations for protective equipment, distributes Hat Trick, Playmaker and Zero Club awards, and provides an insurance plan.

For coaches and officials, USA Hockey conducts clinics and produces training manuals and videos through the Coaching Education Program and the Officiating Education Program. These programs enrich the knowledge of coaches and officials through careful study, training and examination. USA Hockey also promotes uniformity in playing rules and the interpretations of those rules.

USA Hockey has not forgotten parents, supplying this vital segment of the hockey family with a "Parent's Introduction To Youth Hockey" brochure, which includes tips on buying equipment, rules of the game, and the role of parents in youth sports.

USA Hockey also publishes *American Hockey Magazine*, the main communication vehicle for the organization which is sent to the household of every registered member as a benefit of membership.

In December 1994, USA Hockey introduced its official in-line hockey program-USA Hockey InLine-to provide structure and support for the growth of the sport across America. Through valuable membership packages, which include an annual subscription to *USA Hockey InLine Magazine*, competitive playing opportunities, and a variety of educational programs, USA Hockey InLine is dedicated to providing a positive experience for all participants.

USA Hockey serves as a clearinghouse for information to assist local organizations in finding solutions to problems at the grassroots level and annually publishes an "Official Guide" of the USA Hockey by-laws, rules and regulations, officers, board of directors, affiliate associations, and national staff.

THE USA HOCKEY BOOM

Skating Past the Nineties

Looking at the consistently rising numbers for both individual and team registrations, it becomes quite obvious that hockey in the United States is growing rapidly. In the 1990s, these numbers have grown in great strides. In just the last six years, 11,933 teams and 217,334 individuals have become part of USA Hockey. Women's/Girls' teams have quadrupled from 149 teams to 710 teams.

USA Hockey Individual Registration

YEAR	PLAYERS	COACHES	OFFICIALS	TOTAL	+/-
1996-97	383,624	46,473	19,071	449,168	+26,393
1995-96	363,259	43,094	16,422	422,775	+20,242
1994-95	350,007	38,688	13,838	402,533	+55,519
1993-94	303,611	30,985	12,418	347,014	+49,296
1992-93	263,873	23,057	11,788	297,718	+56,237
1991-92	230,201	N/A	11,280	241,481	+36,040
1990-91	195,125	N/A	10,316	205,441	—

USA Hockey first began individual membership registration in 1990.

USA Hockey Team Registration

YEAR	SR./ADULT (OVER 18)	JUNIOR (17-19)	YOUTH (17-UNDER)	WOMEN'S/ GIRLS'	SECONDARY/ COLLEGE	TOTAL	+/-
1996-97	4,238	138	22,502	910	1,961	29,749	+2,847
1995-96	3,948	132	20,385	710	1,727	26,902	+2,347
1994-95	3,641	127	18,865	498	1,424	24,555	+3,405
1993-94	3,434	186	16,046	352	1,132	21,150	+2,513
1992-93	3,089	133	14,026	269	1,120	18,637	+1,966
1991-92	2,663	141	12,646	232	989	16,671	+1,702
1990-91	2,335	204	11,602	149	883	14,969	−325

With the 1994 addition of its official in-line hockey program, USA Hockey InLine, USA Hockey is also providing structure and support for the growth of in-line hockey across America. During the 1996-97 season, USA Hockey InLine saw its membership grow to include more than 85,000 players, coaches, and officials, along with more than 650 leagues.

Chapter 7
USA'S OLYMPIC HOCKEY

A Japanese Bonanza

One hockey game at the 1972 Sapporo Olympics taught 16-year-old Mark Howe as much about history, international politics, and jingoism than he would ever learn at Southfield Lathrup High School in Michigan. He remembers his wise and mature older buddy, Robbie Ftorek, nineteen, insisting they watch the Czechoslovakia-Soviet Union game.

"To this day, I've never seen a hockey game more brutal than that," Howe said later. "The Czech goalie must have broken five sticks over Russian players."

The game was the first Olympic meeting between the two countries since Soviet tanks had invaded Czechoslovakia in 1968 to quash the democratic groundswell that was growing in Prague and other Czech cities. Late in the third period of the 1972 game in Japan, with the Soviets winning 5-2, the Czechs won a faceoff in the Soviet zone. Instead of firing at the Soviet net, Czechoslovakia's best player, Vaclav Nedomansky, turned and rifled the puck into the Soviet bench—a final act of defiance from a very proud man.

International ice hockey's long history of patriotism, passion, and fierce competitiveness is sometimes lost on Americans. The American public still owns the 16-year-old Howe's naiveté about international hockey politics and does not truly appreciate that the

emotional investment other countries put into the sport significantly exceeds our own. Theories abound on why America hasn't had more hockey success on the international stage, but no one disputes that the public doesn't pay enough attention. It's no coincidence that the two international hockey events that stirred Americans' passions most were the 1960 and 1980 Olympics in which U.S. teams won gold medals on their own soil.

The World Championships and World Junior Championships have always seemed more important to the Canadians and Europeans than they have to American fans. But that only partly explains why the United States' results in international competition have

Defenseman Jim McElmury celebrates a goal by Robbie Ftorek (middle). At age twenty, Ftorek, a center, was one of the youngest players on the 1972 U.S. squad. He would go on to become a star in the World Hockey Association.

Mark Howe was just 16 years old when he played for the 1972 U.S. Olympic team that won a silver medal in Sapporo, Japan. By 1980 (above), Howe was already in his seventh professional season and a member of the NHL's Hartford Whalers.

been a mixed bag—glorious highs like gold medals in 1960 and 1980 folded into many torturous lows, such as a 34-year medal drought at the annual World Championships from 1962 to 1996 or the two medals in nineteen years won at the World Junior Championships.

The World Championships, the crowning event of the European season, is a footnote to the Americans. Most players don't appreciate how big the event is until it's too late.

"Canadians are held to a higher standard than we are. They know everyone in their country is watching them," said Ron Wilson, coach of the 1996 U.S. National Team. "We don't think anyone here cares."

Wilson, who played on three U.S. National Teams and coached two others, was struck by the difference in attitude between the Canadians and Americans after the 1996 World Championship. The Canadians had won the silver medal, and the USA had won the bronze—their first medal at the World Championship since 1962.

"We were real proud of winning the bronze medal," Wilson said. "And I saw [Canadian] Paul Kariya and he had the silver medal, and basically that wasn't good enough for him."

Wilson said during the 1996 World Championship that the Team USA general manager, Mike Milbury, a former ESPN analyst who is now general manager of the New York Islanders, convinced ESPN to show scores and highlights on SportsCenter.

"As dumb as this sounds, it really made a difference to the players," Wilson said. "They knew people back home were going to see how they were doing. Players just couldn't say it was no big deal, because people could see that it was a big deal. I think they played better."

Although America's record at the World Championships has been abysmal, its Olympic record is actually better than it appears at first glance. The USA won medals in seven of its first eight Olympic appearances. (They might have won eight of nine if they had been able to raise enough money to attend the 1928 games in St. Moritz.) The Americans had won back-to-back silver medals in 1952 and 1956 before winning the gold in 1960. Howe's 1972 team won the silver medal in Sapporo, Japan, behind the brilliant goaltending of Mike "Lefty" Curran, and coach Bob Johnson's 1976 team finished fourth, losing the bronze on the final day through a loss to Germany.

Only since the Miracle of Lake Placid in 1980 has the U.S. team struggled in Olympic hockey. That's expected to change now that NHL players are competing. The American team should be among the favorites at the 1998 Games in Nagano, Japan. Here's a review of the United States' Olympic participation before 1960:

• **Antwerp, Belgium (1920):** The Winter Games weren't officially added to the Olympic docket until 1924, but the United States did compete in the unofficial Olympic Games in Antwerp. Canada and the United States were by far the most dominant teams. The Americans defeated Switzerland 29-0 in one game. At one point, the Americans had hoped to send only players born in the USA. But realizing their talent level wasn't all that strong, they decided to send some Canadians who were playing for U.S. teams. That's why some talented Canadians like Herb Drury and Frank A. Synott appeared on the U.S. roster. Drury would end up playing in the NHL. The USA's best player was Moose Goheen, who might have been the best player in the tournament. Canada defeated the USA 2-0 in the semifinals en route to the gold. The Americans won the silver.

• **Chamonix, France (1924):** Future NHLer Clarence "Taffy" Abel would help the Americans win the silver medal by scoring 15 goals as a defenseman. But Drury, whose Pittsburgh team would join the National Hockey League the following year, led the Americans in scoring with 22 goals in five games.

• **St. Moritz, Switzerland (1928):** General Douglas MacArthur, then chairman of the United States Olympic Committee, made the final decision not to send an American hockey team to the Games. The University Club of Boston had a very strong team, with future NHLers like George Owen and Myles Lane on the roster. But the team couldn't scrape together the cash needed to make the trip. Several college teams were approached, but only Augsburg College of Minneapolis seemed willing to go. According to research by hockey historian Donald Clark, MacArthur decided that Augsburg, led by five Hanson brothers, "was not representative of American hockey."

• **Lake Placid (1932):** By this time, the Americans had enough talent to discontinue the practice of using a few Canadians to fill the roster. The Americans sent a team of Eastern All-Stars and won a silver medal in a very weak field of entrants. Only Poland and Germany sent teams to be whipped by the Canadians and Americans. Some interesting politics did occur in 1932 because the U.S. Olympic Committee had asked the Amateur Athletic Union (AAU) to take charge of ice hockey. The committee believed the U.S. Amateur Hockey Association had evolved into a weak functioning body. This development would be important in years to come.

The 1932 team was coached by former Harvard coach Alfred Winsor, who had left his mark on hockey in another way. Winsor has been credited with being the first coach to station his defensemen side-by-side, instead of one behind the other. He figured correctly that the side-by-side positioning was better suited for shutting down the always improving passing game. Before 1917 when Winsor made the switch, the thinking was that the first defenseman (known as the point) would meet the forward coming down the ice, and the second defender (known as the counterpoint) would be the safety valve. That system, however, would break down when a clever puck-handler, such as Hobey Baker, simply skated around both defenders.

The 1936 U.S. Olympic hockey team won a bronze medal in Garmish, Germany.

• **Garmish, Germany (1936):** The increase in worldwide interest in hockey was evident when fifteen teams arrived to compete in Garmish. The USA won the bronze medal, despite the fact it gave up only one goal in the final round. The Americans tied Great Britain 0-0, downed the Czechoslovakians 2-1, and then lost to the Canadians 1-0 in a game that featured sixty minutes of overtime. Among those on the American roster was John Garrison, who had played a major role in helping the USA win the 1933 World Championship in Prague along with Gerry Cosby who, as goalie, gave up just one goal in five games.

• **St. Moritz, Switzerland (1948):** The United States' hockey medal streak ended amid the confusion of two teams sent to Switzerland. The Amateur Hockey Association of the United States (AHAUS) had taken root, and it had sent one team to the Games. The AAU had also sent a team. The U.S. Olympic Committee recognized the AAU team, but backed off that stance when the International Ice Hockey Federation threatened to withdraw hockey

Members of the 1952 U.S. Olympic team board a Strato Clipper Pan Am flight to Oslo. Climbing the stairs (left to right): General manager Bob Ridder, Connie Pleban, Reuben Bjorkman, Ken Yackel, Andy Gambucci, John Noah, Arnold Oss, Robert Rampre, James Sedin, and Allan Van.

from the Winter Games if the AHAUS team was not allowed to play. This would be a defining moment in AHAUS history. Among those who would play on that AHAUS team was Jack Riley, coach for the USA Olympic team in Squaw Valley twelve years later.

• **Oslo, Norway (1952):** Having resolved its political differences through a compromise, the USA sent a strong team to Norway and won the silver medal. The Americans finally earned a tie with the Canadians. But a 4-2 loss to the strong Swedish team kept the Americans away from a gold medal. Among the players on the American roster was Len Ceglarski, who went on to have a successful coaching career at Clarkson and Boston College. At Boston College, Ceglarski would continue Snooks Kelly's tradition of recruiting only American players. Also on the American roster was goaltender Dick Desmond, who had played on the strong Dartmouth team, plus Allan Van of St. Paul, Minnesota, whose seven appearances on national teams tie him with Herb Brooks and Mark Johnson for second place on the all-time list. The leading scorer on the U.S. team was Ken Yackel.

The 1956 U.S. Olympic team that competed at Cortina, Italy. Front row (left to right): Frank O'Grady, Bill Cleary, Weldon Olson, John Matchefts, Kenneth Purpur, Dick Meredith, Willard Ikola, and trainer Benny Bertini. Middle row: Manager Bob Ridder, Wimpy Bartnett, Jack Petroske, Captain Gene Campbell, Don Rigazio, John Mayasich, Dick Dougherty, and Dick Rodenheiser. Back row: Coach John Mariucci, Don McKinnon, Wendy Anderson, Gordon Christian, and Ed Sampson.

• **Cortina, Italy (1956):** The Americans, coached by feisty John Mariucci, defeated the archrival Canadians 4-1, but the Soviets arrived to begin their long dominance of international hockey. Two years earlier at the World Championships, the Soviets had the best collection of pure skaters the world had ever seen. They had stunned the Canadians with a 7-2 win in the championship game. The Americans, who hadn't sent a team to that championship, had seen the Soviets at the 1955 World Championships where the Soviets posted a 3-0 win. At Cortina, the Russian power play was too much for the Americans, and they fell 4-0. The Americans were awarded the silver medal, thanks in no small part to the goaltending of Willard Ikola, another player from the Eveleth goaltending factory. Ikola became one of the most successful Minnesota high school coaches, posting a 616-149-36 record and winning eight state titles at Edina High School. Also on the team were John Mayasich, Dick Meredith, and Bill Cleary, who would also play for the 1960 team, plus Wendell Anderson, who would go on to be governor of Minnesota. Among the top players on the 1960 squad was John Matchefts of Eveleth, who was a superb college player at Michigan. He went on to coach at Colorado College and the Air Force Academy.

The 1972 team's accomplishment in Sapporo was considered remarkable at the time because the United States National Team had finished last at the 1971 World Championships. The Americans needed a 5-3 win against Switzerland in a pre-tournament game just to qualify for pool play. The 1972 team never seemed to get the recognition it probably deserved. "We were sandwiched between the boys in '60 and the boys in '80," Curran said years later.

America had the youngest team it had ever brought to the Olympic Games. It included teenagers like Howe and Ftorek, plus a 20-year-old named Henry Boucha, who had been a Minnesota high school legend. It was a team with heart and character, exemplified

Henry Boucha (10) and Keith Christiansen (8) buzz around the Czech goaltender during USA's 5-1 win in Sapporo. Boucha is considered one of the most talented players ever to come out of hockey-rich Minnesota.

by players like Stu Irving, who was in the U.S. military on a combat assignment when he was asked to play for the U.S. Olympic team, and Ron Naslund, who was a quiet leader. The squad also had scorers, such as Tim Sheehy, Kevin Ahearn, and Keith Christiansen.

These players all wanted a spot on that team badly. There was no waffling from these guys about whether it was best for their potential pro careers. Backup goaltender Pete Sears, another Vietnam veteran, quit his job to play for the team.

The gold medalists in 1972 were the Soviets, many of whom played in the famous 1972 Summit Series against NHL All-Stars. Those NHL All-Stars would need a late goal by Paul Henderson to win that eight-game series 4-3-1.

The 1972 Americans lost 6-1 to the Soviets. "It was the best game we played against the Soviets in seven or eight years," coach Murray Williamson said.

Curran's 51-save performance in a 5-1 win against Czechoslovakia was on par with efforts turned in by goaltenders Jack McCartan and Jim Craig in the gold medal-winning campaigns of 1960 and 1980.

Even though Curran had been a member of the U.S. National Team in 1969, 1970, and 1971, it wasn't a given that he would end up as the number-one netminder on Williamson's team. "He was difficult to handle," Williamson said. "We feuded. He was a colorful guy."

Prior to Curran's arrival, *Sports Illustrated* writer Mark Mulvoy had traveled with the team and then left without writing a word. "He just couldn't find much to write about it," Williamson said. "We didn't have any Dennis Rodmans or Charles Barkleys."

Curran's arrival added some sparkle to the team. Curiously, one of the goalies that lost out to Curran in the Olympic cuts was Dave Reece, who would gain ignominy four years later when he would be in goal for the Boston Bruins when Darryl Sittler would set an NHL record of 10 points in a game. He scored six goals against Reece that night. He was a feisty competitor who would come charging out of a goal during a practice session if he thought teammates were shooting too close to his head.

Williamson had too much coaching savvy not to realize that Curran's talent, stubbornness, and experience would all be beneficial for a team that had too many younger players. "Players loved him," Williamson said. "Mostly they loved him because he stood up to me."

Players also realized quickly that Curran knew more about international hockey than anyone else on the roster. Ftorek, an intense competitor even at nineteen, remembered being perplexed to see his netminder starting to roam out of

Tim Sheehy (15) congratulates goaltender Mike "Lefty" Curran after he made 51 saves in a 5-1 win against Czechoslovakia at the 1972 Games in Sapporo. Curran's effort in that game probably rivaled any ever recorded by an American goalie, including Jim Craig's effort against the Soviets in 1980.

his net as soon as the team hit the island of Japan. Curran seemed to have altered his playing style during the flight overseas.

"Lefty, what are you doing?" Ftorek asked him.

"Robbie, these people don't shoot over here, so I cheat," Curran replied. "You just have to trust me."

Ftorek quickly did learn to trust Curran, as did the rest of his teammates. "After the second game I realized he knew what he was doing," Ftorek said. "The European teams didn't shoot. They would make the pass right across the crease and he was always there to stymie them."

Williamson also knew plenty about international hockey. He had coached the United States team at the 1968 Olympics and three other U.S. National Teams. In 1971, he was allowed to watch a Soviet training camp and grew fascinated with the Soviet's dry land training ritual. The 1972 Olympians were rather surprised that their practice routine often included jogging, piggyback races, basketball, tennis, and strength-building exercises.

Tim Sheehy (15) and Henry Boucha (9) wait for the rebound during the important win against the Czechs. Sheehy later signed with New England of the World Hockey Association after the 1972 Olympics, playing seven seasons in the WHA and NHL. He had 177 goals in 433 games.

"The coach's tactic was that we were never going to lose a game because of conditioning," said Tom Mellor, a 1972 defenseman who went on to play briefly with the Detroit Red Wings.

On the final day of the competition, the Americans needed some help to earn a medal. They got it when Finland defeated Sweden and Russia crushed the Czechs. The silver medal would go to the Americans, much to the surprise of most of their opponents who hadn't seen the USA win a medal since 1960.

The 1972 team's lifetime of anonymity probably began when NBC ended its coverage a few minutes before the Americans reached the podium for their medal ceremony. This was an era when networks were paying reasonable amounts for rights to televise the Olympics and didn't feel obliged to provide sunup-to-sundown coverage, as they do today.

"That was the biggest disappointment in my entire career," said defenseman Dick McGlynn, now a Boston attorney.

Years later, NBC host Curt Gowdy told the *Boston Globe* that he had been stunned that the Americans had won the silver medal. "That was the real surprise of the 1972 Olympic Games," Gowdy said.

But he wasn't surprised that the 1972 team's accomplishments were often overlooked in the roll call of U.S. Olympic heroes. "There's an old saying: Finish second and no one remembers who you are," Gowdy said. "That's what America has come to. We hold up our fingers and say, "We're No. 1. That's all we're interested in, in college basketball, college football. That's the desired outcome, gold or No. 1."

But the U.S. players did come back from Japan satisfied with their efforts. They had all performed better than anyone had expected.

Howe, the son of former NHL great Gordie Howe, was the youngest player in U.S. Olympic hockey history. He was a year younger than Jack Kirrane, who was seventeen when he played for the 1948 team. Howe didn't have a point in the tournament, but Williamson said Howe held his own against the older, more experienced international competition.

Howe's presence created a stir; even the Soviet press recognized his legendary name. After the Soviet-USA game, Howe was surrounded by reporters from Izvestia, Pravda, and Tass. They couldn't seem to get enough information about Howe and his relationship with his dad.

"What does your father teach you?" the Russians asked Howe.

"He teaches me to do what the coaches tell me to do," Howe said. "But sometimes he doesn't like what the coaches tell me and he tells me to do something else."

The Soviets loved that answer.

As a 16-year-old, Howe had a perspective about the Olympics that older performers probably couldn't appreciate. Accustomed to an allowance of $10 per

Keith Christiansen receives a silver medal during ceremonies in Sapporo, Japan. Americans missed the medal ceremony because NBC ended its daily Olympic coverage a few minutes before the event took place.

week, he was flabbergasted when team officials gave him $800 living expenses. Empowered by his wealth, he purchased two large suitcases to hold all of his loot.

More than twenty years later, Mark, who went on to become an NHL All-Star, laughed when asked what stood out the most from his Olympic experience. He explained that he and two other players had bought a small television set to watch in the Olympic village.

"They had dubbed Bonanza reruns on every day," Howe said. "I don't think I've ever seen anything as hilarious as Ben Cartwright speaking Japanese."

The innocence of youth was one of the key ingredients of that 1972 team. Williamson told reporters at the Olympics that players, such as Boucha, Howe, and Ftorek, were too young to accept the fact that they would probably lose at the Olympics.

Boucha and Ftorek were among the leading scorers on the team. Both players would sign NHL contracts after the Olympics, and Howe would be in the World Hockey Association.

"Ftorek was one of the hardest-working sonofaguns I've ever seen," said teammate Larry Pleau, now the New York Rangers' assistant general manager. "He wouldn't give you an inch, or a foot, without fighting you for it."

Boucha, a Native American from Warroad, Minnesota, impressed his teammates, just as he had impressed his opponents in Minnesota. Former NHLer Doug Palazarri, now USA Hockey's Senior Director, Youth and Education Programs, remembered a Minnesota high school tournament game when Boucha never left the ice. "When he needed a rest, he went back on defense," Palazzari said.

When Minnesotans talk about the best high school players of all-time, Boucha's name comes up as often as Phil Housley, Neil Broten, or John Mayasich.

"Hank has great hands and real subtle speed," Ftorek said. "It didn't look like he was going fast, but he was really moving."

Any NHL scout or official from Sweden, Finland, or Czechoslovakia who watched the 1972 Olympic tournament and the performances of Boucha, Ftorek, and Howe could undoubtedly see the Americans were coming, and coming hard. But they wouldn't arrive for another eight years.

Chapter 8

T he frosty chill that Bill and Bob Cleary felt as they entered the Denver arena on a February morning in 1960 wasn't emanating from the ice surface. A few days earlier, members of the 1960 Olympic team had learned that coach Jack Riley planned to add the Cleary brothers to the roster. Unhappy with that decision, players agreed upon their own form of protest. The Cleary brothers were going to receive the cold shoulder. To the players, all of whom had been with the team for months, giving the Clearys the silent treatment seemed justified.

"Hardly anyone would speak to us, and we barely got the puck in warm-up," Bill Cleary said.

In many respects, the U.S. team's performance at the 1960 Olympics in Squaw Valley, California, was every bit as remarkable, if not more so, than the Miracle on Ice at the 1980 Olympic Games. First, the Americans had never beaten the Soviets. Second, the Canadians were better than the Soviets. Third, the team hadn't played all that well in the 18-game pre-Olympic tour. And finally, some players didn't like seeing Herb Brooks and Bob Dupuis dropped from the team to make room for the Clearys. Dissension threatened to undermine this team before it even arrived in Squaw Valley.

THE FIRST MIRACLE ON ICE

The 1960 Olympics

Defenseman Jack Kirrane, one of the best U.S. shot blockers in the 1960 Olympic tournament, stops another attempt against the Russians as his goalie Jack McCartan watches the action.

After a players meeting was held in Denver prior to the Clearys arrival, a message delivered to Riley said that the players weren't going to compete if the Clearys were brought in.

"I told [team manager] Jim Claypool, 'To hell with them,'" Riley said. "We'll bring our wives. We've got a nice place in Squaw Valley. We'll have a nice time."

Adding a player late wasn't a novel idea; American and Canadian teams had successfully done so in the past. In 1933, the late addition of Harvard standout John Garrison helped the USA capture the World Championship in Prague, and Riley had watched the Canadians bring in two players just before the 1948 Olympics to help them finish first.

The Clearys had let Riley know, through a message to Riley's brother, that they wanted to play. Everyone knew the Clearys hadn't tried out for the team because they were operating an insurance business and couldn't afford to leave their business for two months. But the Clearys could leave for

The Cleary brothers, Bob and Bill, and the Christian brothers, Roger and Bill, were the top offensive players on the 1960 U.S. Olympic team. There was a competitive rivalry between the two brother combinations because the Christians were from Minnesota and the Clearys were from Massachusetts. In that era, the East vs. West rivalry was prevalent in college and amateur hockey. It remains so even today.

two weeks, which would give them time to play the tournament.

"I've read that I kissed their butts to get them," Riley said. "That's not what happened. They came to me."

A couple of weeks before the tournament began, Riley spoke with hockey guru Walter Brown.

"Walter," Riley said, "do you want to go into the Olympics with a chance to win or no chance to win?"

"I want a chance to win."

"Then I have to bring in the Clearys."

"Do it," Brown had said.

After the tournament, players said they weren't bothered by the addition of John Mayasich or Bill Cleary, whose arrival had been expected from the beginning. Everyone knew Mayasich and Cleary had been the top scorers on the 1956 team in Cortina. The players were more miffed because they knew the Cleary brothers had come as a package deal. Bill Cleary wouldn't come without Bob. At that time, the players didn't believe Bob Cleary deserved to be on the team. That sentiment changed when they watched Bob Cleary play.

"It was pretty controversial," said Roger Christian, one of the top scorers on the 1960 team. "Everyone agreed not to talk to them."

Before their first game, Bill Cleary addressed the tension with a brief, pointed speech: "I didn't come 3,000 miles to lose. We don't have to hug and kiss. I just want you to pass me the puck."

The Christian brothers were among the first to talk to the Clearys. McCartan would also tell his teammates, "We've worked too hard to let this get in the way." Kirrane, a no-nonsense player, said he planned to play in these Olympics, "even if I'm the only guy on the ice."

Players backed off their threat not to compete, but neither Riley nor anyone else on the team could be sure how well this team would jell once the Olympic tournament began. "No one gave us a chance," Bill Cleary said. "I think *Sports Illustrated* picked us last."

Deep down, the American players believed they were capable of winning the tournament. They could look down their bench and see an impressive collection of talent. John Mayasich, a University of Minnesota grad, and Bill Cleary, a Harvard man, were two of the best players ever in college hockey. Billy and Roger Christian were feisty and experienced international players who knew how to create offensive chances. Paul Johnson was a dynamic skater, a breakaway threat every time the puck hit his stick. This was an experienced team. Dick Rodenheiser, Dick Meredith, Weldy Olson, Mayasich, and Cleary had all played for the 1956 U.S. Olympic team, which had won the silver medal.

Then there was Jack McCartan, on loan from the U.S. Army to play goal for coach Jack Riley's Olympic squad. Those on the U.S. team who didn't know McCartan knew of him. In addition to playing goal for the University of Minnesota's hockey team, McCartan had been an all-American third baseman. His career batting average at Minnesota had been .349. In 1956, he had batted .436 with four doubles, six home runs, and 17 RBI in 13 games.

His career 2.95 goals-against average and .908 save percentage still puts him at the top of the school's goaltending leaders. "We all knew he had a great glove hand," Mayasich said.

The 26-year-old Mayasich was a veteran of several international tournaments. To this day, no American player can match Mayasich's record of playing for eight national teams. During the week, he was an advertising executive for a television station, but on weekends he played for the Green Bay Bobcats in the United States Hockey League.

He had been a high-scoring center in college hockey, netting 144 goals in 111 career games at Minnesota. In his senior season, he had 41 goals and 39 assists in 30 games. Opponents simply had no way to shut him down. His moves were too crafty, his shots too hard. He credits former Chicago Blackhawk player Doc Romnes, his coach for just one year at Minnesota, for refining the puck-handling skills that would serve him well for decades.

Playing center on a line with Bill Cleary and John Matchefts at the 1956 Games in Cortina, Mayasich led the Americans in scoring with six goals and four assists. He had a hat trick in the USA's 4-1 win against Canada.

But the Bobcats liked to use Mayasich on defense, because then he could dominate both ends of the ice. Riley, head coach at West Point, also liked Mayasich as a defenseman and let everyone know from the beginning that Mayasich was going to be added to the team right before the Olympics began. Mayasich didn't meet the team until the day before the games began in Squaw Valley.

Yet another product of Eveleth's hockey factory, Mayasich had his own unique

Speedy Tommy Williams of Duluth, Minnesota, was just 19 when Coach Jack Riley picked him as a member of the 1960 Olympic team. He played on a line with Roger and Bill Christian. In 1961, he signed with the Boston Bruins, becoming one of the few Americans to play in the NHL in the 1960s.

As a 17-year-old, Jack Kirrane played for the 1948 U.S. Olympic team. Twelve years later, Kirrane provided veteran leadership as captain of the 1960 gold medal winners.

calling card—a wicked slap shot that would have been the envy of any NHLer except Bobby Hull. "He was way ahead of his time on that slap shot," Cleary said.

Mayasich began experimenting with it during college when Eveleth goaltender Willard Ikola, then playing at the University of Michigan, told him how he had seen another player attempt it. With his skills, Mayasich was able to master the concept just based on Ikola's description.

His slap shot was particularly befuddling to international competitors because it was completely foreign to players outside of North America.

Mayasich remembered when he was playing for the Bobcats in an exhibition game against a Japanese national team, he uncorked a slap shot from center ice that beat the surprised goalkeeper. The goaltender appeared to have pulled a muscle trying to stop the shot. He had fallen in front of the goal and was rolling around on the ice in a fit of hysteria. But when his teammates and the Bobcats moved closer, they saw his hysteria was a fit of laughter, not pain. He had never seen anything like Mayasich's rocket launcher. "It was comical to see them all laughing so hard," Mayasich said.

After the game, Japanese players examined the knob of tape Mayasich had at the top of his stick, thinking that had something to do with the velocity and timing of the shot.

With Mayasich supplying support, the Americans' high-powered offense jelled quickly, in spite of the riff caused by the Cleary brothers' arrival. The team won its first four games in pool play against Czechoslovakia, Australia, Sweden, and Germany. The team was brimming with confidence. The four defensemen—Mayasich, Kirrane, Bob Owen, and Rodney Paavola—were playing well. McCartan was sharp. The offense was clicking.

But the Americans knew they were still the underdog against the vaunted Canadians, whose roster included Harry Sinden, later a coach and general manager in the NHL, and Bobby Rousseau, who would later score 242 NHL goals and win four Stanley Cups as a member of the Montreal Canadiens. The backup Canadian goalie was Cesare Maniago, who would end up in the NHL later that season. The Canadians were coached by Bobby Bauer, a member of the NFL's famous "Kraut Line" with Woody Dumart and Milt Schmidt.

Against Canada, Bob Cleary jammed a rebound past goaltender Don Head on the power play to give the USA a 1-0 lead, and former Minnesota standout Paul Johnson intercepted a pass and streaked up ice to beat Head on a breakaway. The U.S. led by two goals before the end of the second period. Johnson was considered to have as much pure offensive talent as any player to come out of Minnesota in that era. "All the way through high school, he was the scourge," McCartan said. "He could control the game, do anything he wanted."

Canadians winger Jim Connely finally tallied with 5:22 left in the game, but McCartan's strong goaltending preserved the 2-1 victory.

"It was shocking to us," said Sinden, now president of the Boston Bruins. "We were probably favored by seven goals against them."

> **The Americans celebrate a goal at Squaw Valley in 1960. When they played against Czechoslovakia for the gold medal, the outdoor rink was so crowded that spectators were standing in the players' bench area.**

To beat Canada, goaltender Jack McCartan made 38 saves, including 20 in the second period. One wire service report of the game said McCartan seemed to be operating "with radar to smother shots."

"McCartan played well in goal, much like Jim Craig did for the 1980 team," Sinden said.

Team Canada was really the Kitchener-Waterloo Dutchmen, who were Canada's best amateur team. Coming into Squaw Valley, their goal had been to avenge Canada's bronze medal finish at the 1956 Games in Cortina, where they had also lost to the Americans. After being waylaid again by the 1960 U.S. squad, they were bitter. They believed they hadn't played well and blamed McCartan for their undoing.

"Beating the Canadians in hockey," Bill Cleary told the *Associated Press* immediately after the game, "would be like Canada beating us in baseball."

THE FIRST MIRACLE ON ICE

Although not as well remembered as the 1980 Miracle on Ice, the U.S. gold medal victory in the 1960 Olympics demonstrated for the first time that the American hockey program would no longer take a backseat to that of any other nation.

Riley was gracious in victory, telling reporters: "If we played the Canadians 10 games, they'd win nine of them."

He may not have believed that, and the American players certainly didn't. Although the Americans had passed an important test, the Soviets were still favored in their matchup with the USA two days later.

"Though we had beaten the Canadians," McCartan said, "no one would bet his house on beating the Russians. We had never beaten them, and their power play used to do us in all the time."

It was clear the Soviets planned to dominate the sport. The Americans, who had been playing hockey in some form since the 1890s, had always finished behind the Soviets, who had only been competing internationally since 1955. The Soviets had beaten the Americans 4-0 at the 1956 Olympic Games in Cortina, Italy.

Although Jack McCartan never received the attention that Jim Craig did in 1980, his goaltending heroics in 1960 may have been more spectacular. He made 38 saves to beat Canada, including 20 in the second period.

Yet there was cause for optimism: the Soviets had been tied 2-2 by the Swedes, the same Swedes the Americans had whipped 6-1. Roger Christian had netted three goals in that one-sided game, and McCartan had made 36 saves. Ex-Harvard winger Robert McVey, the Clearys' linemate, had also scored for the Americans, who led 4-0 after the first period.

The 1960 game against the Russians drew an overflow crowd to the open-air Blyth Arena at Squaw Valley. The team's trainer, the late Ben Bertini, had to clear the bench to get his players room to sit. Among those thrown out, according to Bill Cleary, was then California governor Pat Brown. "Everyone wanted to carry our skates just to get in," Cleary said.

The Soviets led 2-1 before Bill Christian, assisted by brother Roger, tied the game with a goal at 11:01 of the second period. Russian goaltender Nikolai Puchkov had mistakenly given Bill Christian about two feet of room on the short side, and Christian had ripped a shot about eight inches off the ice. "It was an easy goal," Christian would say later.

For the next twenty-four minutes, the Americans and Soviets fought for every inch of ice, neither side conceding anything.

Perhaps more than anyone else, the Christian brothers wanted this victory against the Soviets. Two years earlier, they had been on the first U.S. team to play inside the Soviet Union during the Cold War. In the four days they spent in Moscow, they were constantly reminded about the Soviets' successful launch of *Sputnik* into outer space in the fall of 1957. Their Soviet hosts had made *Sputnik* centerpieces to place on the tables where the Americans ate.

More than 15,000 Soviet fans had showed up in 1958 to watch the U.S. team lose twice to Soviet teams. The Christians remembered that the hotel, the food, and the conditions were bad. "We hated every minute of it," Bill Christian said.

Now it was 1960, and the games were on American ice. The Christian brothers knew they could pay back the Soviets in grand fashion.

With 5:01 left in the contest, Bill Christian, the U.S. team's smallest player at 5-foot-9, 145 pounds, scored again, set up again by brother Roger and Tommy Williams, his other linemate.

"Tommy had knocked the puck out of the corner and Roger took a shot," Bill remembered. "Puchkov went down. I was getting shoved around in front of the net. The puck came out, and I put it back in, just under Puchkov's head."

A boisterous crowd screamed with delight while the Americans fought off the Soviets in the closing minutes. The puck was in the Americans' end for many of the final

Coach Jack Riley risked player wrath by adding Bill and Bob Cleary late to the 1960 U.S. Olympic roster.

THE CHRISTIANS

Those looking to find a common thread between the successes of the 1960 and 1980 Olympic teams can start with the Christian family of Warroad, Minnesota.

Dave Christian, whose move from forward to defense helped solidify the 1980 U.S. squad, is the son of Bill Christian, who played for the 1960 U.S. team. Bill's brother, Roger, also played for the squad. Another brother, Gordon, played for the U.S. National team in the 1950s.

In 1980, Herb Brooks thought he had enough offense, but he felt he needed help on defense. He thought Christian was smart enough, and talented enough, to handle the switch in positions. That assumption proved correct.

After leading the U.S. team with eight assists in Lake Placid, Dave Christian moved back to forward and enjoyed a standout NHL career, finishing with 340 goals in 1,009 NHL games with Winnipeg, Washington, Boston, St. Louis, and Chicago. He had four seasons in which he netted 30 or more goals and 10 seasons in which he topped 20 goals.

Bill Christian, at 5-foot-9, 145 pounds, was the USA's smallest player at the 1960 Olympics but he scored two big goals in a 3-2 win against the Soviets in Squaw Valley.

minutes, and McCartan was brilliant preserving his country's first hockey win over "the Bear." "Every faceoff seemed to last an eternity," Bill Cleary remembered.

After the game, the teary-eyed Soviet coach, Anatoli Tarasov, entered the American dressing room and kissed Riley on the cheek, and Russian interpreter Roman Kesserlov gave Bill Cleary a bottle of vodka he had to pay off a bet they had made. The vodka still sits unopened in Cleary's Massachusetts home as a memento of the triumph.

Almost twenty years later, Bill Cleary would entertain coach Tarasov at his home overlooking the Charles River in the Boston area. Tarasov would joke that he "ended up in Siberia" because of Cleary and his colleagues.

The visit to Cleary's home was in the spring of 1979, and Tarasov had brought along a bottle of vodka. Before he left, he threw the vodka in the bushes and told Cleary not to retrieve it until the American hockey players won another Olympic gold medal. He probably assumed that wasn't going to happen for many years. Less than a year later, he would be wrong.

Aside from Tarasov, the Russians didn't accept the loss in 1960 very well. A bitter Nikolai Romanov, the Soviet minister of sport, told the assembled media: "Perhaps we would have won on a neutral rink, but naturally it is the right of the spectators to cheer their team as much as they can and we just had to bear that handicap."

The Americans had no time to celebrate because they were scheduled to be on the ice at eight the next morning to face the Czechs for the gold medal. Organizers expected the Canada-Soviet Union game to be for the gold, so the USA-Czech game was scheduled for early Sunday.

The Americans had defeated the Czechs 7-5 in pool play, but they were made uneasy because they had been forced to come from behind to do it. There was no denying they were facing a well-schooled team, quite capable of rendering their victories over Canada and the Soviet Union relatively meaningless.

As if to add some drama to the script, the Americans fell behind 4-3 after two periods. After watching this, Soviet team captain Nikolai Sologubov decided to make a visit to the Americans' dressing room, thereby creating a legend of Olympic competition. He couldn't speak English, and his message was lost until he began using charadelike hand gestures.

"When he put his hand over his mouth we realized he was trying to convince us to take oxygen," Bill Cleary said.

Sologubov believed the oxygen would reenergize the Americans at the high altitude of Squaw Valley, which was a mile above sea level.

When the Americans scored six goals in the third period to upend the Czechs, the media proclaimed Sologubov a true sportsman and saluted his noble gesture as one of the keys to the victory.

But years later, most of the American players weren't so sure how much it really helped the team. Only eight players took the oxygen. "All I know is Roger Christian didn't take oxygen, and he scored three goals in the third period," McCartan said, laughing.

Some question whether Sologubov's gesture was genuinely noble or just an attempt to assure that the archrival Czechs would not finish ahead of the Soviets. If the U.S. won, the Soviets would finish ahead of Czechoslovakia with the bronze or silver medal. On the other hand, Solly, as he was called by the U.S. players, was considered to be friendly toward the Americans.

"I played it up, because I knew it was a good story," Riley recalled. "But it wasn't a big thing in the dressing room."

Bill Cleary, who had played against the Soviets on several occasions, tended to be more idealistic about Sologubov's intentions. "We had played against them so often, I began to see them as friends," Cleary said. "When they sat around and talked, they didn't talk about communism. Like us, they talked about hockey and women."

All the oxygen on mother earth wouldn't have helped the Americans if McCartan hadn't been as brilliant as he was during the tournament. He surrendered just 17 goals in seven games and was clearly the best goaltender in the tournament.

Ironically, McCartan had been cut from the roster three months earlier at the open tryouts. In November, he had tried out in Minneapolis and believed he had played well enough to make the team. When he went down to look at the "cut list" that had been posted by Riley, he whistled to himself over some of the names on the list.

"I thought, they are cutting some pretty good guys, and then it hit me," McCartan said. "These were the guys they were keeping, and my name wasn't on the list."

McCartan was devastated. Walter Bush, then general manager of St. Paul Steers senior team, called and stretched the truth to a U.S. Army general that McCartan was needed as an emergency backup. He really just wanted McCartan for his team, which turned out to be fortunate because McCartan was in game shape when Riley called him a month later.

"That was my plan all along," Riley insisted thirty-six years later. "He was in the army and I knew I could get him back. He was mad at me, and he played great. Hell, they were all mad at me."

Members of the 1960 team say McCartan was the most valuable player of the tournament, although he prefers to modestly say the Americans' success was a case of every player performing to the best of their ability.

Many players did play key roles in the triumph. Kirrane, a stay-at-home defenseman, had been the perfect complement for Mayasich. "He was black and blue from blocking shots," Bill Cleary said. And the American players had been wrong about Bob Cleary, who was among the team's top scorers. The controversy was forgotten, although the team photo with Bob Cleary's head pasted over Herb Brooks's body is a permanent reminder of the upheaval that was present heading into Squaw Valley. The Christian brothers were the first of the players to talk with the Clearys. "After it was all over, I remember us all standing in the shower and the Clearys thanking us for talking to them," Roger said.

There were no invitations to the White House for this team, nor any notoriety that lasted beyond a week. With the NHL boasting only six teams, opportunities for U.S.-born players weren't there.

McCartan and the late Tommy Williams were the only players to go to the NHL. Williams would be considered a successful American pro hockey pioneer. Although his life would never be quite as sweet as it was the day they won the gold medal, he would become the first American to score 20 goals in a season in 1963. But before his career was finished, he would know much discrimination and heartache.

Bill Cleary, who served as head coach at Harvard for 19 years before taking over as athletic director in 1990, had made the decision not to pursue a pro career even before those games. Proud that he was paid only $15 a month to play with the U.S. team, he laments the Olympics are now dominated by highly paid athletes.

"I wouldn't trade my chance to march in the Olympic parade of athletes for 100 Stanley Cup championships," said Cleary. "When it was over, we all went back to our lives. That's the way we wanted it."

As captain, Kirrane would be the one to greet Brundage at the medal ceremony. "Wasn't that ironic given how the bastard treated us in 1948," Riley said. "He said we were pros in 1948. Why weren't we pros in 1960?"

Cleary said he understood the Olympic dream best when he watched Kirrane receive his medal during the traditional medal-presenting ceremony. Kirrane's decision to join the 1960 Olympic team hadn't been as easy as it was in 1948 when he made the Olympic team as a 17-year-old with no responsibilities and no family. Married with three children, Kirrane had to take a leave of absence from his job as a fire fighter to join the team. Later in his fire fighting career, the seniority time he lost to chase his Olympic dream cost him a promotion.

"This is one of the toughest guys you will ever meet," Cleary said. "But when he went up to the podium to get his medal, his knees were shaking and his hands were a pool of water. Seeing him like that is something I will never forget."

When he returned home, Riley took one of his Olympic pictures and sent it to his former Dartmouth coach, Eddie Jeremiah. The inscription read:

To Jerry: Hockey's Greatest Coach:

Words cannot express the tremendous gratitude I owe you. Without your help, Dartmouth, West Point and the Olympics would have been nothing but a dream.

Thanks a million

Jack

Back in Minnesota, Brooks, the last player cut from the 1960 team, watched the gold medal game on television. He was hurt when he had been cut, even though he suspected it was going to happen. He told his roommate, Tommy Williams, that he thought he was in trouble, even though he had been scoring on the pre-Olympic tour. Williams, Brooks, and Bill Christian were the youngest players. "Christian and Williams were better than me," he said later.

When Brooks was cut, he had called home, and his father had told him: "Keep your mouth shut, thank everyone there, and come home." Two weeks later, he and his father were watching the television as his former teammates won the gold medal.

When it became clear that the USA would win, Brooks's father turned to him and said: "It looks like the coach made the right decision."

People less dedicated to their goal might have quit. But Brooks believed he had an Olympic destiny and continued to pursue it with vigor. He would fulfill that destiny twenty years later.

WHAT ARE THEY DOING TODAY?

Members of the USA's 1960 Gold Medal-Winning Olympic Hockey Team:

Roger Christian, Warroad, Minnesota, co-owns hockey equipment company

Bill Christian, Warroad, Minnesota, co-owns hockey equipment company

Bill Cleary, Auburndale, Massachusetts, Harvard athletic director

Bob Cleary, Weston, Massachusetts, insurance company president

Eugene Grazia, West Springfield, Massachusetts, retired teacher, coach

Paul Johnson, Waterloo, Iowa, club owner, Pauly's Place

Jack Kirrane, Brookline, Massachusetts, manager of Harvard's rink

John Mayasich, Lakeland, Minnesota, President of Hubbard Broadcasting, radio division

Jack McCartan, [1]Bloomington, Minnesota, Vancouver Canucks scout

Bob McVey, Wallingford, Connecticut, insurance agent

Richard Meredith, Edina, Minnesota, Vice president of Creative Concepts

Weldon Olson, Findlay, Ohio, retired arena builder

Bob Owen, Topeka, Kansas, retired business consultant

Rodney Paavola, Deceased

Laurence Palmer, Glane, Switzerland, retired investment adviser

Richard Rodenheiser, Framingham, Massachusetts, manager of Loring Arena

Tom Williams, [2]Deceased

1 McCartan played for the New York Rangers in the 1959-60 and 1960-61 seasons.

2 Williams played 13 NHL seasons with Boston, Minnesota, California, and Washington

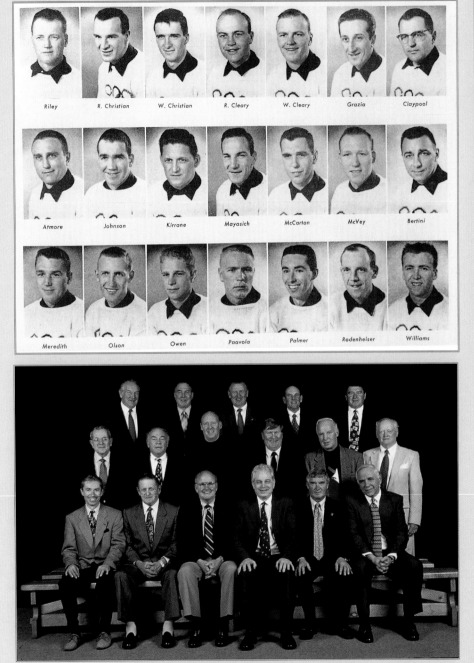

Front row (left to right): Laurence Palmer, Jack Kirrane, Bill Cleary, Robert Owen, Bill Christian, and Jack McCartan. Middle row: James Claypool, Robert Cleary, Robert McVey, Rodney Paavola, Roger Christian, and Coach Jack Riley. Back row: John Mayasich, Paul Johnson, Weldon Olson, Richard Rodenheiser, and Richard Meredith. Not pictured: Eugene Grazia, Tom Williams, and Ben Bertini.

The 1960 Olympics

Chapter 9

What the U.S. hockey team did to the Soviets on the ice at Lake Placid in 1980 hardly compares to what they did to the hearts and minds of American people. "It's the most transcending moment in the history of our sport in this country," gushed Dave Ogrean, executive director of USA Hockey. "For people who were born between 1945 and 1955, they know where they were when John Kennedy was shot, when man walked on the moon, and when the USA beat the Soviet Union in Lake Placid."

No other Olympic performance has touched America the way that hockey team did, not even Jesse Owens's brilliant runs in front of Adolf Hitler in Berlin in 1936. Thanks to the advent of television, Eruzione's goal in 1980 triggered a spontaneous national celebration of amazing proportion. People wept, strangers hugged each other, and groups around the country broke into stirring renditions of "God Bless America" and "The Star-Spangled Banner."

Those in attendance remember the incredible number of American flags that were in the crowd that day, not small

THE 1980 MIRACLE ON ICE

Kicking Stan Laurel's Fanny

Jim Craig makes one of his many big saves in the Olympic competition at Lake Placid. Without Craig's brilliant performance, there would not have been a Miracle on Ice.

flags that fit comfortably in the hands of small children, but mammoth flags that were usually found on 30-foot flag polls. Americans were overcome by patriotism.

"Right after we won I got bags of mail," Eruzione said. "It was like in the movie *Miracle on 34th Street* when they bring in all that mail to Santa. That's what I used to get."

The U.S. team, made up of college players and long-shot pro aspirants like Eruzione and Buzz Schneider, defeated a Russian program that had dominated the Olympics since 1964. The U.S. team beat a Russian team that had seven players from the 1976 Olympic team and one player who had played in three other Olympiads.

Somehow over time, the U.S. team has been miscast as a group of overachievers, even though the core group of players, Mark Johnson, Neal Broten, Mark Pavelich, Ken Morrow, Dave Christian, and Mike Ramsey, also made significant marks in the NHL.

"Maybe we overachieved," Ramsey said. "But we were a damn good hockey team."

The USA had speed, defense, scorers, conditioning, goaltending, and coaching—a complete team, something the Soviets didn't realize until it was too late. The Soviets had expected to win the tournament with the same ease with which they had dispatched all comers at the 1976 Olympics in Innsbruck, Austria. Further buoying their confidence was the 10-3 licking they had applied to the Americans in an exhibition at Madison Square Garden just one week before the world arrived at Lake Placid.

The Americans trailed in six of their seven Olympic wins, including the gold medal game, which they won 4-2 over Finland. In their opener, defenseman Bill Baker scored with 27 seconds left to give the USA a 2-2 tie with Sweden in the opening game of the tournament. Would the Miracle of Lake Placid have occurred if Baker had not scored? Probably not. The tie was important because the Americans had a gloomy history with Sweden. They hadn't beaten the Swedes since 1960. Baker's goal lifted the team's morale like the thrust of a rocket booster.

The Americans then dominated the Czechoslovakians, winning 7-3 with seven different goal scorers. That outcome surprised many, particularly the Czechs, who had entered the tournament with aspirations of at least a silver medal. The Czech team had the Stastny brothers—Petr, Marian, and Anton—who would later defect for a chance to play in the NHL with the Quebec Nordiques.

Then Norway was taken, followed by Romania and West Germany. Coach Herb Brooks had been worried about the Germans, because they had beaten the USA 4-1 in 1976 at Innsbruck, undermining coach Bob Johnson's hope of a bronze medal. They didn't have the talent to compete with the Americans. They weren't fancy, like the Swedes, Czechs, Finns, and Soviets. But they were dangerous because they played hockey as if it was trench warfare. They were tough and determined, not like the German players who the Americans whipped in the 1960s.

The competitive spirit the Germans had unveiled in Innsbruck in 1976 also made the trip to Lake Placid. The Germans claimed a 2-0 lead against the Americans after one period, scoring both goals with shots from beyond the blue line. The first shot was one chance in a thousand, a 70-footer by Horst-Peter Kretschmer that caught Craig off guard. The second goal was a 50-foot shot from the point by Udo Kiessling. Craig was screened on the play.

Enraged by their ineffectiveness, the Americans stepped up their game in the second period. But they weren't able to tie the game until Neal Broten scored with 1:29 remaining in that period. Rob McClanahan and Phil Verchota scored in the third period to complete the 4-2 win.

Although the Americans won, the game didn't help them in the standings. Ironically, at that point in the tournament, the Americans were trying to avoid facing the Soviets. The U.S. was tied with Sweden for first place in the Blue Pool, and the loser of the tiebreaker system would play the Soviets first in the medal round. The Americans want-

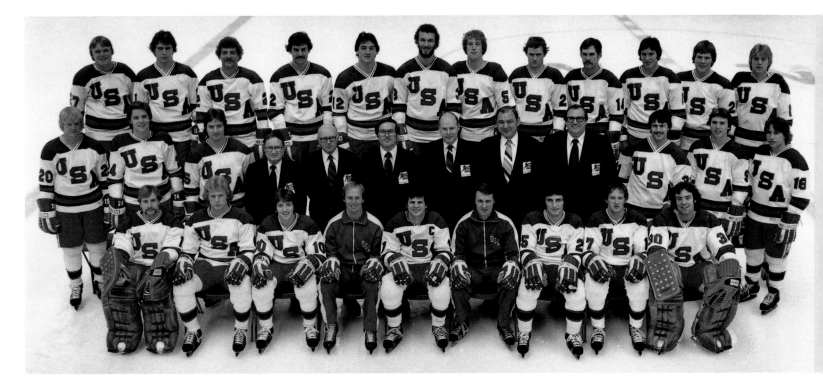

The 1980 U.S. Olympic champions–Front row (left to right): Steve Janaszak, Bill Baker, Mark Johnson, Assistant Coach/Assistant GM Craig Patrick, Captain Mike Eruzione, Coach Herb Brooks, Buzz Schneider, Jack O'Callahan, and Jim Craig. Middle row: Bob Suter, Rob McClanahan, Mark Wells, Equipment Manager Bud Kessel, Physician V. George Nagobads, Trainer Gary Smith, USA Hockey International Chairman Robert Fleming, Team GM Ralph Jasinski, Goalie Coach Warren Strelow, Bruce Horsh, Neal Broten, and Mark Pavelich. Back row: Phil Verchota, Steve Christoff, Les Auge, Dave Delich, Jack Hughes, Ken Morrow, Mike Ramsey, Dave Christian, Ralph Cox, Dave Silk, John Harrington, and Eric Strobel. Horsch, Auge, Delich, Hughes, and Cox didn't make the final roster for Lake Placid.

ed to win the Blue Pool to assure they would play the Finns first and then play the Soviets for the gold medal. Therefore, the U.S. hoped the Czechs would defeat the Swedes in the final Blue Pool game, assuring the United States would win the Blue Pool and face the Finns first. However, the Swedes beat the Czechs, so the United States hoped to beat Germany by seven goals so they would have a better goal differential against the Swedes and win the first tiebreaker and the Blue Pool. But the United States only beat the Germans by a two-goal margin. They would have to play the Soviets first. Destiny awaited.

Brooks wondered whether he had successfully exorcised the players' memories of the humiliating defeat they had suffered in Madison Square Garden at the hands of the Soviets. "Our guys were applauding the Soviets when they were introduced," he recalled.

One of coach Herb Brooks's goals before the Olympics was to "break down the Soviets to mortals." He told his players that the great Boris Mikhailov looked like Stan Laurel of the comedy team Laurel and Hardy. He hoped his players would stop looking at Mikhailov as if he was hockey's Zeus.

"You can beat Stan Laurel, can't you?" Brooks would ask.

The Soviets weren't hockey gods, but they were legends. Mikhailov, goaltender Vladislav Tretiak, Alexander Maltsev, Vladimir Petrov, Vasili Vasiliev, and Valeri Kharlamov were all members of the Soviet team that had played against the NHL All-Stars in the 1972 Summit Series. The NHLers thought they would dominate the Soviets in all eight games. Instead, they needed a goal by Paul Henderson with 34 seconds left in regulation of the final game to win the tournament with a 4-3-1 record.

As expected, the Soviets' Olympic team began an immediate offensive blitzkrieg against the Americans, but the Americans were staying with them. Craig was looking sharp, as sharp as he ever had. The team was gaining confidence as the first period progressed, even if they were getting outshot badly. "When you are an underdog, all you are looking to do is keep the game close so you will have a chance to win it in the end," Mark Johnson would say later.

Eruzione's goal was preserved in the minds of Americans as "The Goal" of American hockey history, but Johnson was the Americans' top scorer in the game against the Soviets and in the tournament. Because of his tremendous skill, teammates called him "Magic" Johnson, comparing him to the NBA superstar. Johnson was as slick with the puck as any player in the tournament.

He was twenty-two years old, yet he probably had as much hockey savvy as some of the veteran Soviets. Though he hadn't played as much as they had, Johnson possessed a sense about the game that other Americans did not. As the son of the legendary American coach Bob Johnson, he had soaked up every bit of insight that was available in every hockey school his father had run and when his father had coached the national team in 1975.

Johnson was a senior at Madison Memorial High School in 1976 when his father, needing a player at the last minute, decided to add his wunderkind son to the Team USA roster for the pre-Olympic tour. Mark held his own on the team, but Bob Johnson felt there would be too much pressure on his son if he took him to the Olympics. Everyone might believe he was there just because his father was the coach.

Although Johnson was probably the best player in college hockey, he had some concerns about making the 1980 Olympic team because Brooks and his dad were bitter rivals. When Brooks was at Minnesota and Johnson was at Wisconsin, they never had anything good to say about each other. "They got along like Germany and France," said agent Art Kaminsky, who considered himself friends with both men.

Mark Johnson said he was never comfortable that he would be on the team until the pre-Olympic tour in Oslo, Norway, when Brooks told him he was counting on him to be a leader as well as a player. Did he really believe Brooks might cut him because of his feud with his father? "Hey," Johnson said, "stranger things have happened in hockey."

But Brooks's desire to win at the Olympics meant more to him than prolonging any feud. He even patched up his considerable differences with Kaminsky, an important step because the agent Kaminsky was going to represent most of the players Brooks wanted for his team. Kaminsky said that prior to their peace accord, Brooks considered him "vermin." Kaminsky jokingly responded: "And I thought he was a maniac."

After Brooks and Kaminsky had each vented their frustrations with the other, they decided to work together, knowing that a successful run at the Olympic Games would be best for all concerned.

On the ice, Mark Johnson lived up to his reputation. He had several big goals, including two against the Russians. He wasn't intimidated by the Russians. Every Sunday, he had played in what his father called the "The Russian Game." His father had Russian jerseys made with all of the top Russian names sewn on the back. Mark Johnson

Goaltender Jim Craig

had played against Mikhailov many times, although the player wearing the jersey never had quite the same talent as the namesake.

With his team trailing 2-1 near the end of the first period, Johnson split two defenders to drive hard to the net after Dave Christian cranked a long shot. Tretiak didn't surrender many rebounds, but this puck bounced off his pads as if it had a spring attached. It went directly to Johnson, who drilled it past him with one second left. The goal gave the USA a major lift going into the second period. After Johnson's goal, Soviet coach Viktor Tikhonov stunned one and all by removing Tretiak and replacing him with Myshkin.

The Americans assumed Tretiak would be back, but he wasn't. Not many coaches would have had the courage to remove a Russian hockey legend from goal after only

THE 1980 MIRACLE ON ICE

one period in the world's most important international hockey tournament, but Tikhonov was no ordinary coach. He was a dictator, as hated as he was successful. Even today, Detroit Red Wing standouts Igor Larionov and Slava Fetisov curse the methods Tikhonov used to keep the Soviets powerful.

Years later, when Johnson found himself playing on the same New Jersey Devils team with Slava Fetisov and Alexei Kasatonov, another member of the 1980 Soviet team, he asked Fetisov why Tikhonov had pulled Tretiak.

Fetisov just shook his head and said two words with his thick Russian accent: "Coach crazy."

Vladimir Myshkin was hardly a second-rate replacement, as he had shut out NHL All-Stars, 6-0, the year before. But clearly, Tretiak's presence had a negative psychological effect on the Americans, an air of invincibility, even if they had scored two goals against him.

Going into the third period, the Americans finally believed they could beat the Soviets. Johnson scored the tying goal on a power play at 8:39 of the third period.

Brooks was short-shifting his players to keep them fresh. Two minutes after Johnson's goal, Eruzione jumped off the bench with a burst of energy. He ended up in the slot, where Pavelich found him with a pass. Eruzione fired a 25-foot wrist shot that skipped through a screen and past Myshkin.

All of America rejoiced.

The celebration that followed the game felt surreal to the players involved. Craig was buried by the crush of his teammates, and sticks and gloves were scattered everywhere. Euphoria reigned, and for the next few hours, players were besieged by well-wishers. Fans lined the short distance between the arena to the media center, forcing the team bus to inch its way toward the press conference. As fans banged on the bus, one player, most seem to think it was Neal Broten, started singing "God Bless America." Other players quickly joined in.

U.S. team physician V. George Nagobads, a native of Latvia, talked with Soviet players after the Olympics. Most of them didn't seem mortally wounded by the loss, although Vasili Vasilyev was perplexed that the U.S. had managed to defeat his strong team.

"What did you give your players to eat or drink so in the third period they can skate like that?" Vasilyev asked. "Last period is always ours. In second period, when we were ahead 3-2, we celebrate."

Nagobads, who speaks some Russian, replied, "It's called the fountain of youth."

Years after the event, it's easier to see that the Soviets badly underestimated the Americans' talent. After soundly beating the United States in Madison Square Garden, the Soviets never entertained the possibility that the Americans would give them a better game in their next meeting.

Also, the Soviets never thought that Craig was capable of playing as well as Tretiak did in his prime. Craig gave the United States the same quality goaltending Jack McCartan had supplied the gold medal-winning 1960 team. Brooks expected no less from Craig, who was his goaltending choice from the beginning.

Craig was a complicated man whose habit of saying the wrong thing at the wrong time made him a lightning rod for controversy. He came across as arrogant, even though those who knew him said he really wasn't like that. Overall, most teammates did like Craig, and all of them respected his ability to play goal. Craig oozed confidence like no goaltender they had ever seen.

Boston University coach Jack Parker recruited Craig out of Massasoit Junior College, actually grabbing him away from Jack Kelley, his former coach, who wanted Craig for his Colby team. Parker was honest with Craig, telling him from the beginning that he had offered a scholarship to Mark Holden of Weymouth, Massachusetts. Parker also had Brian Durocher penciled in as one goaltender. If Holden accepted, Craig wouldn't get a scholarship, as Parker didn't have three scholarships for goaltenders.

"I understand," Craig told Parker. "But I've seen Durocher and I've seen Holden and I'm going to be your goalie."

Holden didn't go to Boston University. Two years later, in 1978, Craig was 16-0-0 with a 3.72 goals-against average and Durocher, grand nephew of baseball legend Leo Durocher, was 14-2-3, as they split duties during Boston University's national championship season in 1978.

"He's the best college goaltender I've seen with the exception of Ken Dryden," Parker said. "[Two-time Olympic coach] Dave Peterson used to tell me that Craig was absolutely perfect technically."

Parker remembered that when he watched Craig practice, it would seem as if "the net had disappeared behind him." Craig's best asset was his confidence. He hated to get beaten by a shooter. "When you are good, and you know you are good, it's the greatest feeling in the world," Parker said. "And Jimmy Craig had that feeling."

Brooks seemed to understand how to push Craig's buttons better than anyone. Just before the Olympics, Brooks told Craig he might have made a mistake by playing him too much. He left the impression that he didn't believe Craig was playing all that well.

"You are playing tired, and your curveball is hanging," Brooks said to him.

That might have devastated some players, but that kind of talk simply fueled Craig, who could transform anger into energy. During the Olympics, he never looked tired.

Brooks was not like any hockey coach these players had experienced before. He was hockey's version of George Patton or Norman Schwarzkopf. In style, he was a combination dictator-philosopher whose instructions forced his players to think as well as act. Every day was an adventure in psychology for the guys wearing the red, white, and blue. "He got inside our heads," Ramsey said.

Backup goaltender Steve Janaszak recalled a nose-to-nose confrontation when Brooks convinced left winger Rob McClanahan to continue playing in the tournament opener against Sweden despite a severe charley horse. Brooks questioned McClanahan's manhood in a curse-filled tirade and called him a "cake eater." McClanahan responded with cursing of his own. The scene was ugly.

The enraged McClanahan went out and played as well as he could with his muscle knotted. "That locker room scene is still vivid in my mind," Janaszak said more than a decade later.

> **Vladislav Tretiak was considered one of the top goaltenders in hockey history. The Americans were stunned when Coach Viktor Tikhonov pulled him from the Soviet-U.S. game in Lake Placid. Years later, Russian Slava Fetisov would say that the Soviet players thought the move was dumb.**

Brooks's attack on McClanahan probably had little to do with McClanahan and more to do with the fact that Americans weren't playing well in their first Olympic test. Brooks tried to unify his team against him, a technique he used on many occasions, and sent a message to his players that the team was going to overcome all obstacles. Players kept a notebook of what they called "Brooksisms." One of them was "This team isn't talented enough to win on talent alone."

Kicking Stan Laurel's Fanny

U.S. players were overcome with emotion after defeating the Soviets at Lake Placid in the 1980 Olympics. Americans had equally patriotic reactions around the country. The *New York Times* reported that people on the Manhattan streets were hugging each other while spectators at a play stood and spontaneously sang "The Star-Spangled Banner."

Before the game against the Soviets, Brooks took out a note card and read a prepared text. "You were born to be a player. You were meant to be here." His players believed him.

Brooks said the 1980 Olympic team members embodied qualities he admired most. "The players had big egos, but they didn't have ego problems. That's why all-star teams traditionally seem to self-destruct. We didn't."

The players' mental toughness was demonstrated when they came back from behind to beat Finland 4-2 to capture the gold medal two days after stunning the Soviets. It's been forgotten by many that if the United States had fallen to Finland, it would not have earned a medal at all, gold or otherwise.

But the American players understood the challenge. Champagne was sent to the American dressing room following the win over the Soviets, and not a single American player touched it.

"If we don't win tomorrow," Craig told the media gathering after the Russian game, "people will forget us."

What made the U.S. team so special was that every player was a hero in his own way. Defenseman Jack O'Callahan's knee was so badly injured in the last exhibition game against the Soviets that he should have headed for surgery and not Lake Placid.

And there was the Conehead line of Mark Pavelich, John Harrington, and Buzz Schneider, named after the Saturday Night Live alien characters. All three players were from Minnesota's Iron Range, and none of them played a style that could be easily copied.

Eruzione recalled their strange play. "They were the only line that stayed intact because no one could play with them," Eruzione says. "I played with them once, and I had no idea what I was doing or where I was going."

Brooks liked to use the Conehead unit when he needed some creativity or a home run swing. When the play looked innocent, that's when the Coneheads were most dangerous.

Craig Patrick said years later that the well-traveled Schneider was probably the unsung hero of the 1980 squad. At twenty-five, he was the oldest player on the team and the only returnee from the 1976 Olympic squad. Playing on his fifth national team, his leadership was probably as important as Eruzione's. Schneider was among the leading scorers in the tournament. He had almost stopped playing hockey when he failed in a tryout with the Pittsburgh Penguins. Before then, Schneider had played briefly in Hershey, Saginaw, Oklahoma City, Birmingham, Hampton, and Europe.

"I was the only player in the Penguins camp without a contract," Schneider said. "They only needed me as a practice body."

Even when the 1980 Olympics ended, the celebration continued. Dave Ogrean, then a young public relations director for USA Hockey, remembered boarding a plane to head home, thinking how nice it would be to catch up on the sleep he lost in the gold medal revelry.

The flight attendant's eyes widened as she noticed his Team USA hockey parka. But Ogrean cut her off with a quick shake of the head. He had just closed his eyes when the flight attendant announced over the public address system: "Ladies and gentleman, in 6C, we have a member of the U.S. gold medal hockey team." The plane filled with applause and hoots of delight.

Mike Eruzione (waving flag) and his American teammates climbed on the medal stand to wave to fans after winning the gold medal at Lake Placid in 1980. Defenseman Ken Morrow (with the beard, far right), would immediately sign with the New York Islanders and win a Stanley Cup.

henever coach Bob Johnson found himself practicing on chopped-up ice in college or the pros, he would call it "Mullen ice."

That meant it was like skating on concrete.

Joe Mullen, the highest-scoring American-born player in NHL history, began his career as a roller hockey player on the streets of Hell's Kitchen in New York City, where the uneven pavement forced players to be strong skaters or else spend the entire season scabbed over from too many spills.

"He has one of the best knacks for the net I've seen," said Pittsburgh Penguins' general manager Craig Patrick, who signed Mullen as a free agent before the 1996-97 season. "He's always focused, and what really amazes me is the balance he has on his skates."

The incredible balance Mullen developed skating in the asphalt jungle was a major reason why he became the first American-born NHL player to reach the 500-goal plateau.

"I'll bet 300 of his goals never hit the back of the net—usually they end up just inches over the line," joked USA Hockey Special Projects Director and 1984 U.S. Olympic Team head coach Lou Vairo, who has known the Mullen family since "Joey was in the stroller."

JOE MULLEN

Deflections. Rebounds. Chip shots through a maze of bodies in front of the net. Pucks caroming off his body. Johnson, who coached Mullen in Calgary and Pittsburgh, would always tell Mullen: "I would go to war with you, Joey."

Mullen is one of those players who can't really explain how he knew exactly where to be to score those 500-plus goals. "Instinct has a lot to do with it," Mullen says.

His brother, Brian, who played for the Winnipeg Jets, New York Rangers, San Jose Sharks, and New York Islanders, believes it goes beyond instinct. "He became a very smart player," Brian says. "Some guys skate a million miles in a game and get nowhere. Joey doesn't waste any energy out there. He has the hockey sense that you can't teach."

Mullen was the one player Herb Brooks wanted but couldn't land for the 1980 U.S. Olympic team. "Joey signed [with the St. Louis Blues] because he needed to help his family," Vairo said.

Mullen has appreciated every dollar he has ever earned because he knows money wasn't plentiful when

he was a youngster. Vairo recalls that when Mullen was growing up, one of the floors in the family's apartment collapsed. "Their bathroom ended up in the alley," Vairo said.

Joey was one of four hockey-playing brothers. Kenny played briefly at Northeastern, and Tom played at American International College. "All the Mullens had hands and brains, and understood the game better than anyone else," Vairo said. "That family had the standards and values that I hope my sons have when they grow up."

One of the highlights of Mullen's career was playing in the 1989 All-Star game against his brother Brian, who was then playing for the New York Rangers. Joey was playing for Calgary at the time. The Mullen boys flew their parents to the game.

"I remember I found out first and my dad put on his New York Rangers jacket and went down to the pub and told all of his buddies that I was playing in the All-Star game," Brian remembered. "Then Joey found out he was going, so my dad put on his Calgary Flames jacket and went down and told his buddies that."

"I really didn't want to take the time to explain to everyone that I wasn't a player, and besides, they wanted me to be a player," said Ogrean, now USA Hockey's executive director. "They wanted to come by and be a part of what had occurred at Lake Placid."

He thought quickly about what player he could pass for and settled on backup goaltender Janaszak, who had been the only team member not to register a minute of playing time at the Olympics. Ogrean figured no one would know Janaszak and signed many cocktail napkins that were passed his way.

Years later, he ran into Janaszak at a luncheon and confessed to the impersonation. He told Janaszak he signed fifteen autographs using his name. "That means there are probably sixteen napkins out there with my autograph," Janaszak joked.

One of Eruzione's favorite Olympic moments occurred years after the gold medal celebration and in Hartford, Connecticut, not Lake Placid, New York. Eruzione was set to drop the puck in a ceremonial pregame NHL face-off between the Hartford Whalers and Quebec Nordiques when the Quebec center addressed the 1980 U.S. Olympic hockey captain by name. "Mike, you fooled us in Lake Placid," said Slovakian Peter Stastny, who had played for Czechoslovakia in 1980.

Eruzione laughed. "He was absolutely right. We were better than anybody thought," Eruzione said.

But superior skill is not why America loved those players as much as they did. Players have said global politics wasn't an issue to them when they were playing against the Soviets in 1980, but it was an issue to those who watched.

The United States' gold medal at the 1960 Olympics may have been just as dramatic, just as emotional, maybe even as unlikely, as the 1980 gold medal. But the 1980 victory was surrounded by political circumstances that weren't present twenty years before. The world had changed dramatically in the two decades between the gold medals. Kennedy and Nikita Khruschev had played a high-stakes game of chicken during the Cuban missile crisis. The arms race had become a dangerous sprint toward mutual destruction. Russia had become a synonym for evil. Therefore, the U.S. victory in 1980 held much symbolism for the American public.

The Soviets had helped create their negative image. After the 1960 debacle at Squaw Valley, they had begun sequestering their athletes, keeping them out of the public eye and therefore constructing a wall of mistrust. To Americans, Russian athletes had lost their humanity. To those who watched international competition on television, Russian athletes were state-run machines. Americans didn't know, or want to know, that Soviet athletes were flesh and marrow human beings who struggled, complained, and fought the system as much as American athletes.

The Soviets' dominance in hockey had humbled everyone, including the mighty Canadians, who didn't compete internationally in the 1970s because they viewed the Russians as professionals. Soviets players were Darth Vader on skates, unemotional soldiers from the evil empire.

Images of athletic Frankensteins created in laboratory experiments were conjured up because Americans couldn't believe that any country could produce better, more dedicated athletes than the United States. Steroids? Blood packing? Performance-enhancing drugs? Americans believed anything was possible with the Soviets.

Remember, the American public of 1980 was disillusioned. Ayatolla Khomeini had kept Americans imprisoned for more than 100 days. The Soviets had invaded Afghanistan. At home, America faced domestic inflation, unemployment, and economic uncertainty. The United States didn't seem to be as mighty on the global scene as it once was—until its hockey team hit the ice.

That's why Americans loved the 1980 hockey team and their victory over the Soviets. They made America feel like it was back in control.

Chapter 10

The United States sent more men to the moon than to the National Hockey League in 1969. Nine Americans made lunar orbits on *Apollo* missions 10, 11, and 12 that year, and astronaut Neal Armstrong took one small step onto the moon. Meanwhile, six men, Bobby Sheehan, Larry Pleau, Doug Roberts, Tracy Pratt, Tommy Williams, and Charlie Burns, were the only Americans who took a giant leap into the NHL.

Canada's stranglehold on NHL roster spots wouldn't loosen for at least another decade until members of the 1980 U.S. Olympic team jumped to the NHL, pushing to 10 percent the number of U.S. citizens on NHL rosters for the first time in NHL history.

In the 1995-96 season, almost 18 percent of all NHL players were American, 25 percent of the league's scoring leaders were American, and 26 percent of the league's starting goaltenders were American. Five of the NHL's general managers—Pittsburgh Penguins' Craig Patrick, New York Islanders' Mike Milbury, New Jersey Devils' Lou Lamoriello, Mighty Ducks of Anaheim's Jack Ferreira, and San Jose Sharks' Dean Lombardi—were born in the United States. Going back one season, in 1995, the New Jersey Devils won the Stanley Cup championship with eleven Americans on their roster.

THE U.S. INVASION

Germs vs. White Corpuscles

Needham, Massachusetts native Robbie Ftorek was among the first stars of the World Hockey Association. In 373 games, he had 218 goals and 307 assists. He was only 5-foot-9, 155 pounds, but he compensated with his feisty playing style.

Minnesota's Bob Dill was a two-sport pro long before Bo Jackson was playing major league baseball and football in the same calendar year. When Dill would finish his hockey season in the 1940s, he grabbed his ball glove and headed for baseball spring training. He played two seasons in the NHL for the New York Rangers, but only advanced as high as AAA minor league baseball.

That level of American participation was never anticipated during the 1950s and 1960s when Tommy Williams was the only U.S. player to gain entrance to Canada's exclusive club for an extended stay. After Frank Brimsek, Doc Romnes, Mike Karakas, Cully Dahlstrom, and John Mariucci had retired, the American NHL presence all but evaporated.

Toronto Star columnist Jim Proudfoot, who began covering the NHL in the 1950s, said when Williams arrived in the league he was viewed as a novelty. "It was like when Sergei Priakin came over here as the first Russian [in 1990]," Proudfoot said. "He was more of a curiosity than anything."

The increased number of American-born NHL players, and growth in the sport overall, can be attributed to several significant factors:

•Bobby Orr's arrival in the NHL spawned a generation of youngsters who were turned on to hockey by watching him dominate in the late 1960s and early 1970s.

•NHL expansion and the arrival of the World Hockey Association in 1972 increased the need for more players and opened the door for more Americans.

•The United States' gold medal performance in Lake Placid enhanced the reputation of the American hockey athlete. After 1980, more youngsters were interested in playing hockey.

•Wayne Gretzky's arrival in the United States in 1988 led to the expansion of hockey into California, Florida, Colorado, Arizona, and Texas.

Evidence suggests prejudice against American players did exist in the NHL for many years. When Eveleth native Aldo Palazzari made the Boston Bruins in 1943, he said players made him feel "like a germ that had just entered the body and all the white corpuscles were ganging up on me."

"One of my own teammates told me, 'Go home and play baseball,'" Palazzari remembered.

New York Rangers general manager Lester Patrick signed St. Paul, Minnesota native Bob Dill before the 1943-44 season. At age twenty-three, Dill registered six goals and 10 assists in 28 games. Dill was also handy with his fists and didn't mind challenging the NHL's toughest players. Before arriving in the NHL, he had survived some memorable minor-league scraps with Bill and Knobby Warwick, who would both end up his teammates in New York.

Dill was the Deion Sanders of the 1940s. In addition to playing in the NHL, he almost made it as a hard-hitting major-league outfielder, advancing as high as the AAA minor-league teams in Minneapolis and Indianapolis.

In his second NHL season, Bob Dill scored nine goals and added five assists in 48 games. But when the regulars came home from World War II, Patrick ordered Dill to the minors. The Boston Bruins had interest in Dill, but Patrick wouldn't release Dill from his contract because he wanted him as a draw for the St. Paul farm team.

"[My dad] believed he could have played another five or six years in the NHL," Bob Dill Jr. said. "He was always ticked at Patrick about that."

Although the late Tommy Williams enjoyed a long NHL career, he too faced some discrimination as an American in the NHL. In the 1965-66 season, Boston Bruins general manager Hap Emms told Williams he wanted to send him to the minors for two weeks to improve his conditioning, even though Williams was second on the team in scoring.

"What gives?" Williams asked.

"Tommy," Emms said, "it's not your fault, but Americans can't play the game."

Williams exploded in anger and told Emms he could take the job and shove it. After listening to Williams's tirade, Emms said he would give Williams another game before

When famed player Eddie Shore owned a Springfield (Massachusetts) team, he became involved in a fight with American Bob Dill, who had become enraged when Shore refused to pay for a season-ending party for the players. The argument ended up requiring police intervention to quell.

Defenseman and University of Minnesota graduate Lou Nanne played his entire eleven-year NHL career with the Minnesota North Stars. He was a co-recipient of the 1988-89 Lester Patrick Trophy, awarded for outstanding service to hockey in the United States.

he sent him down. It's unknown whether Emms really believed what he said, but Williams was so incensed he went out the next game and scored two goals and made two assists against the Canadiens in the Montreal Forum. Emms never did send Williams to the minors.

But others would argue that the vast majority of American players simply weren't talented enough to play in the NHL, on the best six teams in the world. There were about 120 NHL jobs available every year, and competition was fierce. Hockey was to Canada what baseball was to America. Canadian children grew up believing they had a birthright to those jobs.

Another factor inhibited American play, as well: The NHL didn't scout in the United States; it didn't pay particularly well, and the league didn't have the luster or popularity that it enjoys today. Children in Wayne, Michigan, or Edina, Minnesota, or Worchester, Massachusetts, didn't grow up wanting to play in the NHL as they do now.

Some hockey aficionados insist John Mayasich, who played on the 1956 and 1960 Olympic teams, was quite capable of playing in the NHL, but the league never discovered him. "He would have broken the bank if he was playing today," Bill Cleary said. "He would be making millions in the NHL."

Had the NHL discovered Mayasich, it would have needed to make a significant offer to land him. Mayasich had a good job in the television industry and earned extra money playing senior hockey for the Green Bay Bobcats. He probably wouldn't have given up that long-term security for the short-term gratification of playing in the NHL.

The NHL didn't 'wow' players with cash in the fifties, sixties, or early seventies as it does today. In the 1950s, soon-to-be Olympic hero Bill Cleary was offered a contract to play for Montreal, but turned it down to go into the insurance business.

Earlier, the Boston Bruins had an interest in Cleary after his college career. General manager Lynn Patrick offered him about $1,000 to sign and $5,000 to play. Cleary told Patrick he wanted $15,000 as a signing bonus and $10,000 as an annual salary. Patrick came back with an offer of $12,500 to sign, but Cleary heard they were cheating him and decided he wanted no part of pro hockey. Patrick made a final plea, talking about how important it would be to have an American player.

"You have a magic name in this area," Patrick said.

"What you're saying," Cleary replied, "is that I'll be the monkey in the zoo that everyone is coming to see."

Cleary went into the insurance business instead and made more money than he probably would have in the NHL. American college players, with a degree in hand, usually could earn more outside of hockey. Hall of Famer Moose Goheen said no to the Boston Bruins in 1929 because he didn't want to give up his job with the power company. Bob Gaudreau, who played for the 1968 U.S. Olympic team, was one of the top college defensemen of all time, but it made more economic sense for him to use his MBA from Columbia than to seek his fortune in the NHL.

Minnesota graduate Lou Nanne didn't join the NHL for a long time because the Chicago Blackhawks wouldn't pay enough to match what he could earn using his degree from the University of Minnesota. When Nanne graduated in 1963, Blackhawks general manager Tommy Ivan offered him a contract that paid him a $2,000 signing bonus, plus an annual salary of $6,000. Nanne agreed to that figure, even though he was making a little more than that in chemical sales. Later, when Nanne asked for the contract previously agreed upon before he showed up at training camp, Ivan balked. He said the

Blackhawks only awarded contracts after they watched players in training camp. "Not even Bobby Hull got a contract before training camp," Ivan said.

"Bobby Hull doesn't have a college degree, a wife, and a child," said Nanne, who decided to keep the security of his job.

For the next four seasons, the Hawks tried to land Nanne, but the pay gap kept getting wider. In 1967, they were offering $18,500 and he was already making $25,000 in marketing. Not until the Minnesota North Stars got his rights, and Walter Bush began negotiating with Nanne, did a deal get done. It was completed over Frescas at the Dunes Hotel in Las Vegas. "We each wrote our figures down on napkins. It took ten minutes," Bush remembered.

Larry Pleau, with his New England accent, was as American as firecrackers and sparklers on the Fourth of July. He was a 15-year-old sophomore at Lynn English High School in Massachusetts in 1963 when the Montreal Canadiens' Ralph Backstrom discovered him at the Doc O'Connor summer hockey camp. The Canadiens sent Scotty Bowman to woo Pleau. Ralph Backstrom told the director of player personnel, Sam Pollock, that the Rangers were also aware of Pleau.

According to Ron Caron, then a Canadiens' scout, Pollock's response was "take $5 and send him to the movies, because [Rangers' general manager] Emile Francis will get there ahead of Bowman."

The Canadiens wanted Pleau to play junior hockey in Canada and to agree to be placed on their protected list. There was no NHL entry draft in those days. "I didn't even know what junior hockey was," Pleau remembered.

Bowman's pitch worked, and 15-year-old Pleau played for the Notre Dame De'Grace and then joined the Montreal Junior Canadiens for four seasons, playing alongside Serge Savard, Jacques Lemaire, Rogie Vachon, and Carol Vadnais. Another American, Craig Patrick, grandson of Lester Patrick, also played on that squad. Pleau was captain of the Junior Canadiens in his final season.

"People have always asked me how I was treated, and I have to say the Canadiens treated me fairly," Pleau said. "I never had any problems, maybe it was because I followed the same path most the of Canadian players did."

After playing for the United States in the 1968 Olympics in Grenoble, France, Pleau joined the Canadiens, along with Bobby Sheehan from Weymouth, Massachusetts, who had also come up through the Canadian junior system. The Canadiens won the Stanley Cup that season. Sheehan got his name on the Cup because he played in the final. However, Pleau didn't get his name on the Cup because he dressed for some playoff games but never hit the ice.

Sheehan, a 5-foot-7, 157-pound center, played two seasons in Montreal and was then sold to the California Golden Seals, where he played with Craig Patrick. Pleau played parts of three seasons with the Canadiens, finally earning a spot as a fourth-line player and penalty killer.

"My only complaint with the Canadiens was about ice time, but I don't think it had anything to do with me being an American," Pleau said.

Pleau has vivid memories of his second contract negotiation with general manager Pollock because he had the courage to ask for $20,000 per season, after making $15,000 the previous year. He believed he deserved a one-way contract, which assured he would be paid the same salary whether he was playing for the Canadiens or their minor-league affiliate. At that time, it was common to offer players two-way contracts that paid them an NHL salary or a lesser amount if they were shipped to the minors.

Pollock was spitting mad about Pleau's audacity. "Larry," he said, "I want you to go home and think real hard about this. Talk about it with your wife. Let's forget we've

Scouts for the NHL spotted Larry Pleau as a fifteen-year-old playing high school hockey in Lynn, Massachusetts, in 1963. The Montreal Canadiens convinced his parents to send him to Quebec to play junior hockey. He made the NHL in 1969 and was one of the NHL players who jumped to the World Hockey Association in 1972. Today, he is the general manager of the St. Louis Blues.

During the 1960s, Tom Williams was the NHL's novelty player and the only American playing in the league. In 1975-76, after 15 NHL seasons, he retired with 161 goals and 269 assists for 430 points in 663 games.

even had this conversation. Tomorrow you will see things more clearly."

Pleau said he was "nervous as hell" when he came to see Pollock the next day.

"Larry, what do you think today," Pollock said.

"I still think I really deserve $20,000," Pleau said.

"Tell you what I'm going to do," Pollock said. "I'll give you a two-way contract with $14,000 if you are in the minors and $16,000 if you are in the NHL. Or I'll give you a one-way contract for $15,000."

"I'll take the one-way contract," Pleau said.

Negotiating with Pollock was like negotiating with your father. He was always right, and you were always wrong.

After the 1971-72 season, Pleau knew he was always going to struggle for ice time with the Canadiens' talented lineup. The centers were Lemaire, Henri Richard, and Pete Mahovlich, and the left wings in front of Pleau were Frank Mahovlich, Marc Tardif, and Rejean Houle.

At the time, the World Hockey Association was starting to make noise, and the New England Whalers wanted Pleau for his talent and name recognition in the area. The night before Pleau was going to jump to the WHA, he decided to make one final plea to Pollock to trade him to the expansion Vancouver Canucks, who had expressed interest in his talent.

"There will be no WHA ever," Pollock responded to Pleau's ultimatum.

That day, Pleau signed with the Whalers and pocketed a $25,000 signing bonus. His salaries for the three-year deal were to be $25,000, $35,000, and $45,000.

Pollock then traded Pleau's rights to the Toronto Maple Leafs, who tried to convince Pleau to renege on his contract with the Whalers. "If [the Canadiens] would have made that trade earlier, I would have stayed in the NHL," said Pleau, who scored 39 goals in his first WHA season.

When the NHL had expanded from six to twelve teams in 1968, it still didn't seem to need more American players. But the WHA-NHL wars in the 1970s created an explosion of job openings for Americans, particularly college players whose hockey resumes had previously failed to impress NHL teams. The WHA created headlines by signing away NHL stars such as Bobby Hull, Bernie Parent, John McKenzie, and Derek Sanderson, but they also began filling many of their roster spots with Americans.

The New England Whalers won the first Avco Cup with a team coached by former Boston University coach Jack Kelley and a roster that boasted Americans such as Tim Sheehy, Larry Pleau, and Kevin Ahearn.

In a span of six years, from 1967 to 1972, the number of major-league teams, if the WHA could be called that, increased from six to twenty-eight. The NHL had sixteen teams and the WHA had twelve teams. By 1974, the NHL had nineteen teams and the WHA had fourteen teams. Major-league hockey then offered 660 jobs, instead of the 120 that were available just seven years before.

"This wasn't evolution, this was revolution," said Whalers owner Howard Baldwin.

WHA teams in the United States, particularly New England and Minnesota, signed players who had some name recognition in those areas. The Minnesota Fighting Saints, for example, signed 1972 U.S. Olympic hero Mike Curran of International Falls, Minnesota, and 1960 U.S. Olympian Jack McCartan of St. Paul. The Houston Aeros signed Gordie Howe and his two American-born sons, Mark and Marty.

Mark was eighteen when he signed. Although later in his career he would be an all-star NHL defenseman, Mark started his pro career as a left wing. He notched 38 goals in his first season to outscore his 46-year-old father and linemate, who finished with 31.

Mark Howe believed the 1972 U.S. Olympians played a significant role in helping the NHL conclude that there was hockey talent south of the Canadian border. "Up until that point," Mark Howe said, "I don't think anyone in hockey respected the ability of the American player."

The Detroit Red Wings signed U.S. Olympian Robbie Ftorek in 1972, but let him flee to the WHA where he became a star player with the Cincinnati Stingers. Ftorek scored 31 goals in his first WHA season and then followed with season productions of 41, 46, 59, and 38 goals to establish himself as an elite pro player. At age twenty-seven, he moved to the NHL with the Quebec Nordiques.

"He was the Bobby Clarke of the WHA," Pleau said.

Only 5-foot-9 and 170 pounds, Ftorek was always forced to prove he could survive and thrive in a world where opponents were usually a head taller and twenty to forty pounds heavier.

"His size was never a detriment because he was such a smart player," said Jacques Demers, who coached him in Cincinnati and Quebec. "He may have been the most intelligent player I ever coached."

Ftorek's pride was his guide when it came to dealing with the toughness of pro hockey. Demers remembers Ftorek suffered a nasty cut during the WHA All-Star game. Sixty-five stitches were needed to close the wound.

The Cincinnati Stingers' next game was against the Birmingham Bulls, who boasted one of the roughest collections of tough guys pro hockey had ever seen. Demers knew the Bulls would attack Ftorek's wound like tigers after injured prey.

"Robbie knew they were going to kick the crap out of us, but he insisted on playing," Demers said.

When he was coaching in Quebec, Demers named Ftorek captain. It was highly controversial to name an Anglophile as a captain in this French-speaking city, but Ftorek won over the crowd by speaking a few words of French during his first appearance in front of a microphone.

Others to join the NHL included Henry Boucha, who took advantage of a bidding war between the Red Wings and St. Paul Fighting Saints to get a nice contract from Detroit. Craig Sarner, Jim McElmury, and Tom Mellor also played in the NHL, and Mike Curran, Keith Christiansen, Dick McGlynn, Wally Olds, Frank Sanders, and Kevin Ahearn ended up in the WHA.

"The assumption was that Americans couldn't play until they proved they could. It was like every GM was from Missouri and they were saying, 'Show me,'" said Brian Burke, an Edina, Minnesota, native who played college and minor-league hockey in the 1970s. He went on to become an agent, NHL general manager, and the NHL director of hockey operations.

The prevailing NHL attitude during the fifties, sixties, and seventies was similar to the attitude professional boxing judges had about title bouts: to unseat the champion, one had to be unquestionably better, not just marginally better, and ties or close decisions always went to the incumbent. Canadians owned the vast majority of managerial

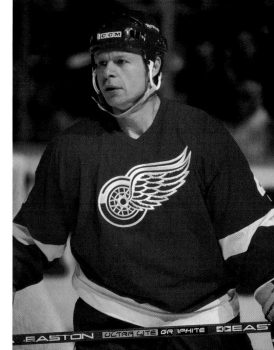

Mark Howe believes the 1972 Olympics played a significant role in convincing the NHL that there was talent in the United States. Howe, goaltender Mike Curran, and center Robbie Ftorek were 1972 Olympians who joined the pro ranks. Howe's career spanned twenty-two seasons, finishing with the Detroit Red Wings in 1995-96.

positions in the NHL, and they were going to dethrone a Canadian player only if the American player was significantly better.

No one fought against that thinking more aggressively than agent Art Kaminsky, who was among the first American-based agents. With a client base made up primarily of college players, Kaminsky was like a salesman who was always forced to jam his foot in the door to get teams to listen.

"It wasn't as much anti-American as it was pro-Canadian," Kaminsky said. "The GMs were all Canadian, the coaches were all Canadian, and the scouts were all Canadian. They just didn't believe there were better players than Canadian players."

An illustration of that attitude, according to Kaminsky, was the NHL's attitude going into the 1972 Summit Series against the Russians. "They didn't think they would lose a game," Kaminsky said. "They thought they were going to go 8-0 and win every game 10-0."

As it turned out, the NHL players needed a memorable goal by Paul Henderson to win that series by a game. The series certainly opened the NHL's eyes to the merits of Russian players, and perhaps there was residual benefit to the American players as well.

In the WHA, American players made a difference. The New England Whalers brought in Harvard's Danny Bolduc and New Hampshire goaltender Cap Raeder late in the 1975-76 season. "I remember we brought in Cap Raeder from the Cape Cod Cubs," said then Whalers coach Harry Neale. "I hadn't heard of him or the Cape Cod Cubs."

Bolduc always played as if his pants were on fire, and his speed put a charge in the Whalers' offense. Raeder, meanwhile, became the starting goaltender in the playoffs, posting 2.27 goals-against average in 14 playoff games. The Whalers, a mediocre regular-season team, came within one win of advancing to the Avco Cup final. "I think it was a preview of what was coming," Kaminsky said. "These guys brought in a lot of enthusiasm, some rah-rah college spirit."

Ironically, the Montreal Canadiens, one of the symbols of Canadian hockey pride, was among the first to see the value in signing Americans. Ron Caron, then the Canadiens' assistant general manager, liked American college defensemen because they were big, strong, and smart.

"The Americans had good goaltenders and defenseman," Caron said. "There was a concern they couldn't play on your first or second line, because they had no creativity with the puck. They were like robots. They could play defense, but they really couldn't score."

In 1972, the Canadiens chose Notre Dame player Bill Nyrop with the sixty-sixth pick in the draft. In 1977, they took New Hampshire defenseman Rod Langway with the thirty-sixth. In 1983, Langway would eventually became the first American to win the Norris Trophy as the league's top defenseman.

Langway was a superb athlete who played linebacker for two years at New Hampshire. At one point, the Dallas Cowboys were interested in him, and Kaminsky has hypothesized that Langway would have been an NFL draft pick had he stuck with football.

> Joe Mullen scored a goal against the Colorado Avalanche on March 14, 1997, to become the first American to score 500 goals in an NHL career. Mullen overcame humble beginnings in New York's Hell's Kitchen to become one of the NHL's premier goal scorers. He first played hockey on roller skates before shifting to the ice.

Nyrop was also a two-sport athlete who played spring football at Notre Dame and earned a spot as Joe Theismann's backup before deciding to concentrate on hockey. When Caron ran into the New Orleans Saints general manager, Jim Finks, in the early 1990s, Finks said Nyrop "could have been an NFL linebacker."

Nyrop helped the Canadiens' win three Stanley Cup championships and then retired at age twenty-six. He came back and played one season with Minnesota in 1981. Nyrop died in 1996 of lung cancer, even though he was a fitness buff and never touched a cigarette in his short life. "That's one of the mysteries of life," Caron said.

Montreal's interest in American players drew the attention of other teams. The Canadiens had a lineup full of Hall of Famers in the 1970s, and they clearly knew something about finding talent.

Yet, the NHL still was moving cautiously toward Americans, and perhaps for good reason. After the WHA arrived, the percentage of American-born players on rosters increased to 4.6 percent, but they weren't producing the level of offensive numbers they were in the WHA. It wasn't until 1979 that Tom Rowe, a native of Lynn, Masssachusetts, became the first American to register a 30-goal season in the NHL. He had 31 goals to break Tommy Williams's record of 23 goals.

Also in the 1978-79 season, Minnesota North Stars' coach Glenn Sonmor decided to make NHL history by starting six Americans. Pete Lopresti was in goal, with Billy Butters, Gary Sargeant, Tom Younghams, Mike Polich, and Jack Carlson.

Germs vs. White Corpuscles

High-scoring forwards such as Livonia, Michigan's Mike Modano have eliminated doubts about the Americans' ability to put the puck in the net. Modano's career includes a 50-goal season with Dallas in 1993-94.

Sonmor told the players just to stay on the ice long enough for photographers to capture the moment on film. "Dump the puck in and come to the bench for the change," Sonmor said.

Problem was the Chicago Blackhawks won the face-off and carried the puck into the North Stars' zone. It seemed as if the Hawks were on a power play.

"It took us forever to get the puck out," said Lopresti.

Sonmor said afterward: "We will never do that again."

Kaminsky recalled that he had difficulty convincing general managers to come out and watch hotshot Minnesota freshman Mike Ramsey before that summer's draft. "I believe Scotty Bowman was the only general manager who came to the U.S. Olympic trials."

Bowman's Buffalo Sabres drafted Ramsey eleventh overall in 1979 to make him the first American to be selected in the first round. Ramsey retired in May of 1996 after 17 seasons in the NHL.

Old habits didn't die easy, even though American players were beginning to make inroads. Kaminsky represented sixteen players on the 1980 Olympic team and was frustrated trying to get some NHL agreements in place before the Games.

"In most cases the offers were so bad, so awful, we didn't even bother," Kaminsky said.

One case involved University of Wisconsin center Mark Johnson, who had been college hockey's best player for two seasons. Before the 1980 Olympic Games, Penguins general manager Baz Bastien offered Johnson a $10,000 signing bonus, plus a three-way contract. He would get one salary if he made the NHL, a lower salary for the American Hockey League, and an even lower salary if he played in the International Hockey League.

After he led the Olympic tournament in scoring and put a gold medal in his trophy collection, Johnson was given a $75,000 signing bonus and a one-way contract. Ramsey,

Jim Craig, Dave Christian, and Rob McClanahan all landed similar deals, which were superior to the ones they would have received before the Miracle on Ice.

The gold medal opened the doors wider for American players and seemed to give renewed credibility to United States hockey. Ken Morrow, Mike Ramsey, and Dave Christian quickly became NHL standouts, and Mark Pavelich, Neal Broten, and Mark Johnson weren't far behind. Christian signed with the Winnipeg Jets immediately after the Games and scored eight goals and 10 assists in the final 15 games of the 1979-80 season. He had 28 goals in his first full season with the Jets.

During the next two years, team registration at the Amateur Hockey Association of the United States was up about 7 percent, and that was probably the maximum that could have been achieved given the number of available rinks. It took time for rink construction to catch up to the hockey enthusiasm that swept over the country. After 1980, NHL teams also approached the draft in a distinctly different way. Bobby Carpenter, a Massachusetts prep star, was selected third overall by the Washington Capitals in 1981 after unprecedented publicity surrounding his performance at St. John's High School.

Would he have been drafted number three overall if the Americans hadn't triumphed in Lake Placid? "Absolutely not," Kaminsky said. "That's an incontrovertible fact. He would have been lucky to be a second-round pick. And I don't care what people will say now. If they weren't all that interested in college players, they weren't suddenly going to develop an interest in high school players overnight."

Mighty Ducks of Anaheim general manager Jack Ferreira disagreed. "He was a great high school player," Ferreira said. "He could play any way you wanted him to play. He could score, he could play tough. He could do it all. He would have gone high no matter what happened in 1980."

Sports Illustrated featured Carpenter on one of its covers as "The Can't-Miss-Kid," and that alone was evidence of the inroads hockey was making in the United States.

In 1980, no U.S. high school player had been drafted in the first two rounds, and in 1981, four high school players, plus Chicago native Chris Chelios, who was about to head to the University of Wisconsin for his freshman season, went in the first two rounds. The tide seemed to be turning, although in dressing rooms, some Canadians didn't know the war was over.

Ex-NHL player Tom Laidlaw, who played for the New York Rangers in the early 1980s after Herb Brooks had brought in a few American college players, remembered American college players still had a stigma attached to them. According to Laidlaw, they were viewed as "milk drinkers" and players "who hadn't paid enough dues."

"The funny thing was I was a college player," said Laidlaw, who went to Northern Michigan. "But I was a Canadian, and no one said anything to me."

As the NHL prepares for its second century of operation, most of the prejudices about Americans have disappeared, particularly those about the American's ability to score. Centers Jeremy Roenick, Pat LaFontaine, Doug Weight, and Mike Modano are among the league's most talented scorers. The NHL still seems to prefer players who play Canadian junior over college, although guys like Chris Chelios, Brian Leetch, Rod Langway, Bryan Smolinski, and others have made it clear that there are many different paths that lead to the final destination.

Some older American players look back at the fifties, sixties, and seventies and wonder whether they would have made the NHL had they owned a different passport. But McCartan, whose NHL career lasted 12 games, isn't among them.

"I was up against Glenn Hall, Jacques Plante, and Gump Worsley," McCartan said. "The bottom line was I wasn't good enough. I wasn't one of the best six goaltenders in the world."

MIKE GRIER

Wendy Grier can't be sure what racial insults, if any, her son Michael endured during his teenage hockey years. She stopped sitting in the stands when he was younger because she couldn't bear to hear them. She would stand at the end of the rink and wonder why some adults had more difficulty than the kids did accepting a talented black hockey player in their midst.

"When we would go to tournaments, there would be name calling," Wendy Grier said. "But we used to tell Mike, 'Just put the puck in the net and answer them that way.'"

Grier's successful fight against discrimination culminated on October 4, 1996, when he played for the Edmonton Oilers against the Buffalo Sabres and became the first black NHLer who was both born and trained in the United States. Most of the previous black NHLers were born in Canada. Val James, who played seven games for Buffalo in the 1981-82 season, was born in Ocala, Florida, but moved to Canada before starting his hockey training. Graeme Townshend, who has 45 NHL games, was trained in the U.S. and played at Rensselear Polytechnic Institute, but he was born in Jamaica.

Grier's arrival in the NHL was an important step for the league and USA Hockey, which had been working with the league to attract more minority players to hockey. Grier and goaltender Doug Bonner were the first African Americans to play on the U.S. National Junior Team in 1995. "I know it's important how I carry myself," Grier said. "I know I can be an inspiration. I can show this isn't just a white man's sport."

Grier began to draw notice when he was drafted 219th overall in the 1993 NHL Entry Draft by the St. Louis Blues as a Massachusetts high school player.

When Blues scout Matt Keator began watching Mike Grier play high school hockey, he knew the youngster had to overcome a major disadvantage to reach the NHL—his size, not his race. "He was 255 pounds when we drafted him," Keator said. "When I first saw him he was an immovable object. He would skate 10 feet, hit someone. Skate 10 more feet and hit someone else."

Boston University coach Jack Parker knew Grier needed to lose weight and add speed when he was brought to the university as a recruited walk-on. But Terriers assistant Blais MacDonald sold Parker on the idea that Grier had the character and drive to be a player.

"Watch him after a game," MacDonald told Parker. "When he comes out of the dressing room, five of his teammates and five from the other team rush to hang out with him."

Grier worked to improve himself at Boston University. He credits the Terriers' conditioning coach, Mike Boyle, for bettering his training habits.

The once blubbery Grier was a muscular 223 pounds when he signed with the Oilers, who acquired his rights from St. Louis. He has a body fat of just 8 percent. The Oilers believe Grier, who played three seasons at Boston University, will mature into a tough power forward who can bring both grit and goals to the lineup.

It's been a remarkable rise for a player who joined a Boston area youth hockey program years ago because he was too large to pass the weight limits for football.

Athletic ability runs in his family. His father, Bobby, is the New England Patriots' director of player development. Pro football Hall of Famer Raymond Berry, who coached with Bobby, used to tell Bobby Grier that his son had great hands.

The elder Grier has always been proud to say his son was a hockey player. "He has been skating since he was four," his father remembered. "He played hockey and soccer because both of those sports would let him play."

Grier has never let any racism he's experienced along the way impede his progress. "Some people did cross the line, but most didn't," Grier said. "I heard more things when I was younger than when I was older."

One racial slur did come his way during an intense game against Boston College. "But his teammates reacted faster than he did," Parker said. "I was mad at Chris Drury for starting a fight until I found out why he did it."

When Mike Grier made his debut with the Edmonton Oilers in the 1996-97 season (opposite page), he became the first black NHLer who was both born and trained in the United States. Mike played at Boston University and was also a member of the U.S National Junior Team (above).

Keator, who still follows Grier's progress, said Grier will never have any difficulty handling whatever opponents hurl his way, even when racism is at the root of the insult.

"If that kind of stuff bothered him, he never would have gotten where he is today," Keator said.

UNSUNG AMERICAN HOCKEY HEROES

Mike Emrick

Growing up in basketball-crazy Indiana, Emrick somehow developed a yearning to be a hockey play-by-play broadcaster. As teenagers, Emrick and friends would travel to Fort Wayne to watch International Hockey League games where Emrick would sit in the highest rows of the Fort Wayne Coliseum and do a broadcast that only he could hear.

He began broadcasting IHL games in Port Huron, Michigan, for $160 a week in the 1970s, and in 1980, he broadcast his first NHL game. Today, as a Fox broadcaster, his voice is synonymous with hockey. "He's a wordsmith," said Fox producer Richie Zyontz. "If you ever heard poetry coming from a hockey announcer, it's Mike Emrick."

Fido Purpur

Born in Grand Forks, North Dakota, in 1916, Purpur caught the hockey world's attention when he jumped from high school hockey to the Minneapolis Millers of the Central League in 1933. He played 15 seasons of pro hockey, including 144 NHL games with the Chicago Blackhawks, Detroit Red Wings, and St. Louis Eagles. Three generations of Purpurs have been involved in U.S. hockey circles. His best NHL season was 1942-43 when he had 13 goals and 16 assists for Chicago.

Bob Paradise

After playing for the 1968 U.S. Olympic team, St. Paul, Minnesota native Paradise went on to register nine seasons in the NHL at a time when few Americans were playing regularly in the world's best league. He was a tough, physical defender who is already a member of the U.S. Hockey Hall of Fame. His best NHL season was 1974-75 with the Pittsburgh Penguins when he had three goals, 15 assists, and 109 penalty minutes in 78 games. He also played with the Minnesota North Stars, Washington Capitals, and Atlanta Flames.

Doug Roberts

When he signed with the Detroit Red Wings in 1965, Roberts, then 23, was one of the first U.S. college players to sign a free agent contract directly with an NHL team. He had played at Michigan State and established school records of 33 assists and 61 points in 1964-65. Versatile enough to play both left wing and defense, Detroit native Roberts survived 10 NHL seasons with Detroit, Cailfornia, Oakland, and Boston. His son, David, played college hockey at Michigan, and now plays for the Vancouver Canucks.

Ed Olson

Marquette, Michigan native Olson made American hockey history when he won the American Hockey League scoring title in 1952-53 by scoring 32 goals and registering 62 assists. He was considered to be the first American-born player to win a pro-scoring crown. Coincidently, Guyle Fielder, who was born in Idaho and trained in Canada, finished second that season to give Americans a one-two finish. Even though Olson had another AHL scoring title to his credit in 1954-55, he never received a real shot at the NHL.

Ken Yackel

A superb all-around athlete, Yackel may have been a victim of the NHL's Canadian bias in the 1950s. After helping the USA win the silver medal at the 1952 Olympics and finishing second in scoring with six goals and three assists, Yackel had a distinguished career in the IHL. He won the IHL scoring championship in 1960-61 with 114 points, and added a 50-goal season for the championship Minneapolis Millers in 1961-62. Even with those credentials, Yackel had only one brief call-up with the Boston Bruins in 1958-59.

Before turning pro, Yackel was a three-sport star at the University of Minnesota where he was an outfielder on the baseball team and a linebacker on the football squad. In 1952, the then-recently married Yackel was about to give up hockey to find a job when John Mariucci, who had just taken over the Minnesota program, talked him into returning to school.

"All that I did later would not have been possible without Mariucci," Yackel would say years later. "I was 22, and married, but John had faith in my abilities."

David E. Kelley

As the son of Boston University coach Jack Kelley, David grew up surrounded by hockey tradition. He played hockey at Princeton, but his real contribution to American hockey culture came as a writer and producer of the television shows *LA Law* and *Chicago Hope*. In an era when hockey still cried for publicity, Kelley was sprinkling hockey references into his shows.

Law firms would be named after old Boston Bruins players, like Stanfield and Hodge. Patients on *Chicago Hope* have been named after goaltenders. "I couldn't have done that with baseball players, like a (Orel) Hershiser or a Roger Clemens, because they were too well-known and it would have distracted from the storyline," said Kelley, who sold his first script to Howard Baldwin, who then owned the Hartford Whalers in addition to a film company.

Kelly O'Leary

had a reputation long before the movie came out," Jeff Carlson jokes.

Kelly O'Leary

Often overshadowed by leading U.S. women's scorer Cammi Granato and all-world goaltender Erin Whitten, O'Leary (left) who plays defense, may be the most indispensible player in the USA women's hockey history. She's one of the world's toughest competitors, and possesses a wicked slap shot and a knack for always making the right play at the right time. She's been a member of six U.S. national teams and made the all-world team three times, including in 1997.

Moe Roberts

Goaltender Roberts, born in Westbury, Connecticut, holds the NHL record for the most years between appearances in an NHL game. He made his NHL debut with the Boston Bruins at age 18. He was summoned from the stands after Boston's regular goaltender Doc Stewart was injured in a game. Roberts only had played a handful of games before making what he thought was his last NHL appearance in 1933-34. But in 1951-52, when he was a trainer with the Chicago Blackhawks, he was forced to play in goal for the Hawks when Harry Lumley was injured. He gave up no goals in one period of work. He was forty-four years old.

The Hanson brothers
(played by Steve and Jeff Carlson, plus Dave Hanson)

Made famous by the 1977 movie entitled *Slap Shot*, the Hanson brothers are synonymous with the 1970s-style hockey. Those movie characters were played by real pro players: Steve and Jeff Carlson, who were originally from Virginia and Minnesota, and Dave Hanson, who was born in Wisconsin. The Carlsons and Hanson were cast in those roles because they were all big, tough minor-league players with great senses of humors.

Another Carlson, Jack, was supposed to play the third Hanson brother. But he had agreed to play with the Edmonton Oilers for the 1975-76 season and was unavailable to play the role. That opened the door for Hanson. The three Carlsons and Dave Hanson actually played together for the World Hockey Association's Minnesota Fighting Saints in 1976-77. Did the movie give the Carlsons a reputation for being hooligans? "We

Mike Lange

As the Pittsburgh Penguins' broadcaster since 1974, Lange has left a mark on the American hockey scene with his colorful play-by-play style. "He beat him like a rented mule," Lange might bellow when a forward scores a goal. A special play? "Buy Sam a drink and get his dog one too," Lange will say. But one phrase has now become part of American hockey culture: "Elvis has just left the building." That means the Penguins have the win in the bag.

Earl Bartholomew

Although the Minneapolis native never received a chance to play in the NHL, Bartholomew was one of the top American-born players in the 1930s and 40s. He scored a game-winning goal to give the Cleveland Barons the 1941 AHL championship. He had 467 points in 523 AHL games and was known as a strong two-way player.

Charles Schulz

Creator of the Peanuts comic strip, Minnesota native Schulz brought attention to hockey in the 1970s by depicting Snoopy and Woodstock playing hockey on a frozen bird feeder. Schulz's fascination with Zamboni machines also is prominent in his strips. He owns two Zamboni machines.

Frank J. Zamboni

In 1949, American businessman Zamboni unveiled the machine that revolutionized ice-cleaning. A famed figure skater took one on tour, and spectators seemed to like the Zamboni as much as the performance. A star was born.

Chapter 11
COLLEGIATE HOCKEY

Dead Gophers and Live Wires

Rivalries remain the lifeblood of college hockey. Above: Boston University versus Boston College.

When legendary goaltender Ken Dryden finally left Cornell in 1969, Boston University coach Jack Kelley offered what turned out to be a premature prayer of gratitude. "Thank God we got rid of Dryden," Kelley growled. "Now all we have to do is beat them." A year later, coaches were still trying to figure out how to beat Cornell. Cornell's 29-0 march to the national championship in the 1969-70 season is the only perfect season ever recorded by an NCAA Division I hockey team.

The year before, the Big Red had graduated four all-Americans, including Dryden. They were said to be rebuilding and weren't considered a prime contender for the national championship.

"But at one of our first meetings, I can remember [coach] Harkness emphatically telling us that we were going to win the national championship," said Brian McCutcheon, the team's leading scorer that season, who later became Cornell's coach.

Coach Ned Harkness has called his 1969-70 Cornell team the "greatest college team ever." At a reunion for the team twenty-five years later, Harkness would sum up that unforgettable season with a single sentence, punctuated with a hearty laugh: "They said Cornell was rebuilding, and we rammed it down their throats."

Harkness's short summation of a special season may explain the lure of college hockey better than a thousand words ever could. No brand of hockey explores rivalries and bragging rights quite like the college game. Since college hockey began in 1896, this one aspect hasn't changed. The puffed-chest feeling Hobey Baker felt when Princeton beat Yale is the same feeling that Jack Parker felt when Boston University beat Boston College and Harkness felt when Cornell beat Harvard in the 1960s, and the same feeling goaltender Steve Shields felt when Michigan beat Michigan State in the 1990s.

College hockey is uniquely American. Boisterous fans, painted faces, raucous student sections, crude taunts, loud pep bands, manic mascots—those aren't elements we've borrowed from Canada. There's a zaniness to college hockey that simply doesn't exist outside college arenas. Where else but in college hockey would some enterprising North Dakota students acknowledge the arrival of the visiting Minnesota Gophers team by throwing a dead gopher on the ice? Where else but in college hockey would you see the Minnesota mascot Goldy the Gopher bodyslam Bucky the Badger to the ice in the pregame festivities?

Nowhere in sports are bragging rights more cherished than in college hockey, and nothing illustrates its lure better than Boston's 45-year-old Beanpot Tournament, which brings together the teams from Harvard, Boston University, Boston College, and Northeastern University for an annual tournament to determine the city's college champion.

David Silk has a 1980 Olympic gold medal stashed away, but in a speech at a Beanpot Tournament luncheon, he said he considers his memory of winning the 1978 Beanpot Championship for Boston University among his most cherished.

"I'll never forget being handed the Beanpot and being able to show it to my family and friends and all those other people in the stands, maybe taunting the other team's band," Silk said.

What Silk enjoyed most about the Beanpot were the bragging rights that accompany a championship. He enjoyed running into his vanquished foes from Harvard, Northeastern, and Boston College at Red Sox games or on the Boston Common and being able to say better luck next time.

That's a feeling absent from international hockey or the NHL. "It's tough to walk up to [Vladimir] Krutov, [Sergei] Makarov, and [Slava] Fetisov and say, 'Hey, sorry about that,'" Silk said.

Parker, head coach at Boston University, says bragging rights were coveted just as much in 1965 as today. He remembers how much he enjoyed beating Boston College 9-2 that season. And he remembers he was both miffed and amused when he heard coach Snooks Kelley talking on the radio, saying the outcome of one game in the 1965-66 season would have been different if Boston College's top player, John Cunniff, had not been sidelined with a severely separated shoulder. "Snooks made it seem as if the loss of John was beyond the scope of imagination," Parker said, laughing.

Parker was actually going with Cunniff's brother to visit John the day of the radio interview. Parker greeted Cunniff, "John, I know you are a helluva player, but do you really think you would have gotten seven or eight against us in that game?"

Rivalries have existed since college hockey was introduced in the United States in 1896. Before then, college athletes were playing what they called "ice polo." The game's objective and strategy were similar to hockey as we know it today, except teams had only five players and used a ball instead of a puck. The ice polo stick resembled the modern-day field hockey stick.

In the summer of 1894, American and Canadian athletes at a tennis tournament at Niagara Falls began talking about what they did in the winter. They discovered they were both playing different versions of the same game and decided to meet the following winter to determine who had the better game.

In the April 1951 issue of the *Brown Alumni Monthly*, Alexander Meikeljohn offered a firsthand account of that Canadian-United States hockey summit of 1895, which was played in Montreal, Ottawa, Kingston, and Toronto. According to Meiklejohn's account, large crowds showed up to watch the ice polo-hockey doubleheader in each city. The U.S. participants included Byron Watson, Bill Jones, and George Matteson of Brown; A. C. Foote and Malcolm Chase of Yale; F. H. Clarkson of Harvard; and Billy Larned of Columbia. C. M. Pope, a reporter for the Associated Press, also accompanied the United States team to the tournament.

The Canadians won all four hockey games—"easily" according to Meiklejohn's remembrances fifty-six years after the event. "Their game was much more highly developed than ours, as shown by their established league, with a regular schedule and big buildings [for] large crowds of spectators," Meikeljohn wrote.

"They had a couple of other advantages [in addition to their] greater skill. First, they used flat-bladed speed skates against our rockers. And second, our hitting stroke with one hand would not move the puck along the ice."

> Northeastern and Harvard are two of the teams competing in the 45-year-old Beanpot Tournament, held annually to determine the city champion of Boston. The schools, along with Boston College and Boston University, battle for bragging rights in one of college hockey's traditional hotbeds.

Beanpot champion Boston University displays its trophy (opposite page and above). Terriers head coach Jack Parker (above, far right), also played in the tournament in the mid-1960s.

The Canadians had an easy time playing polo, although the Americans did manage to win two of the four ice polo matches, while the other two games ended in a tie.

"It was pretty generally agreed among us, as a result of the trip, that the Canadian game was better than ours," Meikeljohn said.

The Americans brought back some Canadian skates and sticks, and before long, collegians abandoned ice polo in favor of ice hockey. In the west, Minnesotans had also picked up Canadian hockey from the Manitobans.

Reporter Pope's attendance at the games turned out to be a benefit. He returned to New York and raised money for building the St. Nicholas Ice Rink, which would become America's hockey center. The American Amateur Hockey Association was also formed in 1896.

The earliest known written documentation of a college hockey game is a newspaper account of a 2-2 tie between Yale and Johns Hopkins. The February 3, 1896, edition of the *Baltimore Sun* states that a game, played at North Avenue Rink, drew "the largest crowd of the season," suggesting there had been other games earlier.

At the turn of the century, the *Spalding Guide to Hockey* said Baltimore was probably "the most enthusiastic ice hockey city in the country." The Baltimore Hockey League was formed in 1897 and included Johns Hopkins University.

Enthusiasm for the sport spilled over into a court battle to decide the 1896-97 championship. (So much for the notion that the litigious side of sports was a modern creation.)

In the championship game for the Northampton Cup, the Maryland Athletic Club led 2-1 over the University of Maryland. With only a few minutes remaining in the game, the college players scored what they considered the tying goal. The shot appeared to be too high to many, including the Maryland Athletic Club players. Following a heated argument, referee G. B. Macrae of the New York Athletic Club ruled that it was a goal and signaled for overtime to begin. Taking advantage of their momentum, the college players scored again to win 3-2, or so they thought.

The Maryland Athletic Club protested the referee's decision to the league's governing body, which heard testimony from those attending the game. The ruling: the shot was high and the Maryland Athletic Club was the winner. The Spalding Guide said the University of Maryland student body reacted "with great indignation" and sought legal vindication. The school retained three prominent Baltimore attorneys, who argued passionately before Justice Bailey. On October 16, 1897, seven months after the game was played, Justice Bailey ruled in favor of the University of Maryland. In his decision, he said the "umpire's decision on the question of goals should be final."

College hockey in Hobey Baker's day was well attended and actually well chronicled in newspapers. By the 1930s, college hockey started to enjoy immense popularity, particularly on the East Coast, where a Harvard-Yale game drew 14,000 fans to Boston Garden in March 1930. College hockey had also spread to the West Coast campuses of USC, UCLA, Loyola, and California. "Some of the best college hockey in the country was played out west," hockey historian Don Clark has said.

And where did those schools go to look for players? Eveleth, Minnesota, of course.

Former Eveleth postmaster Gilbert Finnegan documented that in one season during the depression, 147 Eveleth-born players were playing in various leagues and schools around the country. At a national Amateur Athletic Union tournament in Chicago in 1935, about 33 percent of the players on the eight teams were from Eveleth. One team at that tournament, St. Cloud Teachers College, used only Eveleth players to amass a record of 45-7-0 in three seasons from 1933 to 1936.

But college hockey as we know it today didn't really take shape until after World War II. Hockey enthusiasm was high after the war. At Harvard's open tryout in 1946, about 180 students showed up, a mixture of the traditional students and veterans in their mid to late twenties who had come home from the war and wanted to pick up where they had left off.

Eddie Jeremiah's Dartmouth College teams from 1942 to 1946 were the first college hockey dynasty of the modern era. During one stretch, Dartmouth won 46 consecutive games, a college record. Throughout the 1940s, they were considered invincible by most of their rivals.

"Being on Jerry's team was like being with a smash Broadway musical," one of his former players, Jim Malone, said when Jeremiah retired in 1967. "It was a long run."

Dartmouth's dominance ended when the NCAA began crowning the national champions in Colorado Springs at the Broadmoor World Arena in 1948. The University of Michigan defeated Dartmouth in the first championship game in 1948, not long after several Dartmouth players had returned from the Olympic debacle in St. Moritz, Switzerland.

The loss to the Wolverines was bitter for Dartmouth because of a controversial Michigan goal that was allowed at the end of the second period. According to news accounts of the game, Dartmouth was leading 4-3 late in the period when the Wolverines took three consecutive penalties. Under the rules, the Wolverines could have a substitute player on the ice for the third penalized player, and his penalty time wouldn't start until the first penalized player's time had expired. But the timekeeper was unfamiliar with the rules and allowed the third penalized player, Michigan captain Connie Hill, back on the ice when the first penalty expired.

Realizing something was amiss, the timekeeper blew the whistle to get the referee's attention. According to news accounts, players on both teams stopped competing, including Dartmouth goaltender Dick Desmond. He wasn't all that concerned when a Michigan player's shot whizzed past him and into the net after the whistle blew. The goal was disallowed, and Hill was returned to the box.

But between the first and second period, NCAA officials decided to allow the goal, making it a 4-4 tie. Dartmouth captain Bill Riley, brother of 1960 Olympic coach Jack Riley, was so incensed by what he considered an outrageous ruling that he didn't want to return to the ice. Other Dartmouth players felt the same way. But they came back and played, only to lose the game in the third period.

In 1949, Boston College defeated Dartmouth for the national title. Dartmouth had such strong hockey teams in that era no one would have guessed that it would be 1981 before they would return to the semifinals.

Dartmouth's experiences cemented the idea that western teams had an unfair advantage because many were using older Canadian players. Teams from the west won eighteen of the first twenty national championships. Vic Heyliger's Michigan team won six more (1951, 1952, 1953, 1955, 1956, and 1964); Denver won five (1958, 1960, 1961, 1968, and 1969) and was a runner-up in 1963 and 1964.

Minnesota coach John Mariucci, who primarily used players straight out of the Minnesota high schools, was particularly incensed about playing against the older

Canadians. Those older Canadians included Colorado College's Jack Smith, who was thirty-six. Teammates called him the Silver Fox.

"Tony Frasca was thirty when he was coaching at Colorado College and he had players older than he was," said USA Hockey's Art Berglund, who played at Colorado College. "Only the real good Americans got to play."

Given today's rigid NCAA eligibility guidelines, it's difficult to fathom that the University of Michigan's 1957 NCAA runner-up team actually used a player, Wally Maxwell, who had played two games for the Toronto Maple Leafs in the 1952-53 season.

"There were games when the only American on the ice was the referee," said Bob Ridder, whose ties to USA Hockey brought him to many games.

Teams from the east also didn't like playing the game in Colorado Springs every year, believing it was also a disadvantage to them. In 1958, NCAA officials decided to play the championship game in a different venue every year. Most believe it was Mariucci's lobbying that paved the way for that change.

At one point, Mariucci vowed to never play Denver University because of all the older Canadians Murray Armstrong was using on his roster. The night before, Colorado College's line of Ike Scott, Bob McCusker, and Red Hay had physically dominated the young Minnesota team. (Colorado College also had Cy Whiteside, who would eventually become one of the toughest competitors ever to play in the International Hockey League.)

Not many of Mariucci's players really wanted to take the ice against the Colorado College team. After losing the game 7-2, Mariucci launched into another sermon about how overage players shouldn't be allowed in the game. Denver University's coach, Murray Armstrong, hearing about Mariucci's comment from a reporter, said that Mariucci should be ignored because he "was just a paper salesman." Mariucci was, in fact, a part-time coach who also worked for a paper company. But that didn't stop the anger from rising in Mariucci's face when he read Armstrong's comments.

"I will never play Denver again," he said to everyone within earshot.

Mariucci had enough influence to convince Michigan State, University of Michigan, Michigan Tech, and University of North Dakota to abandon the existing Western

As head coach at Dartmouth, Eddie Jeremiah built a college hockey dynasty in the 1940s.

Intercollegiate Hockey Association in favor of an informal league in which mandatory scheduling wasn't required. Eventually, Denver University and Colorado College ended up in the league, but Mariucci still wouldn't play Denver for many years.

Fate would bring them both to the NCAA tournament in 1961. As the Gophers were exiting the plane, Mariucci handed Canadian-born, but naturalized U.S. citizen, Lou Nanne a sign to carry. It read: "We fry Canadian bacon."

Acknowledging he had one Canadian-born player on his team, Mariucci introduced his team at the NCAA banquet as "19 future presidents and one future prime minister."

With many of the top Canadians playing for Denver, Michigan, and other schools in the west, western teams continued to dominate the NCAA tournament. "Then, Ned Harkness and Jack Kelley changed things," said Jack Parker, the current Boston University coach.

Harkness at Cornell and Kelley at Boston University began recruiting more Canadians and started to compete favorably with the teams in the west.

With Canadian Ken Dryden in goal, Cornell won the NCAA title in 1967 by defeating Boston University. The Big Red were finalists in 1969 and won the title again in 1970. Kelley's Boston University teams won back-to-back titles in 1971 and 1972. The Terriers are the last team to record consecutive championships.

But the unbeaten 1969-70 Cornell team is the one most remembered. "You win a lot of lunch money by asking people who the goaltender was on that team," McCutcheon said. "Most people would be willing to bet that Dryden was the goaltender."

But Dryden had graduated the year

Hall of Famer Ken Dryden was one of the most dominant goaltenders in NCAA history, but he wasn't the goalie who led Cornell to the undefeated season. That was Brian Cropper.

before and had signed with the Montreal Canadiens. (His last year at Cornell, they had lost the championship to Denver.) The following fall, Cornell's goaltending chores transferred from Dryden, who was 6-foot-4 and 210 pounds, to Brian Cropper, who was 5-foot-5 and 125 pounds.

Another key member of the 1969-70 team was Dan Lodboa, a jet-propelled, 5-foot-9 scorer whom Harkness had switched from wing to defense, much to the displeasure of Lodboa. But that move proved to be one of the keys to the season. In the 6-4 win against Clarkson in the NCAA championship game, Lodboa scored three goals in the third period to break a 3-3 tie. He had 24 goals that season.

"He was my Bobby Orr," Harkness has often said. "Boa was the greatest hockey player I ever coached. The greatest I ever saw."

Cornell had six one-goal wins during their season, including a 3-2 win against Clarkson in the Eastern College Athletic Conference championship game, in which John Hughes scored with 14 seconds left to notch victory number 27.

"I don't remember us talking about the streak much," McCutcheon said. "But we went into every game expecting to win."

Since then, only the 1992-93 Maine Black Bears (42-1-2) have come close to matching Cornell's feat. The Black Bears were led by Paul Kariya, a Canadian who is now a star with the Mighty Ducks of Anaheim. The goalies on the 1992-93 Maine team were Mike Dunham and Garth Snow, both of whom have left their mark in the U.S. national program. Dunham had been spectacular in helping Team USA win a bronze at the 1992 World Junior Championship. He and Garth Snow would play on the 1994 U.S. Olympic team and are now both playing in the NHL.

In the Black Bears' 1992-93 championship season, Snow posted a 21-0-1 record with a 2.08 goals-against average, and Dunham was 21-1-1 with a 2.65 goals-against average. Other important members of that team were twins Peter and Chris Ferraro from Port Jefferson, New York, both drafted by the New York Rangers and both teammates on that 1992 U.S. National Junior Team.

In 1994, Maine and Michigan played one of the most thrilling NCAA tournament games when the Black Bears defeated the Wolverines 4-3 in the national semifinals.

The contest became the longest NCAA tournament game in men's hockey history when Shermerhorn scored 28 seconds into the third overtime. The official time log totalled 100 minutes and 28 seconds. Previously, the longest tournament game was 97 minutes, 11 seconds, when Bowling Green beat Minnesota-Duluth 5-4 on Gino Cavallini's goal in the 1984 NCAA final.

The Michigan-Maine game had been an open-throttle marathon with numerous breakaways and odd-man rushes. Maine goaltender Blair Allison made 47 saves and Michigan's Marty Turco stopped 52 shots.

"I hate to call that game a test because that would mean somebody failed," said Maine coach Shawn Walsh. "And no one failed in this game."

It had drama, emotion, and heartache. It was college hockey at its best. Not all of the players on the ice were NHL-caliber, but each was representing his school's honor as if his life depended upon the outcome.

Harvard athletic director Bill Cleary said some of his favorite coaching moments involved players who weren't stars. Cleary's favorite Beanpot story occurred in 1977 when he recruited a soccer-tennis player to replace one of his injured hockey warriors.

Lyman Bullard had played some junior varsity hockey, but was known as a tennis and soccer player. He had two very attractive qualities: he was an athlete, and he roomed with Harvard goalie Brian Petrovek, which meant that coach Cleary knew where to find him.

"Bullard answered the phone when I called and assumed I had called to talk to Brian," Cleary said. "I remember he wished me luck in the Beanpot, and then I asked him, 'How would you like to wear the Harvard colors and play with us in the Beanpot?' He let out this tremendous whoop."

Bullard actually scored a goal and added two assists as Harvard won the tournament. "Those were the only two games he ever played," Cleary said. "He never expected to be called up. But he was an athlete and he was ready. That's what college sports are all about."

WORLD JUNIORS

Minutes after his U.S. team lost 2-0 to Canada at the 1997 World Junior Championship, U.S. coach Jeff Jackson said matter-of-factly that his team had outplayed the Canadians.

Perhaps surprised by the words pouring from his mouth, Jackson added: "I don't ever remember when a U.S. coach has been able to say that."

By earning only the third medal in the USA's rather bleak World Junior Championship history, Jackson's 1997 team had proved it could compete with the Canadians. Considering Canada had won an unprecedented five consecutive World Junior Championships, it is a small step, but a very important one, according to Jackson, who is USA Hockey's national teams coach.

"We are no longer afraid to play the Canadians," Jackson said.

Team cohesiveness, frequently lacking in previous U.S. National Teams, was crucial to the USA's success.

Dave Peterson coached the 1986 U.S. National Junior Team to a bronze medal at the World Junior Championships in Hamilton, Ontario. It was USA's first medal in world junior competition.

Canada's top player, Alyn McCauley, called the championship game against USA "a life and death struggle" until the end.

USA Hockey's national junior program has come light years since it began in 1976, with no one truly understanding its significance.

"We had some growing pains," said National Team director Art Berglund. "They didn't know who we were. It has taken time to get where we are now."

The team's rise among contenders began in 1985 at Hamilton, Ontario, when the Americans claimed a bronze medal—their first World Junior Championship medal.

"I still think if Mike Richter didn't get blood poisoning we would have won the silver medal," said Dave Peterson, who coached that team before moving up to coach the USA's Olympic teams in 1988 and 1992.

Pro scouts saw that the 1985 team symbolized America's rise in hockey. Brian Leetch, Jimmy Carson, Steve Leach, Craig Janney, Scott Young, and Richter were among the future NHLers who dotted that roster.

"In 1985, it was the first time we started to get full cooperation from all the [college] coaches," Peterson said. "We got almost all of the players we wanted."

Though the team was loaded with offensive stars, Richter was the key to success. He was 3-1 with a 2.60 goals-against average. He also had a nasty bout with blood poisoning and he was out of the lineup when the U.S. squad lost to Finland.

Another hero on the 1985 team was former Miami-Ohio player Greg Dornbach, who never reached the NHL. "He was a good centerman. He did a lot of little things for us," Peterson said.

Following the tradition of University of Wisconsin star Richter, University of Minnesota star Robb Stauber was the USA's goaltending hero the following year in Czechoslovakia. Though the USA didn't win a medal, Stauber recorded the first win for the U.S. junior program against the Russians. He also beat the Czechoslovakians. Scott Young and Darren Turcotte, both of whom now play in the NHL, were the offensive leaders with a combined 13 goals in seven games.

The USA's national junior alumni list reads like the Who's Who of American NHL stars: Phoenix Coyote Jeremy Roenick, Dallas Star Mike Modano, Phoenix Coyote Keith Tkachuk, Edmonton Oiler Doug Weight,

Chicago Blackhawk Chris Chelios, and New York Islander Scott Lachance and Bryan Berard.

Among the best players to ever wear a USA uniform was Leetch, who played on three World Junior Teams. "He played very well, but the first year he couldn't do all the things he could later," Peterson said. "But really every year he has been a bright and shining light. He is such a great skater."

Roenick was the first American to win a World Junior scoring title. He won in 1989 when competition included Russians Alexander Mogilny and Pavel Bure, now star players for the Vancouver Canucks.

"That gave me a lot of confidence," said Roenick. "I played with [Dallas Star] Mike Modano and [Mighty Duck of Anaheim] Joe Sacco. Who couldn't score with those guys?"

Berglund said the USA had known many good young players, but Roenick's performance stood out. "He was such a dynamic player in that tournament," Berglund said.

Doug Weight outpointed megaprospect Eric Lindros to win the 1991 World Junior Championship scoring title in Saskatoon, Saskatchewan. Kevin Constantine, now head coach in Pittsburgh, said Weight outplayed Lindros in that tournament.

"Doug Weight was the best forward," said Constantine, who coached the USA. "And he was the best defensive forward of all those getting points."

A native of Roseville, Michigan, Weight said the USA players believed they proved a point when they tied Canada 4-4.

"It was ridiculous how we were talked about before the tournament," Weight said. "[The Canadian press] was talking about us being a tuneup for teams, a chance for Canada to get its lines together."

Weight had two goals and six assists in a 19-1 win against Norway. "Everything I shot or passed ended up in the goal," Weight said. "I didn't play that well. My wingers Keith Tkachuk and Chris Gotziaman buried everything for me."

The bronze medal-winning 1992 U.S. team—with Tkachuk, Chris and Peter Ferraro, and Scott LaChance—was one of the USA's best.

Again the spotlight was on the goaltender, in this case University of Maine's Mike Dunham. "When Mike

New York Islanders defenseman Bryan Berard, the NHL's 1997 Rookie of the Year, was a member of the U.S. National Junior Team.

Dunham was in goal," said the USA coach Walt Kyle, "the team expected to win."

Remembering the tournament, Dunham said: "The puck seemed the size of basketball to me. I was on one of those rolls where I felt I could stop anything."

Dunham was the tournament's Most Valuable Goaltender. "We had a great team, but let's face it, if he doesn't play like he does, we don't win a medal," Kyle said.

Many top American coaches and players have participated in the World Junior Championships without winning a medal. Lou Vairo was coach of five World Junior teams. Among the honor roll of players who graced his lineups: Phil Housley, Dave Christian, John Vanbiesbrouck, Mike Ramsey, Chris Chelios, Tom Kurvers, and Kelly Miller.

Miller played twice for Vairo, serving as captain on one team. "I screwed up when I didn't pick him for the 1984 Olympic team. And you can write that," Vairo said.

In terms of visibility, the U.S. junior team has come a long way. Vairo remembers when he was hired by USA Hockey in 1978. His first assignment was to attend the college coaches convention and convince the fraternity the U.S. junior program was worthwhile.

"I told them, 'Give us your players and we will give you back a better player,'" Vairo said. "The experience these players get can't be found anywhere else."

Almost two decades later that still holds true.

Chapter 12

THE RISE OF WOMEN'S HOCKEY

Targets on Their Backs

The Granato family in Downers Grove, Illinois, has always loved hockey—the way the Kennedys love politics and the Jacksons love music. Older brothers Tony, Don, and Rob made a joyful journey to Schroeder Park every morning to play hockey, so naturally younger sister Cammi did the same. From breakfast to bedtime, she skated alongside her brothers in one of America's true equal opportunity pickup games.

"I never realized I was the only girl until later," Cammi said.

Those innocent, fun-filled games at the park were Granato's first steps on what would be a difficult climb to the top of women's ice hockey. Once she left Schroeder Park, Granato soon discovered some players, and a surprising number of adults, didn't want to see a girl playing what they considered a boys' game. She was treated as an interloper, an outsider, a minority trying to gain entrance to an exclusive club. All the

Cammi Granato battles a Chinese forward for the puck at the 1997 Women's World Ice Hockey Championship. She is the highest-scoring forward in USA women's international hockey history and the younger sister of San Jose Sharks' right wing Tony Granato.

affirmative action legislation in America couldn't protect Granato when she went into the corners with a boy who didn't believe she belonged on the ice.

When her peewee team was informed that girls weren't welcome at a peewee tournament in Kitchener, Ontario, team officials listed Cammi Granato as "Carl" Granato. "I wore a baseball cap pulled down," Granato recalled.

At the peewee national boys' tournament, Granato scored a goal and was immediately decked by an opposing player. Her linemate, Jeff Jestadt, popped her assailant with such force that he's probably still feeling it. "I was lucky, because it was like I had nineteen brothers out there looking out for me," Cammi said.

Once, her cousin Bob Granato switched jerseys with Cammi because the opposing team's players were threatening to single out her number 21 for special abuse. Imagine their surprise when number 21 turned out to be 6 feet tall, and not 5-foot-6.

When Granato entered bantam hockey, where checking is allowed, she was subjected to a higher degree of danger. One opposing coach told Granato's coach that if Cammi played, "We will break her shoulders."

"I did play the game," Granato said, "but my coach made me stay out of the corners."

By this time, Granato's parents were beginning to believe the game was becoming too dangerous for their daughter, especially since it seemed as if she had a target pinned to her back. Her next stop would be midget hockey, which could sometimes deteriorate into hand-to-hand combat. But Granato was beginning to reach the conclusion that she needed to give up boy's hockey for a different reason: she was weary of the insults and the suggestions that she was somehow unusual because she liked hockey.

Cammi Granato became a star women's player at Providence College, scoring 89 goals over her junior and senior seasons—a school record.

"I was a junior in high school and I wanted to be accepted as a female," Granato said. "I was fed up with the stares, the whispers, and tired of hearing the stuff guys would say to me. That's at a time in life when you need some confidence and acceptance."

Almost a decade later, Granato's confidence and acceptance levels befit her status as a world-class athlete. As Granato developed into a star women's player at Providence College, netting a school record 89 goals over her junior and senior seasons, she watched U.S. women's hockey develop a far greater acceptance than it did when top players like Karyn Bye, Kelly Dyer, Erin Whitten, and Kelly O'Leary were growing up in the sport. In the past seven years alone, the number of registered female hockey players with USA Hockey has jumped from 5,573 to 23,010—more than 400 percent.

Women's college hockey is also improving dramatically, as evidenced by the 1996 Eastern College Athletic Conference championship game between New Hampshire and Providence. The Wildcats defeated Providence 3-2, but it took five overtimes. The elapsed time of 145 minutes, 35 seconds made it the longest ice hockey game in NCAA history. The previous record of 102 minutes, 19 seconds was set December 21, 1968, when North Dakota defeated Minnesota 5-4 in a men's game.

New Hampshire sophomore Brandy Fisher drove home a rebound for the game-winner after Providence netminder Meghan Smith had stopped Dottie Carlin's initial shot from the point.

"I've coached in three World Championships and I've never seen a game like this," said New Hampshire coach Karen Kay. "I don't think anybody at this game can say they have ever seen a better hockey game, men's or women's."

New Hampshire's win ended Providence's four-year hold on the Eastern College Athletic Conference title and completed a 24-0-2 season for the Wildcats. Goaltender Dina Solimini also tied New Hampshire's school record for wins in a career, previously held by Cathy Narsiff and Erin Whitten.

The most important period for the sport's growth may have occurred in 1990 when the first International Ice Hockey Federation Women's World Championship was played in Ottawa. The Americans finished second to the Canadians, losing 5-3 in the championship game. The publicity surrounding that event was crucial to helping land women's hockey in the 1998 Olympics in Nagano. USA Hockey executive committee member Bob Allen had also lobbied long and passionately to expand the women's national program as had Walter Bush, USA Hockey president and chairman of the Women's Committee for the International Ice Hockey Federation.

In 1992, Minnesota became the first state to recognize girls' hockey as a varsity sport. Today, there are ninety schools in the state with girls' varsity ice hockey teams.

"The women's game has been elevated by leaps and bounds," said goaltender Kelly Dyer, a four-time member of the U.S. National Team.

Dyer was the goaltender in the first World Championship gold medal game in 1990. That tournament ignited passions for women's hockey more than any other previous experience. The level of play, and player enthusiasm, proved women were ready to take their sport to a higher level.

"I remember looking at the crowd of 10,000 and saying, 'This is amazing,'" said Granato, who was eighteen at the time. "We were used to playing in front of 200 people."

The Americans actually took a 2-0 lead in the gold medal game before the Canadians came from behind to win in front of the home fans. The Canadians outshot the Americans 41-10, although Team USA dominated the first period.

"I'll never forget when Canada got its first goal, my whole rib cage was vibrating from the force of their [the Canadian fans'] cheering," said Dyer, named most valuable player of that gold medal game.

What the Americans learned in Ottawa was that their top players, such as Granato, Bye, O'Leary, Dyer, and others, could compete evenly with the Canadians. But they couldn't match the Canadians' depth. It was the same lament that the American men had when they played the Canadians in the Canada Cup series.

In the first Women's World Championship, full body checking was allowed. After watching that event, International Ice Hockey Federation officials decided body checking slowed the game, and the Women's World Championship has been played under no-check rules since 1992. Most players applauded the decision. It wasn't that they minded being

During the 1990s, Kelly O'Leary has been among the world's top defenders in women's ice hockey. She has helped pave the way for the rapid rise in popularity of women's programs. In the past seven years, the number of women registered with USA Hockey has increased more than 400 percent.

hit, but the women hit so much that the game was very slow in the third period because players were weary from hitting and getting hit for two periods.

The no-checking edict allowed the women to sharpen their passing and shooting skills. As a result, the international games became quicker, particularly in the third period.

"But if you are watching, it probably still seems like there is some checking out there," Bye says. "Sometimes it's hard to tell whether it was a collision or a check."

The Canada-United States rivalry has developed an intensity and physical texture, even without checking. These athletes aren't like the women's hockey players of the turn of the century, who played in long skirts, wool sweaters, and stocking caps. Women's hockey was actually played in Canada in 1892, even before the men's college game developed in the United States. The modesty of women's apparel at that time dictated that female athletes develop their own unique style. *A Brief History of Women's Hockey*, released by Canadian Hockey, states women would "protect pucks under their skirts" as they stickhandled down the ice and goaltenders would spread their skirts across the goal line to stop the puck. In the early twentieth century, that style was undoubtedly just as effective as Patrick Roy's butterfly is today.

Dyer, hired by Louisville Hockey in 1995 to help them develop a full line of hockey equipment designed specifically for women, said that in the early years women goaltenders would sew a lead lining to the hems of their skirts to help them stop the puck. "Considering how high the skirts are worn now that wouldn't be much help today," Dyer joked.

Erin Whitten was the first female goaltender to post a win in a men's professional game. In goal for the Toledo Storm, Whitten came on to relieve starter Alain Harvey. She was credited with a 6-5 win against the Dayton Bombers in an East Coast Hockey League game on October 30, 1993.

Canada had some very serious, very prominent women's teams even before World War I. Women's hockey in America developed slower than in Canada, although by the 1920s there were several serious college teams. Hall of Famer Bill Stewart, who guided the 1937-38 Chicago Blackhawks to the Stanley Cup championship, coached the 1924 Radcliffe women's team. "My grandfather said they were a lovely group," said Bill Stewart III, laughing.

But the depression, followed by World War II, stifled the growth of women's hockey in Canada and the United States. In terms of structure and recognition, women's hockey didn't regenerate in the United States until the 1980s when USA Hockey began crowning champions in girls' peewee (11 and 12) and midget (15 and 16) age groups. At the same time, women's college hockey was beginning to gain a foothold. When the Eastern College Athletic Conference began holding playoffs to crown what was really the national champion, U.S. women's hockey was here to stay.

Erin Whitten and Kelly Dyer have both become important figures in American women's hockey history because they brought more awareness to female players by signing with men's minor-league teams. The forays of these goaltenders into men's professional hockey suggests how many light years women's hockey athletes have traveled in a short time.

Canadian goaltender Manon Rheaume broke the gender barrier by appearing in an NHL exhibition game for the Tampa Bay Lightning against the St. Louis Blues in 1992. At the time, Whitten played for the University of New Hampshire. "I hope she makes it because maybe I will be next," Whitten told *USA Today*.

Fourteen months later, Whitten was playing for the Toledo Storm in the East Coast Hockey League. On October 30, 1993, she made hockey history by becoming the first female goaltender to record a win in a pro game. Replacing the injured Alain Harvey in the second period of a game against the Dayton Bombers, Whitten stopped 15 of 19 shots to record a 6-5 win.

"I'm in the record books and that's great," Whitten said. "But that's not what I'm concerned about. I'm just doing what I love to do."

When she entered the game, the score was tied 1-1. Whitten impressed teammates with her grit and determination. "Erin is developing more rapidly than we had anticipated," Storm coach Chris McSorley said at the time. "We feel strongly that she can be a solid backup for this team."

McSorley had signed Whitten after her impressive four-day tryout with the Adrirondack Red Wings of the American Hockey League. It was an appropriate launching pad for Whitten, who was lured into the sport by the Red Wings' prominence in her hometown of Glen Falls, New York. After one day of practice with the Red Wings, she was drawing favorable comparisons to Rheaume.

"This is not a marketing scheme," Adirondack coach Newell Brown said. "She deserves to play. This is not something where we're sacrificing the integrity of the game."

His initial scouting assessment of Whitten supported that statement. "She's quick and agile moving around the net. You'd think at this level, a female goaltender might flinch. But at the end of practice, players were drilling the net and she was standing in and making the save. Whether she is good enough to play

U.S. goaltender Erin Whitten readies for a slap shot from the point during the 1997 Women's World Ice Hockey Championship in Kitchener, Ontario. Whitten played for Flint (Michigan) in the Colonial League during the 1996-97 season.

Karyn Bye owns one of the hardest shots in the world of women's hockey. When she was a youngster playing on boys' teams, she would list her name as "K. L. Bye" to prevent opponents from going out of their way to check her.

at this level, I doubt. But she's worthy of a game. I have no reservations about giving her ice time."

Whitten received that playing time in an exhibition game against the Cornwall Aces. She received a standing ovation from the crowd when it was announced she was entering the game in the second period. She surrendered a goal to Paul Brousseau when she was screened on the first shot she faced, but her instincts, talent, and training quickly overcame the nervousness she was feeling that night. She stopped 10 of 12 shots, including a dazzling stop when Niklas Andersson and Pat Nadeau came down the ice on a two-on-one break. When Andersson batted a rebound out of the air toward the net, Whitten spun post to post to rob him with a glove save. The crowd erupted in delight.

"I was nervous before she played because I'm the father—I've been nervous since she was eight years old," quipped her father, Peter, after the game.

Whitten said her focus wasn't shaken by the first goal. "I had pumped myself up for that one period," she said. "I don't know what would have happened had I played more than that."

Mental preparation was always one of Whitten's strong suits. As a young player in Glens Falls, New York, she needed mental toughness to compete against the boys, although Whitten says she never really experienced any gender bashing until she began playing for Glens Falls High School. Before that, her teammates, many of whom had played in front of her for many years, had no problem with a girl being their starting goaltender. But the taunting in high school didn't prevent Whitten from leading her team to the Division II state semi-final where they lost 4-2 to Salmon River, the eventual state champion.

Peter Whitten said he never worried about seeing his daughter play against boys. "She learned to take care of herself," the elder Whitten said. "She wouldn't let anyone intimidate her."

Accustomed to playing against boys, Whitten was surprised to discover during her junior year in high school that women's varsity college hockey actually existed. Teams in the Eastern College Athletic Conference, which had been crowning a champion every year since 1984, wanted Whitten, but she wasn't sure she wanted ECAC hockey. "I was skeptical," Whitten said. "I thought about playing Division III men's hockey."

But Whitten never regretted her decision to play women's college hockey, where she was able to develop into an elite-level netminder. In four years at New Hampshire, Erin posted a 51-14-4 record, with a 2.62 goals-against average. She won two ECAC titles, the women's version of the national championship.

Another member of that New Hampshire team was Karyn Bye, who is also considered among the world's best players. Bye, who grew up in River Falls, Wisconsin, and Kelly O'Leary are said to have two of the hardest shots in women's international hockey. As a youngster, Karyn Bye would have her name listed as K. L. Bye on the scoresheets at tournaments just to prevent players from taking the usual "extra runs" at her. But her years of playing tough hockey against the boys paid off for her when she made the boys' high school team as a regular center.

Bye was a novelty in high school, and the River Falls parents would often make the opposing team's parents guess which player was the girl. Given that Bye had short hair and everyone was wearing a full face shield, it was very difficult for anyone to say for sure, especially since her talent level was on par with most of the boys on the team.

So the opposing team's parents would say the girl was the player with the long hair, who happened to be a boy with a mustache. "They would all say, 'Oh, my God,'" Bye recalled.

U.S. players congratulate Vicki Movsessian after she scored a goal against China at the 1997 Women's World Ice Hockey Championship in Kitchener, Ontario.

Kelly Dyer also played boys' high school hockey at Acton-Boxboro in Massachusetts, first as one of the backups to Tom Barrasso, who would jump directly from high school to the NHL with the Buffalo Sabres in 1983. As a senior, Dyer would earn a chance to play eight games.

Dyer started out in the Boxboro figure skating program, the same program where Nancy Kerrigan began her skating career. But Dyer quickly discovered she liked diving for loose pucks more than she liked cranking up for double axles.

By the time she reached Northeastern University in 1985, Dyer was receiving considerable recognition as perhaps the world's best female netminder. (Erin Whitten hadn't yet reached high school, and Manon Rheaume was still four years away from earning any notoriety.) Dyer posted a 47-6-2 record at Northeastern, with 10 career shutouts and a career goals-against average of 2.01.

"She was so awesome," said Granato who played against her in college. "It was like playing against Mike Richter. She was intimidating. Just her presence was intimidating."

At 5-foot-11, Dyer was physically imposing to most of her competitors. Her pro opportunities didn't come immediately after college. She played for the Assabet Valley women's senior team in Massachusetts and helped them win two USA Hockey national titles, while keeping in shape for international competition. Dyer was 4-1 in the first Women's World Championship with a 3.60 goals-against average. In her international career, she is 8-1 with a 1.91 goals-against average.

Her performance in international competition drew some notice from minor-league mens' teams. Dyer followed Rheaume and Whitten as the third woman to play in the minors when she appeared in a Sunshine League game for the West Palm Beach Blaze on January 4, 1994. She played nine games that season and posted a 3-0 record and 5.25 goals-against average. In the 1995-96 season, she played nine games, posting a 3.41 goals-against average. Dyer signed with the Louisville River Frogs of the East Coast Hockey League in 1995-96, but didn't play. She's been helping out as a coach for the United States' young goaltenders since retiring from international competition in 1976.

Dyer says it's still difficult for her to believe that women are going to play in the Olympics, just eight years after their first World Championship tour-

Kelly Dyer was the first dominant goaltender in women's hockey. At 5-foot-11, she was an intimidating presence in the net. She posted a record of 47-6-2 while playing for the women's team at Northeastern.

nament. "I don't think this would have happened without [USA Hockey president] Walter Bush using his influence to get it done," Dyer said.

In preparing for the women's first Olympic experience, USA Hockey executive director Dave Ogrean put a premium on making sure the right coach was picked. There would be no rewards for past service and no political favors repaid. He wanted the best available candidate. That turned out to be Ben Smith, head coach of the men's hockey team at Northeastern University.

Much to Ogrean's delight, Ben Smith's dream to be a head U.S. Olympic hockey coach had no gender bias attached. When presented with the opportunity to coach the U.S. Women's National Team in its first Olympic appearance, Smith willingly gave up his job coaching Northeastern's men's team. He accepted a three-year deal, which extends beyond the Olympics to give him an opportunity to set up a training plan for the future.

"How could I pass up the opportunity of a lifetime?" Smith asked. "I look forward to this experience with as much anticipation as anything I've done in my life."

Smith was Dave Peterson's assistant for the men's team at the 1988 Olympic Games in Calgary. He also has an extensive international background as an assistant at the Men's World Championships and the World Junior Championships.

"In 22 years of playing hockey, Ben Smith is absolutely the best coach I have ever had," said Kelly O'Leary, a five-time member of the U.S. Women's National Team. O'Leary said she was thinking of retiring until Smith coached her in the summer of 1996. "I felt like I was six years old again," she said. "I never enjoyed the game so much."

Smith's appointment did raise some eyebrows, because there were women candidates for the job. "I don't view this situation as a man coaching a women's sport," Smith said. "I'm a hockey coach, a person with a solid background coaching athletes in international competition."

USA Hockey officials hired Smith with the belief that he's capable of helping the United States move past Canada.

"You only get one opportunity to do things for the first time," said USA Hockey executive director Dave Ogrean. "It's our objective to challenge for the first-ever Olympic gold medal."

For the Olympic team, the sport's old guard, such as Granato, Bye, and O'Leary, will merge with younger players, such as Stephanie O'Sullivan, sister of Calgary Flames defenseman Chris O'Sullivan, and Tara Mounsey, who burst onto the international scene as an 18-year-old star in 1996. A puck-carrying defenseman, she was Brown University's prize recruit.

"She [Mounsey] is a complete player," Smith said. "Her vision of the game is really what sets her apart from most young players. She sees the ice offensively and defensively, which is something other players don't do at this age."

Smith is a practical coach, with many colors to his personality. His style plays well with his elite-level hockey players. They are amused with his frequent use of video to illustrate points, although his choices often date him. He was making a point using the movie *Butch Cassidy and the Sundance Kid* when he realized that none of his players had seen it. Using a Jackie Gleason "Honeymooners" episode to explain a problem with his national team's offense received a more favorable response.

Smith had compared the women's reluctance to shoot the puck to Ed Norton sitting down to write. He would crack his knuckles, prepare his paper, stretch his shoulders—and then never quite get down to the actual writing. "That used to drive Ralph Cramden nuts," Smith said, perhaps suggesting that it was also making him nuts that the women did all the preparation and then never shot the puck.

Minutes before a United States game against Sweden, bystanders were probably surprised to hear Smith joking around about how the United States could have a strong team if there was "mixed doubles" version of hockey.

"How about that for an Olympic concept," Smith said to *The Hockey News* columnist Jack Falla. "Let's see, I'll have to play Chris Bailey with Chris Chelios and Cammi Granato can center Keith Tkachuk. What do you think?"

Actually, Cammi would probably prefer to center her brother, Tony, who came back from brain surgery in seven months to play the 1996-97 season with the San Jose Sharks. Cammi has always idolized her brother, who seems to like doting on her. "She is the most natural athlete in the family," Tony says.

Even though Tony is seven years her senior, they are very close. They often talk by phone. "I try to copy his work ethic," Cammi says. "He's a leader and a team player. He taught me a lot. I listen more to advice he gives me than I do anyone else."

The Granatos, Cammi included, have played some summer hockey together in the past, although the closeness of family gets in the way, according to Cammi. If someone touches their younger sister, the Granato boys get riled up.

"It's a little ridiculous," Cammi says, laughing. "A minute into the game, and they are all kicked out. I tell them, 'You gotta just let me play. I can handle it.'"

Like most of the other U.S. women's players, she has already proven that many times.

Chapter 13

As USA Hockey began preparing for the 1996 World Cup of Hockey, it was immediately clear this wasn't 1976. At the first Canada Cup two decades before, Team USA's ability to compete with Canadians and Russians was akin to David trying to best Goliath on a day when David's aim wasn't true. The Americans had blue-collar players like Mike Milbury, Larry Pleau, and Lou Nanne competing against Hall of Famers like Guy Lafleur, Bryan Trottier, Darryl Sittler, and Bobby Orr.

The American team's coaches were Canadians Harry Neale and Bob Pulford because no Americans were coaching in either the NHL or WHA. "We had a great bunch of guys on that team, but our talent level was minimal," Neale recalled. "And we were going up against a monstrous Canadian team. Their defense was Larry Robinson, Serge Savard, Guy Lapointe, Denis Potvin, and Orr."

Who was the sixth defenseman?

"Does it really matter?" Neale said, laughing.

The Americans actually played their best game against the Canadians, losing by a respectable 4-2 verdict. But even though the score was close, the Americans knew they were no match for the Canadians. When the Americans had pulled their goaltender in

INSIDE THE WAR ROOM

Assembling the 1996 World Cup Team

an attempt to tie the game in the closing minutes, the point men were Milbury and Nanne. Milbury had three games of NHL experience, and naturalized-citizen Nanne, then thirty-five, had netted only three goals in his previous season's 79 games. "Can you imagine us trying to tie that game?" Milbury asked.

Planning for 1996, the choices were far more attractive. When word leaked out that the World Cup would replace the Canada Cup, the media had already reported that Team USA's chances of winning the championship were much better than they had been in previous Canada Cups, including 1991 when the Americans finished second to Canada. That 1991 team, although possessing some skill, really couldn't come close to the talent the United States could put on the ice in 1996. With a potential defense of Chris Chelios, Brian Leetch, Gary Suter, Mathieu Schneider, Phil Housley, and the

Team captain Brian Leetch provided valuable leadership on defense for the U.S. squad. Whenever the game was on the line, Coach Ron Wilson had Leetch on the ice. Leetch received the Conn Smythe Trophy as Most Valuable Player in the 1994 Stanley Cup playoffs for the champion New York Rangers.

Team USA featured quality and depth in its defense corps, including New York City native Mathieu Schneider.

Hatcher brothers, Derian and Kevin, Team USA could have the best blue line corps in the tournament. John Vanbiesbrouck and Mike Richter looked like a great goaltending duo to lead the charge. And the group of forwards included Pat LaFontaine, Jeremy Roenick, Brett Hull, and Keith Tkachuk, whose 50 goals the previous NHL season showed he was ready to compete with Brendan Shanahan for the title of the league's best power foward.

The tournament plan designed by Bush, DeGregorio, Ogrean, and Petrovek was simple: they wanted to make sure they had the right people in the right jobs, from the men choosing the players and the guys packing the equipment to the elite, high-salaried athletes who would be skating up and down the wings.

The candidate pool for team general manager came down to the five Americans: San Jose Sharks' Dean Lombardi, Pittsburgh Penguins' Craig Patrick, Anaheim's Jack Ferreira, New York Islanders' general manager and coach Mike Milbury, and Lou Lamoriello, who was president and general manager of the New Jersey Devils.

When meeting to discuss who should be the general manager, the group considered all the names but unanimously chose to pursue Lamoriello.

"You just knew Lou would see this like chasing the Holy Grail," Ogrean said. "You knew he would be possessed by it. He would stay up nights scheming to win it. That was the kind of guy we wanted."

When Lamoriello was offered the job, he had one important question.

"What are the conditions?" he asked.

"There are no conditions," Ogrean replied.

Ogrean knew Lamoriello would want unchallenged control. As Devils president, Lamoriello had a reputation for being a man who operated the team as if every dollar was his own. He had the eye of an accountant and the soul of an IRS investigator. He was a shrewd, detail-oriented CEO with hunting dog's toughness and the patience to build a house by himself, one brick, one nail, one shingle at a time. He took pride in the tidiness of his ship and his knowledge of all the miscellanies that go into managing a successful team and business.

The media might have preferred either Ferreira or Milbury only because both were usually more open with the press and more quotable. Lamoriello had a firm approach to management: information was available on a need-to-know basis. If fewer people knew, leaks were less likely. Nothing seemed to bother Lamoriello more than to see his team's linen waving in public. But Lamoriello was also among the hardest-working executives on the planet. He was known as an excellent judge of talent and tough negotiator.

Brian Burke, of the NHL's hockey operations, said he'd never met anyone who believed in discipline more than Lamoriello. Burke, who played for Lamoriello at Providence, recalled Lamoriello gave him no relief when he overslept and was late for a Christmas Day practice after taking some freshmen to midnight mass. After the practice, Lamoriello skated Burke until he was near exhaustion. Then he told him he would skate at 4 A.M. throughout the Christmas vacation.

"All nine days, he was there on the ice with his whistle," Burke said. "But you know, I haven't been late since."

During Burke's senior season, he was summoned to Lamoriello's office. The coach informed him that he had arranged for Burke to take the LSAT test so that he could enter law school.

"Coach," Burke said, "I haven't made up my mind whether that's what I'm going to do. I may try to play pro hockey.

"I'm not asking you whether you want to," Lamoriello said. "I'm telling you that's what you are going to do."

Pat LaFontaine was one of a group of experienced veterans forming the nucleus of Team USA's offense. Born in St. Louis, LaFontaine began his NHL career in 1983-84.

Burke did as his coach had demanded, and when he graduated from Harvard Law School, he was mighty thankful Lamoriello had been so forceful. "When Lou is involved, there are just two hands on the steering wheel and they are both his," Burke said.

No matter who was chosen general manager for the U.S. team, USA Hockey was prepared to give him complete control. The World Cup was to be played with NHL players, and USA Hockey's thinking was that an NHL person should pick and coach the team of American stars. "Lou Lamoriello didn't need me calling him up and telling him who should be on the team," Ogrean said. "He knows better than we do. It's his job to know that league."

Lamoriello was named general manager on March 7 and announced his roster on April 15 without creating a stir. There were some mild surprises, but nothing that would cause any second-guessing. Craig Janney, an excellent playmaker, was missing. Eric Weinrich and Craig Wolanin, both of whom had played defense for Team USA at the 1991 Canada Cup, weren't there, and neither was Kevin Stevens, who had struggled all season in an effort to regain the form that allowed him to net back-to-back 50-goal seasons in 1991-92 and 1992-93. Lamoriello did raise some eyebrows by taking Shawn Chambers, a Devils' defenseman who really hadn't gained much notoriety during his 10 NHL seasons.

The roster had some potential problem spots: Doug Weight, Bryan Smolinski, Mike Modano, and Jeremy Roenick were all heading into Group II free agency and might not have contracts when camp began August 15. But the NHL Players' Association executive director, Bob Goodenow, said insurance would be available to cover players who weren't under contract.

The announcement of the roster simply reaffirmed that Team USA had a chance to win. At the roster press conference, Jeremy Roenick, who hadn't even been officially named to the team, churned passions in Canada by predicting the USA would win the tournament. Publicly, Lamoriello didn't seem to appreciate Roenick's brash comments. The coach in Lamoriello didn't like Roenick providing their opponents with inflammatory comments to fasten to their bulletin board for inspiration. But USA Hockey officials were pleased that a leading American player would enter this tournament believing his country was going to win. Shedding the country's hockey inferiority complex was an important piece of the American plan for success. The country's history against Canada was one-sided:

- At the World Junior Championships, an annual tournament for the world's best teenage players, Team USA had gone 2-18-2 against Canada since 1976.
- At the World Championships, the United States hadn't defeated Canada since 1985.
- In the Canada Cup, the forerunner of the World Cup, Team USA was 0-7-1 against Canada since 1976.

The Americans really hadn't defeated the Canadians in a meaningful game since the gold medal-winning 1960 U.S. Olympic team had beaten Bobby Bauer's Canadian team at Squaw Valley, California.

When coaching candidates for the 1996 team were discussed, there was one chief requirement—a belief that the USA should win this tournament. Being competitive was no longer good enough for the American program. The leading candidate from the beginning seemed to be Ron Wilson, the feisty, quick-witted coach of the Mighty Ducks of Anaheim.

At the World Championship in Vienna, Wilson had told a foreign journalist that he would be named coach of Team USA for the World Cup. When the report was published in *USA Today*, word spread quickly that Lamoriello wasn't happy. But no one believed Wilson wouldn't get the job. He had been Lamoriello's star at Providence. "He was the coach's pet," Burke joked. "I'm surprised Lou didn't name one of his sons Ron."

Wilson had a right to believe the job should be his: he had just coached the USA to the bronze medal in Vienna, the first medal the USA had earned at the World Championships in thirty-four years. He also had more international experience than just about anyone who could have wanted the job: he played for U.S. National Teams in 1975, 1981, 1983, and 1987 and was an assistant coach for Team USA when it finished second at the 1990 Goodwill Games. Under his command, the United States finished fourth at the World Championship in 1994. Then, in the spring 1996, an overtime goal by Brian Rolston gave Team USA a win over Russia for the bronze medal.

USA Hockey's Art Berglund had taken a liking to Wilson when he was just starting his coaching career. Berglund had given Wilson opportunities that other young coaches weren't getting. "He comes from coaching genes," Berglund would say. "And he proves himself at every level he reaches."

Mike Modano was among the NHL players heading toward Group II free agency who might not have been under contract when camp was to begin in August. But the NHL Players' Association granted insurance to the players, thus enabling them to play for Team USA.

Wilson had grown up with NHL. His late father, Larry, and his uncle, Johnny, were both NHL players and coaches. Larry had played six seasons in the NHL and coached one season with the Detroit Red Wings, while Johnny had played 13 seasons and had a lengthy coaching career, with tours of duty in Detroit, Los Angeles, Colorado, and Pittsburgh.

Ron Wilson's coaching style could best be described as a cross between Toe Blake and Jerry Seinfeld—a classic hockey mind combined with a walking comedy show. On one hand, he's a demanding coach who has no difficulty telling a player when they aren't working hard enough to please him. On the other hand, he's a standup comedian who keeps his players loose with his sharp wit.

When budding superstar Paul Kariya showed up for his first Mighty Ducks of Anaheim camp, he started calling his new coach "Mr. Wilson."

Ron immediately started calling Kariya "Dennis."

Finally, Kariya, who still has a touch of shyness in him, could stand it no longer. "Why," he asked Wilson, "do you call me Dennis?"

"Dennis the Menace calls Mr. Wilson 'Mr. Wilson,'" his coach answered. "I'm Ron, or you can call me Coach, but don't ever call me Mr. Wilson."

Burke, who has known Wilson since they both showed up as freshman players at Providence College, said it was clear even back in college that Wilson was headed for a career as a coach. His understanding of the game far exceeded that of the average college player. His playing ability

also exceeded that of the average hockey player. Burke had heard all the stories about Wilson being a phenom who had scored 100 points in his last season in high school. He was skeptical when he saw the runt-sized Wilson for the first time. Wilson was 5-foot-9 and 160 pounds.

"If he had 100 points, I figured it must not have been much of a league," Burke said. "But when he hit the ice, you could see what kind of player he was. He had two dazzling scoring chances the first time he hit the ice at Providence."

Lamoriello didn't name Wilson as coach until June 27, two full months after the roster had been released. Lamoriello never offered any public explanation as to why he waited until June to name his coach. It was assumed that Lou was just being Lou, waiting until the last minute to make sure no one had been overlooked.

At the opening meeting with his American players before the World Cup, Ron Wilson asked a rhetorical question about what each of them would be willing to do to win the championship. Wilson, a veteran of many international tournaments, knew the Canadians were always willing to do whatever it took.

Forward Brian Rolston was a late, but important, addition to Team USA's World Cup roster.

One name that had circulated in the hockey community as a possible coach for the USA's team was Mike Keenan, the St. Louis Blues' general manager and coach. Keenan let it be known that he was in the process of obtaining his U.S. citizenship. The word was he was lobbying to be the coach, but there is no evidence to suggest Lamoriello ever came close to giving him the job. Lou was merely doing what Lou Lamoriello does, moving methodically through the process he felt was necessary to assure he had the right man for the job. Although Wilson had been more successful in international hockey than any U.S coach since Herb Brooks, he had not coached players of this caliber, at least not so many on one team. Lamoriello wanted to be sure. Real sure.

Part of the American plan for this World Cup was to raise expectations from the coaching staff on down. When Lamoriello was interviewing for Wilson's assistants, he had one specific question he wanted answered. "I asked all of them: 'Do you believe you can win?'" said Lou Lamoriello.

Wilson always believed he could win, even though three weeks after the coaching staff was named, the good ship USA began to spring its first leak. Modano had agreed to a new contract, and Weight and Smolinski were satisfied with their insurance protection. But agent Neil Abbott said publicly that Roenick wouldn't play in the World Cup if he didn't have a contract.

INSIDE THE WAR ROOM

"You know how badly he wants to play," Abbott told the press. "But I told him you have to listen to me on this call."

Abbott believed the insurance wouldn't cover Roenick for short-term injury, nor would it compensate him if a general manager changed his mind about giving Roenick a long-term deal if Roenick severely broke his leg in a World Cup game. Abbott was looking for a five-year deal worth $20 to $22 million. He advised Roenick not to risk that payoff by participating in the World Cup.

Meanwhile, late in July, Chelios told a photographer he might not play in the World Cup. When a reporter called USA Hockey to ask about Chelios's comments, USA Hockey officials said it was the first time they'd heard that Chelios was thinking about not playing. A call to Chelios confirmed he probably wouldn't play. The official reason: his groin injury hadn't healed, but those close to Chelios knew him better than that. No groin injury would keep Chelios out of the World Cup. Something else was bothering him.

A few days later, Vanbiesbrouck withdrew from the tournament because he needed surgery to repair a small cartilage tear in his right shoulder. Guy Hebert was named to replace him. With Mike Richter, Jim Carey, and Hebert, the Americans were still comfortable with their goaltending situation.

When Roenick was traded to the Phoenix Coyotes just before the start of the World Cup, there was reason to believe he would play. But inexplicably, the Coyotes had made the deal without even talking to Roenick's agent. After the first meeting between Abbott and the Coyotes, it was clear they were miles apart on annual salary figures. Roenick wanted $4.5 million per season, and the Coyotes were offering roughly $3 million per season.

Abbott killed any optimistic thoughts about Roenick playing when he said, "We are not going to let the World Cup put any pressure on us."

The loss of Roenick and Vanbiesbrouck wasn't nearly as critical as it would have been in previous Canada Cups. It wasn't as if Canada was getting every player it wanted. Mario Lemieux didn't want to put any more miles on his weathered body, and Ray Bourque simply said he wasn't playing. Al MacInnis had an elbow injury that was going to keep him out of action. And Ron Francis was injured during the World Cup pre-tournament schedule.

Keith Tkachuk joined Team USA after a 50-goal season for the 1995-96 Winnipeg Jets.

But when Chelios didn't show up for the start of training camp on August 15, there was much concern. The team needed Chelios, more for his attitude than for his impressive array of defensive talents. "It was the Mark Messier factor," assistant coach Keith Allain said.

Messier had become the symbol for why Canada succeeded in international competition. Aside from his skill and speed, Messier can bring an intangible contribution to a team, one that simply can't be measured in any statistical fashion. Opponents detest playing against Messier because they can't comfortably predict his limits. There is a calculated recklessness to his play—an edge and an unpredictability to his performance. He will do whatever it takes to win. Legend has it that Messier once pinned teammate Kent Nilsson against a wall to make a point about defensive hockey. Keenan once called Messier "the greatest leader in professional sports." No one could really argue; Messier had conquered as many opponents with his glares as his goals.

Chelios is the U.S. answer to Messier. He is a Norris Trophy winner and a leader, who ranks among the NHL's top ten players. His playing style is nuclear; no opponent wants to be within miles of him when his core overheats. ESPN color analyst Bill Clement once said of Chelios, "He protects the goal as if his children's lives were at stake."

"We felt we had to have him," Allain would say later. "Keith Tkachuk was like that, but he was younger and didn't have Chelios's experience."

As everyone quickly suspected, Chelios's reasons for not coming extended well beyond his healing groin injury. He was trying to negotiate a contract extension, and perhaps more important, he really hadn't enjoyed his previous experiences in the Canada Cup.

Lamoriello wasn't the only person trying to convince Chelios to report to training camp. Captain Brian Leetch called him, and his longtime buddy Gary Suter, a fellow University of Wisconsin alum, also did some lobbying. "This training camp isn't like USA Hockey training camps of the past," Suter told him.

That was true. USA Hockey had decided from the beginning that it would not run this team on a shoestring budget. Ogrean and Lamoriello both agreed Team USA had to be a class act at the World Cup. Bush, DeGregorio, and Ogrean gave Petrovek the assignment of making sure that the players received first-class treatment and that logistics never were barriers to success. "He was perfect for that assignment because he is the most organized person I have ever known," Ogrean said.

Players knew immediately that things were different when Petrovek sent each of the players' children a USA jersey with their dad's name on the back. Wives all received gift bags. The gifts weren't nearly as important as the message: times had changed.

Even without Chelios, the Americans looked very impressive in the training camp. A 3-1 exhibition game loss to Canada in Vancouver didn't dampen their spirits. The following night, the Americans defeated Canada 7-5 in a fight-marred game in San Jose.

After John Vanbiesbrouck withdrew from the tournament because he needed surgery to repair his right shoulder, Team USA was still comfortable with its goaltending situation. It turned to Mike Richter (above), Jim Carey, and Vanbiesbrouck's replacement on the roster, Guy Hebert.

In past USA-Canada encounters, if the Canadians couldn't vanquish the Americans with their skill, they would turn the game into a physical war. That was one area where they were always superior. Either the Americans couldn't compete with the physical challenge, or the Americans would take ill-advised penalties and the Canadians would beat them with power play goals.

The Canadian team went to the physical game in San Jose, and much to everyone's surprise, it had no effect on the USA. "Once I saw that, I knew we had a chance," Allain said.

The team lost a pre-tournament game to the Russians in Detroit, but no one was overly concerned. The Americans knew they could beat the Russians when it mattered. The game turned out to be significant in that Pavel Bure, who suffered a kidney injury after being checked, was knocked out of the tournament.

Before the American team went out west, word began to circulate that Chelios was going to play. He decided he would come to Providence on the day of the last pre-tournament game against Slovakia.

On the drive from the airport to the practice, Chelios quizzed team services director Rick Minch.

"They aren't expecting me to play right away, are they?" Chelios asked.

"Oh no, not at all," Minch replied.

Chelios arrived at the Providence rink during the morning skate. After meeting with head coach Ron Wilson on the ice for a brief chat, Chelios took a couple of laps around the rink and participated in a couple of drills. He wasn't on the ice more than a half hour when he skated over to Wilson and said: "I'm ready to go tonight."

The final piece of the puzzle was a snug fit. Wilson surveyed his roster that day and realized the team was even better than he had hoped it would be.

The significant difference between this American squad and the one that had finished second at the 1991 Canada Cup was size and strength on the wings. In 1991, the USA didn't have power forwards like Tkachuk, Bill Guerin, Adam Deadmarsh, and John LeClair.

They were the players the late Bob Johnson used to dream about when he was coaching at Wisconsin or with the Calgary Flames, or when he was executive director of USA Hockey. Back when Johnson would watch Monday Night Football and muse about what kind of hockey players the NFL stars would make, he had asked, "Can you imagine John Elway as a tough left winger?" If only Elway and others had been exposed to the sport at a young age.

In the 1980s, after the Miracle at Lake Placid, U.S. hockey finally started winning more battles against football coaches in the recruitment of top athletes. Big, strong athletes like Tkachuk, LeClair, and Guerin stayed with hockey instead of accepting a spot on their high school's linebacking corps.

Because Chris Chelios was negotiating a contract with the Blackhawks, he wasn't sure he wanted to play in the World Cup. After Brian Leetch and others convinced him to join the team, he arrived as his usual, dedicated self.

"I grew up in Boston wanting to be like Cam Neely," Tkachuk said.

That meant he wanted to bang along the boards as much as he wanted to score goals. He wanted to be tough and gritty. Just like the tough kids in Canada, he wanted to be a force.

When the American players came together for the training camp in Providence, they seemed to sense that the playing field against the Canadians had been leveled since the 1991 Canada Cup.

In 1991, Doug Weight had just left Lake Superior State, John LeClair had just left Vermont, Tkachuk was a 19-year-old Olympic aspirant, Adam Deadmarsh was sixteen, and Derian Hatcher was a 6-foot-4, 200-pound teenager, who hadn't yet grown into his body. He looked so uncoordinated when he lumbered up the ice, NHL scouts compared him to a big puppy dog whose feet never seemed to be quite in harmony with the rest of his body.

Five years later, Derian Hatcher was a chiseled 6-foot-5, 225 pounds and a feared open-ice hitter. At twenty-four, he had worn the "C" as captain of the Dallas Stars.

"When I showed up at training camp, I couldn't believe how much talent was in the dressing room," Hatcher said. "And I couldn't believe how many big guys there were."

Doug Weight was another intimidating presence in the pre-tournament games. His savvy and talent didn't surprise Wilson because he had coached in the west, where

Weight had ruled in the previous season. "Even when his team was out of the playoffs, he competed as if every game was a playoff game," Wilson said.

Weight had played all 82 games, despite suffering a broken nose, badly-bruised ribs, a hip pointer, and several facial cuts. His refusal to yield isn't surprising to those who knew him when he was playing junior hockey in Michigan. Even when he was just stickhandling around kitchen chairs, he knew he wanted to be an NHLer. Those who marvel at Weight's ability to control a puck on the ice should have seen him with a ping-pong ball on linoleum.

Doug Weight, Sr., recalled that his son started at about age four, stickhandling with an undersized stick through his suburban Detroit home for hours at a time. The young Weight would zip from room to room at parent-unnerving speeds while trying to master a tiny ball that rebelled against him every step he took.

"If you ever tried to control a ping-pong ball, you know that after about the fourth hit, it's [gone]," the elder Weight said. "But I remember he never broke anything. He developed a great touch with the puck."

Adam Deadmarsh's eligibility for the World Cup team was a stroke of good fortune for the Americans. He wasn't sitting on the fence when it came time to choose his hockey allegiance. He was sitting on the border.

The Colorado Avalanche right winger grew up in Fruitvale, British Columbia, right across the United States-Canadian border. His father was Canadian. His mother was American. He played youth hockey in Canada. He played junior hockey in Portland, Oregon. It's fair to say he had an identity crisis when it came to international hockey. "I really didn't know what to do at first," Deadmarsh said.

Dual citizen Brett Hull (above) was verbally tarred and feathered in Canada for his decision to play with the USA instead of Canada. Hull said he decided to play with Team USA because, as a young player, the 1986 U.S. National Team wanted him and Canada didn't. Adam Deadmarsh (right) grew up in Fruitvale, British Columbia, near the U.S.-Canadian border. He played in programs in both countries, but eventually found his way to the U.S. National Junior Team and later to Team USA.

He played for the Canadian National Under-17 Team in Japan, but the following year he opted to join the U.S. National Junior Team, a decision that probably played a role in his quick ascension to the rank of National Hockey League standout. Deadmarsh was one of the key contributors in the Avalanche's run to the 1996 Stanley Cup championship.

"He was Canadian-trained, but I think playing for us certainly helped his development," said Berglund, who helped recruit Deadmarsh to the U.S. junior program. "I don't think I've ever seen a player improve as much as he has in a short time. He has the speed, the power, and scoring touch. And he's fearless."

Deadmarsh has admitted he might not have received the same experience had he chosen to try out for the Canada junior

program, whose abundance of talent made his future less certain.

He made the U.S. National Junior Team at seventeen, and not many 17-year-olds make the Canadian National Junior Team. NHL scouts took note of how well he played for Team USA in his three World Junior appearances. His three appearances on the U.S. National Junior Team also puts him on a very short list.

"He had the talent, and we could provide him with the opportunity," Berglund said. "And he had become pretty Americanized while playing in Portland."

Early into training camp, Wilson began to like what he saw with this team. He liked the line of Tkachuk, Modano, and Guerin. He liked Weight centering Hull. He liked Derian Hatcher anywhere, anytime. "I can't believe how quickly we are coming together," John LeClair said.

The lineup was sorting itself out. But right before the first game, Wilson still had some decisions to make. The first one wasn't that difficult: he could wait for Roenick no longer. He was dropped from the roster and Brian Rolston, the hero from the bronze medal-winning 1996 U.S. National Team, was added.

It would be more difficult to tell one of his defensemen that he wouldn't be playing. Wilson was probably the first U.S. coach to tell a consistent 80-point NHL defenseman that he couldn't make Team USA. That's how far the American program had come.

Phil Housley seemed stunned when he ran into equipment manager Bob Webster following his meeting with Wilson.

"Webbie, they told me I'm the seventh defenseman," Housley said. He looked Webster in the eye. "And you know what," Housley continued, "on this team, I am the seventh defenseman."

Power winger Bill Guerin (left), with his size and strength, was the kind of player the Americans had always lacked in previous international competition. Another forward, John LeClair (right), outperformed his more famous Philadelphia Flyers linemate Eric Lindros in the World Cup. Leading the tournament in goal-scoring, LeClair's size and strength were also important factors in helping the Americans deal with the Lindros-led Canadians.

DRIVING

Mike Richter scrambles out of his net to freeze the puck against Canada. He was one of the top U.S. performers at the World Cup, carving out a place in American hockey history, just as goaltenders Jack McCartan and Jim Craig had done.

When Team USA's World Cup training camp began in Providence, Rhode Island, the highly organized Lou Lamoriello brought in a white coach's board divided by a line in the middle. On one side, Lamoriello had written a long list of points he would raise with players at the opening meeting. The other side Lamoriello had left blank so that coach Ron Wilson could jot down an outline of his opening remarks.

"What are you going to say?" Lamoriello asked his coach.

"I have some points I want to make, but I really don't know what I will say until I get there," Wilson replied. "I'm usually better when I'm unrehearsed. I'm at my best when it comes from the heart."

Chapter 14
THE BUS

A World Cup Breakthrough

"Can you at least give me an idea?" Lamoriello persisted.

"Lou," Wilson said finally, "you are just going to have to trust me on this."

Wilson knew his address to the team was important. Coaches need the skills of a strategist, counselor, teacher, and psychologist. Sometimes the difference between winning and losing comes down to the coach's mastery of the skills good used-car salesmen use to close deals. A coach has to convince players to buy his ideas and plans, even if some of them have a lot of miles on them. That was indeed true at the World Cup, where Wilson would have to quickly sell a team-oriented concept to star players, many

of whom didn't know much about him except that his Mighty Ducks of Anaheim team had yet to make the NHL playoffs.

But Wilson was an engaging speaker, and not long into his opening talk, players began to believe this was a guy who they could follow. Wilson told them that the days of America coming to international tournaments with a goal of being respectable were over. This team would enter the tournament to win—anything less would be considered failure.

He challenged each player to ponder what he would be willing to do to win the World Cup. "If USA-Canada were tied 2-2 with two minutes to go in Game 3, what would you be willing to do?" Wilson asked "We all know that Mark Messier will do anything it takes for Canada to win in that situation."

He looked at Brian Leetch, the captain of the USA's World Cup team, and asked rhetorically if Leetch would be willing to tangle with Messier, his New York Rangers teammate, if the game was on the line.

He looked at John LeClair and asked whether LeClair would go after his teammate with the Philadelphia Flyers, Eric Lindros, if the game was tied 2-2 in the final two minutes.

Wilson had another message as well, one he would repeat over the next few weeks: He compared hockey's history to a bus ride, with Canadians always in the driver's seat and Americans always asked to ride in the back of the bus.

During preparation for the World Cup, Ron Wilson used many motivational tools, including showing film clips of *Rocky*. He wanted to get his players fired up with the idea that they were underdogs about to become champions.

"I started out in the luggage compartment," said Wilson, who was the only American college player on the Toronto Maple Leafs in the 1978-79 season. "Some of you are closer to the front now. But the Americans have never driven. Now it's time for us to drive the bus."

Wilson saw some nods. Before arriving in Providence, he and USA Hockey officials knew the team was talented enough to win. Now he was confident they were hungry enough to win. Canadians had long understood the importance of sacrificing personal agendas for the sake of winning. Starting with the national junior team, top Canadian players appreciate that playing on all-star teams requires sacrifice. Through the years, top Canadian players have accepted third and fourth-line assignments without complaint. Colorado Avalanche star Joe Sakic had won the Hart Trophy as the NHL playoff's most valuable player in June, but when the World Cup started, he was probably going to be on the third line. He would accept that because he had been taught since he was a child that there was no room in the Canadian program for those who didn't want to do what was best for the team.

With the United States finally possessing as much talent as Canada, Wilson knew it was important for the American players to share that philosophy. He preached his gospel with honesty, with humor, and above all, with all the charm he could muster.

"What Ron does well is sell his program," said Keith Allain, who along with John Cuniff and Paul Holmgren was an assistant coach for Team USA. "He doesn't jam it down your throat."

Wilson quickly won over the leaders of the team—Brian Leetch, Keith Tkachuk, and Joel Otto, among others. Bonding with Hull was very important to the American cause. Five years before at the Canada Cup, Hull hadn't mixed well with coach Tim Taylor, who had taken over after Bob Johnson was diagnosed with a brain tumor. During the 1991 tournament, the Hull-Taylor relationship was always a lit fuse, always in the back of everyone's mind, always a threat to detonate in someone's face. Publicly, Wilson said he wasn't going to let history influence his program. Privately, Wilson wanted to make sure he and Hull were reading from the same page.

"I just told him great players have to play their best against the best competition," Wilson said. "I told him we needed him to be among our best players."

The meeting was important for Hull, who wasn't shy about saying he didn't appreciate his experience at the 1991 Canada Cup. "Ron just told me he wanted me to be part of what was going on. That's all I needed," said Hull.

Harmony and togetherness were important to the Americans, especially since the team had to face the Canadians in the first game. Even though the Americans could lose that game and still win the tournament, the first game was very important to their collective psyche. The Americans had never beaten Canada in a tournament where the best NHL players were competing. The first game, played in Philadelphia, would not necessarily give them a

Brian Leetch, the U.S. captain, was one of Team USA's leaders won over by the coaching style and tactics of Ron Wilson.

home ice advantage because Flyers' captain Eric Lindros played for Canada. Philadelphia fans might have a difficult time rooting against big number 88.

The pre-tournament game against Russia in Detroit had taught the Americans not to take home ice advantage for granted. Red Wings Sergei Fedorov, Slava Kozlov, and Igor Larionov were in the Russian lineup, and the majority of fans were rooting for the Russians. Some American players were miffed.

Wilson was, too, although publicly he said: "You can't expect fans to root against a player who they will be cheering for in two weeks."

The importance of the first pool play game against Canada was evident before it was 20 seconds old. Keith Tkachuk broke Claude Lemieux's nose in a fight. Both players were ejected because their fight had been a secondary bout. The physical play continued when Derian Hatcher decked Lindros behind the net. The symbolism was more important than the hit. It let the Canadians know that this tournament wasn't going to be like the Canada Cup of 1976 or 1991.

"You don't have to tell Hatcher to do things like that," Holmgren said. "He just knows."

The Americans trailed 2-1 after one period, but Doug Weight's goal at 3:27 of the second period tied the score and restored the USA's confidence. Even if Lindros was the Flyers' most important captain since Bobby Clarke, Philadelphia fans were clearly pro-American. They cheered enthusiastically when Scott Young's goal at 10:48 put the USA ahead for good. Canada's hopes for tying the game were hurt when Hull scored on a blistering 20-footer early in the third period. At the time, Wayne Gretzky was in the

The impressive play of Derian Hatcher was one of the surprises for the U.S. team. Rarely caught out of position, Hatcher had a strong physical presence in the series. His stay-at-home style made him a logical partner for Brian Leetch.

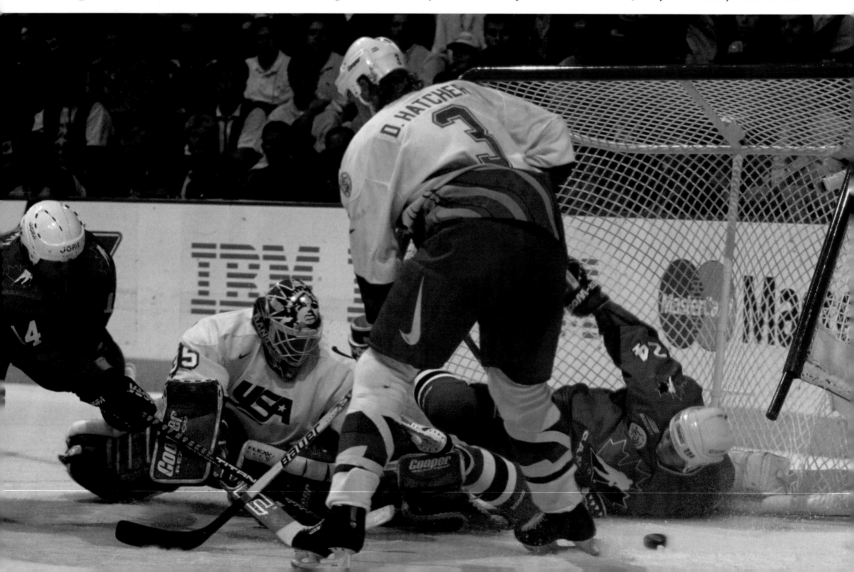

penalty box for hooking. Team USA won 5-3. It seemed appropriate that USA Hockey had finally removed one of its Canadian shackles in the city where the United States' independence was born.

"After this, maybe we can expect to beat them, instead of hoping to beat them," Wilson said.

Hull had played a major role in the game with two goals and two assists. It was clear he and Wilson were reading from the same page. He genuinely liked Wilson.

"Ron does a good job of finding allies in the room," Allain said. "Once he does that, then he can tease players into performing if that's what is necessary."

Chelios's presence also had the desired effect. Living up to his reputation, Chelios had put his team ahead of all other considerations and had left a woman at the altar to attend the game. Actually, he left her at the receiving line. His sister, Eleni, was getting married in Chicago a few hours before Chelios was scheduled to face-off against the Canadians in Philadelphia. But the fact that it wasn't Chris getting married didn't make it any easier for him to slip out. His sister and her new husband, Don, were understanding, but Chelios' father, Gus, wasn't very happy about his decision to be at the Core States Center instead of the reception.

USA Hockey had arranged for a private jet to transport Chelios to the Philadelphia airport where he was picked up and rushed to the arena. He showed up fifteen minutes before the opening face-off.

"My dad's still not talking to me," Chelios said after the game. "This one is going to take time to heal." Teammates told Chelios if family harmony wasn't restored after the World Cup, they would all petition his father to get him pardoned.

Though Chelios believed Team USA would be competitive at the tournament, even he was impressed by the team's chemistry. Chelios had watched the U.S. program take major steps since he was a 1984 U.S. Olympian. He saw them adding large elite warriors who could play hockey the way he liked to play hockey.

"We had some tough players on past teams, like Chris Nilan, but no offense to help him; he wasn't a scorer," said Chelios.

Having ticked off his father to play the first game, Chelios said afterwards, "If we don't win this, I'm going to be real disappointed."

Next up was a Labor Day tilt with the Russians and a game against the Slovakians the next day. For some reason, the loss to the Russians in Detroit meant nothing to the Americans. Somehow they knew they were a much better team than the Russians, even though on paper the Russians had just as many elite players. They expected to beat the Russians and they did, 5-2, with Pat LaFontaine registering a goal and two assists.

LaFontaine said he never thought he would see the day when he was cheered in Madison Square Garden. The Garden fans lined up solidly behind the surprisingly confident Americans, including LaFontaine, who was never a favorite when he played for the hated New York Islanders.

The surprising aspect of Team USA's play was not that they won over Canada and Russia, but how they played to win. The USA players took charge in both games and never acted as if they considered the possibility of losing. Russian defenseman Darius Kasparaitis said Team USA disrupted the Russians' offensive movement with relentless fore-checking. The day before, American players had said the Russians were no longer timid European-style

Pat LaFontaine had been booed in Madison Square Garden while a member of the New York Islanders, but he was cheered when Team USA squared off against the Russians.

Mike Modano (center) and Keith Tkachuk (left) help push out an intruding Russian as U.S. goaltender Mike Richter covers up the rebound.

players. They had proven they could survive a rough style of play, and that's what Team USA gave them.

"It's tough to play," Kasparaitis said, "when you have to look around all the time to see who is on your back."

Just as had been expected, the USA's tough collection of physical wingers, including roomies Tkachuk and Guerin, were having a major impact. Players like LaFontaine and Hull had more freedom to move because guys like Tkachuk, Deadmarsh, and Guerin were holding up the opposition or making them pay a price along the boards.

The still unsigned Jeremy Roenick was at the game against Russia. He was the American who had predicted a victory, so obviously it gnawed at him not to be playing. "No question I would like to be playing," Roenick said. "But sometimes you have to put business before your heart."

The win over Russia meant the USA had the number-one seed, regardless of how they did against the Slovakians. Wilson rested key players, but they destroyed the Slovakians anyway, 9-3. That meant they would have a bye in the first round.

The team was humming. Team harmony was exceptional, and everyone was having fun. Players were razzing Tkachuk regularly about his bout with Lemieux. Posted on the wall of Team USA's dressing room was a New York Athletic Commission boxing scorecard for the Tkachuk-Lemieux tussle. Tkachuk had been credited with a 10-1 decision. The card also noted that all of Tkachuk's previous fights had been with "undersized amateur opponents" and that Tkachuk "had the potential to be a thug." Guys loved the humor—Lemieux wasn't one of the most popular men in hockey.

Every move the coaching staff made was working. Placing Mike Modano on a line with Keith Tkachuk and Bill Guerin was like asking a sheep to party with two wolves. Modano is mellow. Tkachuk and Guerin are maniacal. "Before the game, they look like they want to pound me to get me more intense," Modano said, a smile crossing his lips.

But the Tkachuk-Modano-Guerin trio, mismatched in terms of personality, proved to be an excellent blend on the ice, particularly against Slovakia. Tkachuk had three goals and an assist, Modano had two goals and an assist, and Bill Guerin had an assist, a slashing penalty, and multitude of hits and dirty looks that intimidated the Slovaks. To opponents, playing against Guerin was like entering a radiation zone—prolonged exposure was ill-advised.

Tkachuk is a throwback to the 1950s when the leading scorer on an NHL team was usually the toughest player as well. Gordie Howe, Maurice "Rocket" Richard, Milt Schmidt—all of them were captains who could score, hit, fight, and control the game in any number of different ways. Although he was never captain, Hull's father, Bobby, was the same way. Tkachuk is the 1990s version of those players, right down to his willingness to do whatever it takes to be successful.

The way Modano handled the ribbing he took from Guerin and Tkachuk was indicative of how close-knit the American team had become. Guerin and Tkachuk helped keep everyone loose. In Philadelphia, they put on a synchronized swimming exhibition in the jacuzzi.

Bill Guerin was one-third of a line that was particulary effective against Slovakia. Along with Keith Tkachuk and Mike Modano, the trio registered five goals in the victory.

After the win over Slovakia, Wilson gave his players a day off as a reward for their stellar play. Chelios and Hull competed in a charity golf event in Chicago. Others lounged around. Pat LaFontaine flew home to Buffalo so he could walk his daughter to her first day of school. Players wouldn't have been surprised if Tkachuk and Guerin had spent the day wishing there had been a game to play. These guys were born to spend their life on a rink.

Having earned the bye, the Americans wouldn't play again until six days later when they faced the Russians in Ottawa. The Americans were ready for the Russians. But they weren't ready for Ottawa's fans.

One sign of how far USA Hockey's program had come was that Uncle Sam had surpassed Boris Mikhailov on Canada's list of leading hockey villains.

Remember Mikhailov had outraged fans by laughing in Bobby Clarke's face after the Russians had whipped Canada's NHL All-Stars twenty years ago. In 1996, he coached the Russian team against the Americans in the game in Ottawa, and the Canadian fans cheered his players as if they were born in Moose Jaw, not Moscow.

When Team USA coach Ron Wilson entered the postgame press conference after the United States defeated Russia 5-2, he had a right to act as if he didn't know where he was.

"Let's make this quick," Wilson joked. "It's a long flight from Moscow to Philadelphia."

Pat LaFontaine celebrates a goal in the 1996 World Cup of Hockey.

Don Cherry, color analyst for Hockey Night in Canada, told a reporter he was disappointed the Canadians had cheered the Russians. "If we were bombed by Iraq," Cherry said, "who would come to our defense? The Russians?"

Ottawa might as well have been Moscow to Brett Hull, who was booed unmercifully by the fans. The Canadians reacted to him as if he had become hockey's Benedict Arnold. Fans started chanting "traitor, traitor, traitor" after the Canadian-born Hull scored his second goal to give Team USA a 4-1 lead at 14:48 of the second period.

This fan reaction was at most bizarre and at the very least unexpected. After all, Hull had played for the USA in 1991 without abuse, and that was after he had won the Hart Trophy as the NHL's most valuable player. Born in Belleville, Ontario, and raised in Winnipeg and Vancouver, Hull had the right to play for either Canada or the USA because his mother was a U.S. citizen. In 1986, when both the USA and Canada had scouted Hull for their national teams, only the USA had wanted him. Hull hadn't forgotten that.

"When I was a sophomore in college, [Canada's] Dave King and [the USA's] Dave Peterson came to watch me play," Hull said. "Dave King said I was no good or whatever. He didn't come and see me afterward, but Peterson did."

Although Hull says he's no super patriot, his only regret was that he had but two goals to give to his chosen country. The Ottawa fans' booing and taunting bothered him. "It wasn't like I high-sticked anyone," Hull said.

Team Canada, meanwhile, was struggling just to reach the final round. The Canadians needed a goal by Theo Fleury with 12.5 seconds left in second overtime to win a semifinal game against Sweden. Canada recovered after blowing a two-goal lead in the third period.

Watching that game from his hotel room, Wilson was definitely cheering for Canada. Everyone in USA Hockey believed it was important to face Canada in the final. If they won the tournament without beating Canada in the best-of-three series, doubters would suggest their triumph was a matter of good fortune, not good playing.

This final series against the Canadians was meant to happen. At a press conference before the first game of the final series, Wilson downplayed the nationalistic significance of the tournament. He insisted that it was team versus team, not country versus country. These next two or three games, he said, were merely twenty guys playing against another twenty guys. He made it sound as if the Americans and Canadians were just playing a pickup game.

As Wilson left the press conference, an American journalist stopped him for a private conversation. "I just wanted to be able to call you a liar to your face," the journalist joked. "There's no way you believed any of the words that just came out of your mouth."

Wilson laughed. "Well, what did you want to me say? That I wanted to kick Canada's ass? That would be great with all of those Canadian journalists sitting there. I couldn't exactly say that, could I?"

No, he couldn't, even though it was the truth. He may have been born in Windsor, Ontario, but Wilson was probably as nationalistic as any player on the team, maybe more so. He respected the Canadians. He admired the Canadians. But he had been on too many U.S. teams that were hammered by the Canadians not to appreciate an opportunity to wave Old Glory in their faces.

But in game one in Philadelphia, Canada showed it wouldn't easily abdicate its title as the hockey world's undisputed ruler. Steve Yzerman scored at 10:37 of overtime to give Canada a 4-3 win against Team USA.

"It's like a heavyweight fight," Wilson said. "They are the reigning champ. We didn't use our knockout punch. They got off the ropes and beat us."

Yzerman's game-winner was a fluttering shot from a bad angle that fell into the net after goaltender Mike Richter hit it with his glove. "I think the shot was going wide until Mike Richter hit it," Yzerman said.

Team USA had forced overtime after a goal by John LeClair with 6.3 seconds remaining in regulation. The goal was actually netted by Canadian defenseman Eric Desjardins, who accidently knocked the puck through his own goaltender. Moments before, linesman Kevin Collins had waved Mark Messier out of the face-off circle. With Adam Graves in his place, the USA's Joel Otto won the draw, and the USA gained possession for a final drive to the net. LeClair was credited with the goal because he was battling in front of the net.

Then Yzerman scored in overtime. Adding insult to the loss was the fact that Collins had missed an offsides call that should have stopped the play before Yzerman scored.

Fate seemed to have sided against the Americans. Although the Canadians were gracious in triumph, they had to be thinking, same old Americans. They can't find a savior when the game is on the line. Haven't we seen this before?

Doug Weight is tripped by a Slovakian player during the World Cup. A Michigan native, Weight started playing against Canadian teams when he was just a peewee player. His feisty style of play was a perfect fit for the U.S. squad, making Weight a key contributor to the U.S. triumph.

U.S. goaltender Mike Richter makes the save against Canada. The Americans had learned to defeat the Russians, but facing the Canadians was still a psychological challenge.

But Wilson wasn't panicking, nor were his players. They embraced the idea that Canada had barely beaten them on a night when the Americans had been mediocre at best. The Canadians had actually paid the ultimate compliment by throwing a trap defense against the Americans in game one. They had clogged up the neutral zone like it was New York's Lincoln Tunnel at rush hour.

For years the Canadians had attacked the Americans in waves, believing they would eventually shake the Americans' confidence. Now, out of respect for the Americans' aggressive fore-checking and talent, they were sitting back, playing defense and waiting for their chances. Instead of attacking like sharks as they usually did, the Canadians were lying in the weeds like equally dangerous snakes.

The loss brought a sense of reality back to the Americans, who had known no adversity until Yzerman's shot crossed the line. But it didn't undermine their confidence. They believed they could win two games in Montreal, even if it was a mecca for Canadian hockey. The Americans expected game two to be different, and it was.

If the old script had been followed, the Canadians would have closed out the Americans in the second game. Instead, the Americans defeated the Canadians 5-2.

Team USA produced its best effort against the Canadians since the United States shocked Canada en route to the 1960 Olympic gold medal. Canada's favorite ex-patriot, Hull, had scored a key goal at 15:24 of the second period to put Team USA ahead 3-2. He got the breakaway when Adam Foote's shot hit Chelios and deflected directly to Hull, who scooted down the ice the way his father, Bobby, had done so many times at Chicago Stadium. Hullie, who had played well defensively throughout the tournament, had been hanging out like a school yard cherry picker when the puck found him.

"I would like to say Hullie was cheating on that play," Wilson joked. "But I should say 'anticipating.'"

Canada played without its leader, Mark Messier, who was sidelined with the flu. Because of his previous history of playing with illness and injury, it was presumed Messier's symptoms were quite severe. With Messier bedridden, the Canadians were sluggish. The Americans countered the Canadian defensive scheme by pounding their defense.

Team USA goaltender Mike Richter made 35 saves to shut down Canada's offense. Richter was sharpest in the third period when Canada outshot the United States, 18-8. "He took [the Game 1] loss hard," Wilson said. "I think he felt he let the team down."

Canada's head coach, Glen Sather, gave Lindros more ice time with the hope he might step up and replace Messier as an offensive force and leader. The Americans had gone after Lindros. Tkachuk was nose to nose with Lindros on a couple of occasions, and Hatcher was in his face.

Chelios went after Lindros at every opportunity. He and Lindros swung sticks and traded jabs. Obscenities spewed from their lips. Taunts rose from their mouths. They were like two gladiators, only the forum was in Montreal, not Rome.

One verbal exchange while both men were in the penalty box nearly escalated into an ugly scene. Later, both men said it was simply the emotions of the battle. "I don't think Chelios ever goes ten minutes without yakking at someone," Lindros said.

On a night when Canada was looking for Lindros to lead the charge, it was his American-born Philadelphia Flyers linemate, John LeClair, who was the important offensive player with two goals in the game. "He doesn't need Eric to be a great hockey player," Wilson said.

LeClair may be unique in that the hockey world thought he had arrived as a player before he actually believed he had arrived as a player. Usually it's the other way around.

He started to get noticed as a member of the Montreal Canadiens in the 1993 playoffs when he scored back-to-back playoff goals in the Stanley Cup finals against the Los Angeles Kings. The Canadiens coach, Jacques Demers, talked glowingly about his potential, and the hockey world began believing he was an elite power winger. Demers compared him to Kevin Stevens, who at the time was still a tenacious, fast, high-scoring winger.

"When I look back at those playoffs, I just don't see it," LeClair says candidly. "I only had four goals [in 20 playoff games]. It wasn't like I stole the show. We won by teamwork. If you look at it, I don't think I played all that outstanding."

The following season, he finished with 19 goals in 74 games. LeClair believes his arrival didn't occur until the lockout season of 1994-95 when he

John LeClair was Team USA's second-leading scorer in the World Cup with 10 points in 7 games.

was dealt to Philadelphia with Eric Desjardins and Gilbert Dionne for Mark Recchi. "I was in a rut and that trade changed my career around," LeClair said.

In the World Cup, he proved himself to be among the world's best players. Heading into game three, he looked as if he had a chance to be named the tournament's most valuable player if Team USA won.

"Both teams have one hand on the World Cup," Wilson said after the second game. "It will be a slugfest to see who can get the other one on it."

The third game was billed as Canada's most important since its 1972 showdown with the Soviet Union. Canada fell behind 3-1 in that series before rallying to win 4-3-1, capturing the title on Moscow's soil in perhaps the most dramatic series in hockey history.

"We've all experienced that kind of pressure," Gretzky said. "People want to win so badly. This is a way of life in Canada. We're taught and expected to win. There's a great deal of pressure on everyone. We're more scared not to win. No one wants to be known as the team that lost, and that's the difference between this country and a lot of other countries."

Mike Richter wanted to battle the best in World Cup competition, even if it meant defending goal against his New York Rangers teammate, Mark Messier.

The day before the game, Messier said he would play in game three, as if anyone really doubted he would. The Canadian media tried to coax him into guaranteeing a victory as he had during the 1994 playoffs. That moment may define Messier's whole career. With the Rangers trailing 3-2 in a best-of-seven series, he guaranteed the Rangers would defeat the New Jersey Devils. He then went out and scored a hat trick to make sure it happened. In New York sports lore, his guarantee will be forever lumped with Joe Namath's prediction that his New York Jets would beat the Baltimore Colts in the 1969 Super Bowl, and the myth or reality of Babe Ruth calling his home run hit.

But Messier offered no such guarantee in 1996. "I wish I could," he said.

Richter, Messier's teammate during the NHL season, said he was glad Messier would be playing. "We want to beat the best," he said.

When the Americans took the ice for game three in Montreal, they were greeted by a multitude of Canadian flags. The province was divided over the issue of Quebec independence, but it was unified in the belief that Team Canada needed its support.

"We have to beat the lion in the lion's den," Wilson said before the game.

No miracle was required to win the World Cup of Hockey that day. The Americans had beaten the Canadians twice in this tournament, and they really believed they could do it a third time.

"In the past, we said we could beat Canada," said Edmonton Oilers' center Doug Weight. "But when we were in our hotel room, all alone, did we really believe it? Maybe not, but this team believed it."

They believed it when the Canadians were peppering goaltender Mike Richter with shot after shot in the second period. They believed it when the USA's Keith Tkachuk, who may be the NHL's best power winger, received a controversial game misconduct for slashing Adam Foote. They believed it even when Foote scored with 7:10 left to give Canada a 2-1 lead. After Foote scored, Chicago Blackhawks' winger Tony Amonte and Philadelphia Flyers' winger John LeClair started chirping on the bench.

"We're still going to win," LeClair said.

Amonte was even emphatic. "We're still in control," he said.

Knowing the Canadian program always shows tapes of past Canadian successes to players before playing a big international game, Wilson had brought in film clips of *Rocky II* for his players. That's the movie where Rocky and Apollo Creed are both down, and Rocky rises off the canvas to win the championship.

Less than four minutes after Foote scored, the Americans began to remove themselves from the canvas. Brett Hull redirected Derian Hatcher's shot from the point past goaltender Curtis Joseph for what looked like the tying goal. But the referee indicated the goal would be reviewed by the replay official. Was Hull's stick above his shoulders? If it was, the goal would be disallowed. Hull was so nervous that he kept chirping at the officials that he hadn't even touched the puck. But the replay would show he had, but his stick wasn't too high.

Emotions boiled over on the bench, and Wilson suddenly realized that his team was in the 2-2 tie that he had talked about the first day of training camp.

"This is what we talked about," he shouted at players. "It's 2-2. We know what to do, and the Canadians don't. They thought they would be up 5-1 at this point."

The LeClair-Smolinski-Amonte line was up next for the Americans. That trio had been the USA's best all-around line in the tournament. Bryan Smolinski had been an unsung hero, doing a job at both ends of the ice. LeClair was leading the tournament in goals. Amonte was the designated hero. When he left the bench, it seemed as if his skates were barely touching the ice. He skimmed the surface of the ice like he had been expelled from a torpedo tube. He honed in on a point in front of the net as if his conversation with Wilson had preordained what was about to occur. The puck was on his stick, and in a flash, he tucked it in under the cross bar with a shot that flew upward like it had been lofted with a seven-iron.

The U.S. bench was a cauldron of emotion after Tony Amonte scored the game-winning goal with 2:35 left in the deciding World Cup game against Canada.

The American bench boiled over. But again, the play would be reviewed because the referee thought Amonte might have kicked it in. The replays confirmed the goal, and for the second time in a minute, the American bench got to celebrate a goal.

Wilson quickly rechanneled his players' emotions, reminding them that 2:35 remained in the game. In the final two minutes, Wilson chose to use Leetch and Derian Hatcher as his two primary defensemen. Given that Chelios was available, it showed the respect Wilson had for Hatcher.

Much to the surprise of 28 million Canadians, Team Canada would not pull off any last-minute heroics to turn defeat into victory.

Symbolism was available for those who needed it. With 47 seconds left, Mark Messier and Wayne Gretzky, two icons of Canadian hockey, misfired on a goal that would have tied the game 3-3. Messier had made a perfect pass to Gretzky, who was all alone in the goalmouth. Gretzky had probably redirected that same Messier pass into the goal a hundred times, but this time he couldn't handle it, and the puck skipped away. A second later Derian Hatcher swatted the puck 180 feet down the ice and into the empty Canadian net. Adam Deadmarsh added another empty-net goal to make the final score 5-2.

When time expired, sticks went skyward and gloves were tossed all over the ice. Keith Tkachuk was carrying an American flag when he came back on the ice. Tears, laughter, relief—the gamut of human emotions was available for inspection on the Molson Centre ice.

This wasn't Lake Placid. No political implications were present. There would be no trip to The White House, no interruption of normal programming to tell the world of this victory, no appearances on "Good Morning America." Dan Rather would not be leading the "CBS Evening News" with an analysis of their triumph. But everyone in the hockey world understood the significance of this moment.

Several hundred miles away, University of Michigan coach Red Berenson would watch and cheer and understand. When the NHL had just one American, one college player, and no Europeans, he was the college player. That was his link to the majority of players on the U.S. squad. "Everyone would just look at you sideways," Berenson said. "I was considered an intellectual geek."

Mike Modano's mother, Karen, understood the significance because she had spent far too many hours and dollars transporting her son to hockey tournaments. Once a group of parents sat down to determine how much they spent on hockey in one season. As the dollars began staring them in the face, they quit adding, figuring it was better not to know. "Sometimes you had to make the hockey payment before the house payment," Karen Modano remembered.

Of course, coach Ron Wilson understood because he was a veteran of foreign hockey wars. He had been on teams where none of the players believed they had a chance against the Canadians.

After the celebration had moved from the ice to the dressing room, Wilson knew that it would be impossible to have a moment alone with his players once the door had opened and relatives and press were allowed in. Amid the shouting and hoopla, he had a moment of quiet to tell of his winter knights they had deserved their victory. He left them with only one final thought.

It was Independence Day. The Americans were driving the bus.

Chris Chelios carries the World Cup. The victory verified what the veteran NHL defenseman had believed since his days as an Olympian in 1984—that the U.S. program had taken major steps toward successfully competing with the best in the world.

CELEBRATE!

Jubilant Americans (above) celebrate USA's most significant hockey triumph over Canada since the Americans nipped the Canadians 2-1 at the 1960 Olympics in Squaw Valley. Left photo: Doug Weight (left) and Tony Amonte proudly show off the trophy. Right photo: Mike Richter receives a motorcycle as the most valuable player of the tournament.

1996 World Cup Statistics

Team USA Game-by-Game Results

Date	Result		Location	Round
August 31	Team USA 5,	Team Canada 3	Philadelphia, Pa.	Preliminary Round
September 2	Team USA 5,	Team Russia 2	New York, N.Y.	Preliminary Round
September 3	Team USA 9,	Team Slovakia 3	New York, N.Y.	Preliminary Round
September 8	Team USA 5,	Team Russia 2	Ottawa, Ontario	Semifinal Round
September 10	Team Canada 4,	Team USA 3 (OT)	Philadelphia, Pa.	Championship Game #1
September 12	Team USA 5,	Team Canada 2	Montreal, Quebec	Championship Game #2
September 14	Team USA 5,	Team Canada 2	Montreal, Quebec	Championship Game #3

Top Ten Scoring Leaders

PLAYER	TEAM	GP	G	A	PTS	+/-	PIM	PP	SH	GW	OT	S	PCTG
Brett Hull	United States	7	7	4	11	4	4	3	1	2	0	27	25.9
John LeClair	United States	7	6	4	10	9	6	1	0	0	0	23	26.1
Mats Sundin	Sweden	4	4	3	7	5	4	1	0	2	0	26	15.4
Doug Weight	United States	7	3	4	7	3	12	1	0	0	0	11	27.3
Wayne Gretzky	Canada	8	3	4	7	6-	2	2	0	0	0	19	15.8
Brian Leetch	United States	7	0	7	7	10	4	0	0	0	0	11	.0
Paul Coffey	Canada	8	0	7	7	3-	12	0	0	0	0	14	.0
Keith Tkachuk	United States	7	5	1	6	6	44	1	0	2	0	15	33.3
Theoren Fleury	Canada	8	4	2	6	2	8	1	0	1	1	23	17.4
Sergei Fedorov	Russia	5	3	3	6	2-	2	1	0	1	0	13	23.1

Team USA Scoring

POS	NO.	PLAYER	GP	G	A	PTS	+/-	PIM	PP	SH	GW	OT	S	PCTG
R	15	Brett Hull	7	7	4	11	4	4	3	1	2	0	27	25.9
L	10	John LeClair	7	6	4	10	9	6	1	0	0	0	23	26.1
C	19	Doug Weight	7	3	4	7	3	12	1	0	0	0	11	27.3
D	2	Brian Leetch	7	0	7	7	10	4	0	0	0	0	11	.0
L	17	Keith Tkachuk	7	5	1	6	6	44	1	0	2	0	15	33.3
C	9	Mike Modano	7	2	4	6	5	4	0	0	0	0	17	11.8
R	11	Tony Amonte	7	2	4	6	6	6	0	0	2	0	10	20.0
D	3	Derian Hatcher	6	3	2	5	8	10	0	0	0	0	10	30.0
C	8	Bryan Smolinski	6	0	5	5	7	0	0	0	0	0	9	.0
C	16	Pat LaFontaine	5	2	2	4	4	2	0	1	0	0	4	50.0
R	21	Scott Young	7	2	2	4	2	4	0	0	0	0	11	18.2
C	18	Adam Deadmarsh	7	2	2	4	1	8	0	0	0	0	10	20.0
D	7	Chris Chelios	7	0	4	4	7	10	0	0	0	0	7	.0
C	29	Joel Otto	7	1	2	3	4	6	0	0	0	0	6	16.7
D	4	Kevin Hatcher	7	0	3	3	5	4	0	0	0	0	13	.0
D	5	Mathieu Schneider	7	2	0	2	1	8	0	0	0	0	10	20.0
D	20	Gary Suter	6	0	2	2	6	6	0	0	0	0	7	.0
R	12	Bill Guerin	7	0	2	2	3	17	0	0	0	0	7	.0
D	6	Phil Housley	1	0	1	1	1	0	0	0	0	0	0	.0
C	14	Shawn McEachern	1	0	1	1	1	0	0	0	0	0	3	.0
D	28	Shawn Chambers	1	0	0	0	0	0	0	0	0	0	0	.0
G	31	Guy Hebert	1	0	0	0	0	0	0	0	0	0	0	.0
L	25	Brian Rolston	1	0	0	0	0	0	0	0	0	0	5	.0
C	22	Steve Konowalchuk	1	0	0	0	1-	0	0	0	0	0	0	.0
G	35	Mike Richter	6	0	0	0	0	0	0	0	0	0	0	.0

Team USA Goaltending

SW#	GOALTENDER	GPI	MINS	AVG	W	L	T	EN	SO	GA	SA	SV%	G	A	PIM
35	Mike Richter	6	370	2.43	5	1	0	0	0	15	194	.923	0	0	0
31	Guy Hebert	1	60	3.00	1	0	0	0	0	3	31	.903	0	0	0
	USA Totals	7	431	2.51	6	1	0	0	0	18	225	.920			

EPILOGUE

Canadians wax poetic about their hockey tradition, speaking in eloquent prose about frozen ponds, frigid toes, and marathon games of shinny in such magical-sounding outposts as Moose Jaw, Red Deer, and Flin Flon. Hockey's history is entwined with Canada's heritage, like those vines that add life to the outfield walls at Chicago's Wrigley Field.

While it is true hockey doesn't hold the same place of esteem in American history, it is just as true that America's hockey tradition didn't begin with Emilio Estevez and Disney's Mighty Ducks movie. For more than 100 years, some Americans have had a devotion to the game as strong as any found north of the 48th parallel.

Even when Canadians owned 99 percent of NHL jobs, some Americans had as much reverence for hockey as anyone in Guelph or Sudbury. Almost thirty years ago, some of us were stuffing our pant legs with the padding from a recently deceased sofa in order to be properly outfitted for a hockey game on the frozen tennis court at Monroe Elementary school in Wayne, Michigan. Forget Bobby Hull. For those of us who played at Monroe in the 1960s, nothing brought you nearer to God than a close encounter with Bobby McGinley's slap shot.

America's hockey tradition isn't about towns and programs as much as it is about people and what they were willing to do to play a sport that many Americans treated as a novelty until the 1990s. Many of the heroes of American hockey are those who have never worn an NHL sweater. They are the mothers, fathers, referees, coaches, players, and league directors who put in time and kept the passion for hockey burning for years when the flame could have easily gone out. Those who don't recognize the dedication U.S. citizens have to the sport should know that five decades ago defenseman Manny Cotlow of Minnesota played fifty minutes in an American Association game hours after marrying his sweetheart.

They should know that thirty years ago Bob Caldwell volunteered to be a coach after reading an article in a newspaper about a hockey team for troubled youths and ended up as a major force in the Acton-Boxboro program in Massachusetts, which has produced five NHL players and two Olympians.

They should know that Joe Vernon, back in the 1960s, religiously awakened before 5 A.M. so he could get to the local rink early and light the stove that warmed youngsters of Saratoga Springs, New York, as they showed up for early practices.

Loving hockey in America has always meant paying a price greater than that paid by athletes in other sports. Midnight practices, outrageous costs, six-hour drives to find quality competition, and high-mileage automobiles with low resale value are all symbols of America's hockey tradition.

Guy and Lisa LaChance drove ninety minutes one way every day to transport their future NHL son, Scott, from his Connecticut home to Springfield, Massachusetts, for practice.

Wally Roenick sacrificed opportunities for career advancement so he could move his family from Virginia to Massachusetts where the hockey was better. He knew his son, Jeremy, needed better competition to become an NHLer. Before the move, Jeremy had commuted from Virginia to New Jersey to play for a junior team. "We would put him on People's Express every Friday for about $59 one way to New Jersey," Wally Roenick said. "But sometimes we had to send him to Boston or Detroit. We probably spent $25,000 that season."

Expense has been no object for Americans who love hockey. Noted hockey writer Jack Falla put a rink up in his backyard for many years, and International Hockey League commissioner Bob Ufer celebrated a new contract with the players' association by inviting rival negotiators to play against him on his pond.

America's hockey tradition is a salute to perseverance, the willingness to keep the faith, even when surrounded by many nonbelievers.

Most of those who attended the USA Hockey World Cup victory party at the Montreal Chateau Champlain understood that, none more so than Jack Leetch, who seemed to enjoy watching his All-Star son Brian and the rest of the American players celebrate their victory with huge Havana cigars and plenty of strutting.

Long before he had fathered an All-Star NHL defenseman, he had been a good player at Boston College. Jack Leetch was a tough competitor and dedicated man who embraced weightlifting long before it was the norm. But when the 1964 U.S. Olympic team was chosen, the team's general manager, Walter Bush, had to tell Leetch he was cut from the team.

"He thanked me for the opportunity we had given him," Bush remembered. "And I remember he said: 'I hope I have a son someday who will wear the USA uniform.'"

Although Jack hadn't made the Olympic team, he had passed along his love of the game to his son. Brian Leetch was also a standout baseball pitcher, once breaking the Avon Old Farms school record for strikeouts in a game, surpassing a mark that had been set by future major-league pitcher Juan Nieves. But when it came time to choose between sports, Brian Leetch embraced his father's game. And when the United States was trying to hold a lead against Canada in the final minute of the World Cup, Brian Leetch, the team's captain, was America's white knight, winning a major battle in the name of his country's hockey pride.

What can be said about the American hockey tradition? Only this—we have loved hockey when loving it wasn't easy.

INDEX

PHOTO CREDITS